SO YOU WANNA BE A ROCK & ROLL STAR

JAKE, DAN, AND JOHN

SO YOU WANNA BE A ROCK & ROLL STAR

How I Machine-Gunned

a Roomful of Record Executives

and Other True Tales from

a Drummer's Life

JACOB SLICHTER

Broadway Books
New York

BROADWAY BOOKS and its logo, a letter B bisected on the diagonal, are trademarks of Random House, Inc.

Visit our website at www.broadwaybooks.com

First trade paperback edition published 2005.

Portions of chapters VIII, XII, and XVI appeared in slightly different form on National Public Radio's *Morning Edition*.

Photo Credits: page ii, Marina Chavez; page 239, Dana Collins; page 257, Gavin Roberts

"Closing Time" and "Made to Last." Words and Music by Dan Wilson. © 1998 WB Music Corp. and Semidelicious Music. All Rights Administered by WB Music Corp. Lyrics reprinted by Permission of Warner Bros. Publications. All Rights Reserved.

Book design by Chris Welch

The Library of Congress has cataloged the hardcover edition as:
Slichter, Jacob.
So you wanna be a rock & roll star : how I machine-gunned a roomful of record executives and other true tales from a drummer's life / Jacob Slichter.—1st ed.
    p.   cm.
ISBN 978-0-7679-1471-0
1. Slichter, Jacob. 2. Rock musicians—United States—Biography.
I. Title: So you wanna be a rock and roll star. II. Title.

ML419.S62A3 2004
781.66'092—dc22
[B]   2004043540

14

FOR MY PARENTS

CONTENTS

When my friends introduce me to their friends, it often goes like this:

"Bob, this is Jake. Jake's a rock star!"

Bob looks me over. "Really?"

"Well, I don't know if I'd call myself a—"

My friend continues. "Jake's the drummer in Semisonic."

Bob smiles and shrugs. "Semisonic? Never heard of you."

"Most people don't know who we—"

"Jake, don't be so modest! Come on, Bob, you know Semisonic. You heard them all the time on the radio. Remember that song 'Closing Time'?"

"Wow, you wrote 'Closing Time'?"

"No, I'm the drummer."

Bob divides "Closing Time" by "drummer" and remains moderately impressed. "So, you're a rock star. What's that like?" Before I can answer, his smile reveals an imagination already at work, most likely reveling in the kind of visions I myself have had.

Perhaps you, too, have entertained such air-guitar fantasies—rocking out in front of thousands of cheering fans and shouting "THANK YOU!" into the microphone. In your rock-star daydreams, you are your most confident self: On stage, you lean back with closed eyes as your right hand windmills over your head and down across the strings of your guitar. In front of the camera, you cock your head to the side and melt the lens with a mysterious smile. Before the interviewer's microphone, you uncork a sparkling wit. Life is a wellspring of adoration from a world of fawning strangers. You can see yourself walking down the street, stopping to sign autographs with breezy self-assurance as your song plays on a nearby radio. (The DJ at the station loves you, too.)

As I waited through my teenage years and beyond for the chance to realize those bright fantasies, I also had darker ones, perhaps also familiar to you. I imagined a lonely and depressing world where a struggling band sells the rights to its music for a pittance, only to watch the record company (run by an evil genius) rake in millions. Perhaps stardom would be a vacuous existence where the quest for a meaningful life and the enjoyment of friendships were replaced by snorting cocaine and staring in the mirror. These rival visions of the rock world each contain elements of truth, but neither of them is as strange as the reality that eventually transformed my life.

Rocking on stage in front of thousands, as I did many times, was an unsurpassable thrill—all the more so because I had survived panic attacks on tiny club stages in front of a few dozen. Signing an autograph, which I've done thousands of times, required trial and error before I learned how to do it without feeling like an idiot. I learned about the unfair arrangements that underlie record deals and the countless ways that success is bought and sold. Instead of becoming outraged, though, I felt the myopia and illogic of the music business slowly become my own. When my bandmates and I received platinum record awards for having sold one million albums, the mood among those gathered for the occasion was somber. Why? Because we hadn't sold three million.

This book is a drummer's-eye view of that strange world, which, like all reality, is both better and worse than fantasy. Here is your chance to see what it's like to sit behind the drum set facing the camera on Letterman; eavesdrop on arguments in recording studios; walk along backstage hallways past Prince, Sheryl Crow, Whitney Houston, Garth Brooks, and Courtney Love; try on endless racks of expensive clothing; star in rock videos, even if they are ones that few people will ever see; stretch out in the back lounge of a tour bus; shake hands with the power brokers of radio; suffer the idiotic opinions of record executives; drink Champagne at the Grammys; sit through an anxiety-filled interview with Howard Stern; travel the world wondering if you're famous, kind of famous, soon to be really famous, or a wannabe; and most of all, to enjoy the rush that is found on stage in front of 200 people at a bar in Minneapolis, 10,000 in an arena in Mexico City, or 100,000 on an open field in Glastonbury, England.

Along with my bandmates Dan Wilson and John Munson, I did all of that. From some stages I threw my drumsticks into a swarm of reaching hands, and on other stages I dodged flying bottles and mud. My band was signed to record deals, dropped from them, and then picked up again. I rode in limousines, paraded down red carpets in front of flashing cameras, signed those countless autographs, and even checked into hotels using an alias. In five years, I rose from anonymity—working as an office temp—to something like stardom—being hailed by a stranger in Paris and asked, "Are you the drummer for Everclear?"

No, I'm the drummer for Semisonic, and this is my story.

SO YOU WANNA

WANNA

BE A

ROCK & ROLL

STAR

Chapter 1

JUMP START

t's never snowed in Minnesota during the month of July. The boundary waters up north, however, have tasted light accumulations in August and June, and as for the months in between, keep those winter boots handy. From autumn to spring, Minnesota is a frozen soundscape of snowplows, snow shovels, windshield scrapers, and auto ignitions laboring to turn over. Once, to get into my ice-entombed car, I needed a rubber mallet, seventy-five feet of extension cord, and a blow dryer. The long brutal winters, however, are sometimes credited with fostering Minneapolis's vital music scene. Without such horrible weather keeping them inside with their guitars, the theory goes, the world might never have heard of Bob Dylan, Prince, the Suburbs, the Replacements, Husker Du, Babes in Toyland, the Time, Soul Asylum, or the Jayhawks.

It takes more than blizzards and musicians to sustain this thriving scene. It takes fans, and the fans in the Twin Cities are famous for pushing their cars out of snowdrifts, driving down to Minneapolis's prized rock club, First Avenue, and lining up around the block in subzero temperatures on a weekday night to get through the doors before the tickets sell out. Those fans and the bands they love make a potent combination. I'll never forget watching Soul Asylum rule the stage while the body heat from the crowd of 2,000 thawed my frozen jaw. With their amplifiers turned up past the breaking point, the band spilled back and forth across the stage and brought the crowd seesawing with them, as if we were all on the deck of a ship. Singer Dave Pirner whipped his long hair in circles and screamed, "I want somebody to shove! I need somebody to shove! I want somebody to shove me!" An overexcited fan launched a cup of beer from twenty rows back, and it soared over the crowd and exploded on Karl Mueller's bass guitar. Pirner pointed into the crowd and shouted into the mike. "We're gonna find out who fuckin' threw that, and when we do, we're gonna kick your ass. And everyone here's gonna help us do it!" The crowd roared its approval.

I was a musician in my early thirties, still living under the cloud of disappointment that had followed me since graduating six years earlier from Harvard, a place for which I was poorly prepared and which in every regard had annihilated my self-confidence. I had intended to major in music, but after completing a year of study at the Berklee College of Music, for which Harvard's music department had promised me credit, I received a cold letter from the chairman of the department rescinding this promise and inviting me to find another course of study. I wandered from major to major, eventually settling on Afro-American studies, where I quietly explored my interests in race, politics, music, and literature. I entertained visions of graduate school, but such daydreaming was brought to an abrupt end when I opened the envelope containing the miserable grade given to my senior thesis, and the accompanying terse comments on its shabbiness. I graduated with a lackluster record and threw my diploma in a storage box. So much for plan B; back to plan A—rock stardom.

I proceeded with a move to San Francisco. I worked at various day jobs—selling synthesizers and drum machines at Guitar Center, making copies and filing them for executives at Chevron, and then administering the office of Saint Gregory's Episcopal

Church—and wrote songs at night, recording them in my bedroom. Alas, songwriting vexed me. The emotions that I longed to put into words and music proved beyond my reach whenever I laid my fingers on a guitar, piano keyboard, or pen. I wanted to address themes of social justice through the poetry of personal reflection. What I ended up with were a stack of legal pads filled with half-finished lyrics, manuscript paper with half-finished melodies, and a cassette of the twelve songs I managed to write in five years. The extent of my public performances was also minimal, spanning a period of three months during which my friend Hal Movius and I performed on the stages of the Paradise Lounge and the Hotel Utah. On these five or six occasions, we were applauded thoughtfully by a few strangers and enthusiastically by twenty members of Saint Gregory's Church.

I left San Francisco with little to show for my musical aspirations and hoped the legendary scene in Minneapolis would be the launch pad for a career that had not yet gotten off the ground. I knew a number of musicians in town, but for the most part I continued to do what I had done in San Francisco—work a day job and write and record songs in my basement studio at night, playing the drums, keyboards, and making use of my fledgling skills on guitar. The rare feat of finishing a song was cause for celebration. I'd listen to the recording for days, triumphant at first and then mortified by its shortcomings—my sugary melodies and lyrics, my inept guitar playing, and most of all my quavering baritone voice. As I lay in bed at night, I'd hear another page tearing off of my life's shortening calendar. I was running out of time, hair, and dignity. The mantle of failure weighed on me, no place more than at my day job downtown, where I attended to the photocopying and envelope-stuffing needs of executives who sold retirement plans.

"So, Jake, I hear you're a musician. What kind of music do you play?"

"It's . . . hard to describe."

"I see. Where do you play?"

"I have a studio in my basement."

"Good for you. I need five hundred copies of this report stapled and collated by the end of the day."

By contrast, my closest friends in town had no day jobs; they had a record deal with A&M Records. Dan Wilson, a friend of mine from college, his brother Matt, John Munson, and Elaine Harris were the members of Trip Shakespeare, a rock band whose dark psychedelic sound entranced fans around the country, and especially in the Midwest, where they performed for capacity crowds at the Metro in Chicago, the Shadow in Kansas City, and First Avenue in Minneapolis. To dine out with Dan, John, Matt, or Elaine was an exciting chance to be seen with a rock star who needed an unlisted phone number. It was also an occasion to silently compare career stats between them and me: one record deal to none, four albums to none, tens of thousands of fans to none.

Dan was the closest of these friends. I had met him during our freshman week at Harvard, when he heard me playing the drums in a dormitory common room. He stuck his head in the door and said, "I'll be back with my bass." (He played bass in college and later switched to guitar.) We jammed for several hours that day and in the following weeks. Our musical tastes ran in different directions—I stuck to soul and funk, while Dan was more excited by English rock and punk—so it wasn't until our senior year that we played in a band together.

It was with Dan that I moved to San Francisco, following the trail of his girlfriend, Diane. Dan and I shared an apartment, where I saw his exhausting focus firsthand. A Phi Beta Kappa, he had graduated Harvard *summa cum laude* and won the Louis Sudler Prize in the Arts, awarded to the senior who demonstrates outstanding artistic achievement, which in Dan's case was not in music but painting. In San Francisco, he carried on a double artistic life, painting and songwriting, in addition to working various day jobs. Even his days off began with a double shot of espresso and then proceeded with a furious pace of activity that was unsettling to watch, especially given my meager output. The sound of his pen scrawling across the pages of his journal could keep me from reading. (Today, the snap of his fingers on a computer keyboard can make one twitch.) In conversation, his eyes focused into an intent gaze and often he'd hold up his hand like a stop sign. Then, having remembered some forgotten task, he'd get up and disappear for a twenty-minute flurry of phone calls. Upon returning to the room, he might sit down and stare at me.

"Jake, I have a question for you."

"Yes."

"How would you like to go with me to look at some photographs at the museum, get a bowl of fish soup, drop in on Diane, and then get the new R.E.M. album on the way home?" Even his mornings off intimidated me. We had planned to start a new band together, but it never happened. Within two years, Dan returned to his hometown of Minneapolis to join Trip Shakespeare, which his brother Matt had started. While touring and recording, he continued his parallel career as a painter and had two successful gallery shows in Minneapolis.

The occasion of Dan and Diane's wedding provided my first opportunity to visit Minneapolis and glimpse its famed music scene for myself. In three days, I met a dozen musicians, several of whom encouraged me to relocate to the Twin Cities. The following year, I did, and before long I was standing in the crowd at First Avenue, awed by the spectacle of Dave Pirner promising revenge on behalf of his beer-splattered bass player.

I got to know Dan's bandmate John after moving to Minneapolis, when for a brief time we shared an apartment. He had dropped out of college, where he had studied Chinese, to play in bands and make records. John's days started slowly, and it wasn't unusual for me to return from my day job to find him sitting on the couch, luxuriating in a pair of flannel-lined jeans and a soft wool sweater, stroking his cat, and savoring a cigarette and a glass of merlot while listening to Charles Mingus. As evening arrived, he might stand up and yawn and then, after gliding through the streets in a battered but well-heated 1967 Sedan de Ville, drop in on a friend unannounced. Occasionally, without consulting the weather forecast, he would disappear into the woods on the Canadian border for solo camping trips whose length was never predetermined. His friends held their breath waiting for his return, and when he resurfaced to knock on a friend's door at bedtime, he would walk in, sit down in the living room, and recount with nonchalance nearly freezing to death in his tent and his subsequent escape from a blizzard.

As apartment sharing goes, it's hard to say which threatened me more, Dan's harrying productivity or John's alarming commitment to relaxation. John's casual manner, however, belied the fact that he was the best musician in any of the Minneapolis rock bands. There was no question in my mind that he was better on bass than anyone else was on guitar, piano, or drums. In addition to that, he was a gifted producer whose talents were in constant demand. For a man who seemed to ease through life, John had produced several albums and EPs for Minneapolis bands and singer/songwriters—this in addition to rehearsing, touring, and recording with Trip Shakespeare. Indeed, it was hard to reconcile the volume of his studio accomplishments and the long hours of practice apparent in his bass playing with the same John Munson who held court in local restaurants, bars, and rock clubs, and, during the summer, on the golf course.

Both Dan and John served as mentors for my musical pursuits, listening to my songs and basement recordings, and giving me advice and encouragement. The two of them turned me on to new music, introduced me to other musicians around town, and encouraged me to write more songs and perform them, but I continued to flounder.

Then, in the summer of 1992, a friend of ours, Heather Keena, asked John and Dan to play at her college graduation party. She suggested they ask me to play drums, perhaps in the interest of keeping a low-key affair intended for friends from escalating into a madhouse of Trip Shakespeare fans. This was a great opportunity to show off my drumming, my greatest strength as a musician and, as Dan stressed, something I had long ignored. I would be seen and heard playing with two stars of the Minneapolis scene, the two best musicians I knew.

Hours before the party, Dan with his guitar and John with his bass joined me in my basement, and we learned a dozen sixties and seventies covers. That night, the three of us climbed up onto the small stage at the 400 Bar and slammed through "In Dreams" by Roy Orbison, "Drift Away" by Dobie Gray, and whatever other songs we could remember from our afternoon rehearsal. Dan's brother Matt played with us for a song, and Dave Pirner of Soul Asylum joined us for "Dancing in the Moonlight" by King Harvest. Sharing the stage with these local luminaries was a rush, as were the cheers that greeted our strong performance.

This impromptu set was such a success that in the ensuing weeks the three of us recorded some new songs of Dan's (with small contributions from me)—songs that suited the bare textures of our trio more than the ornamented arrangements of Trip Shakespeare. The recordings turned out great, and Dan and John thought our trio would make an interesting side project. Dan named our band Pleasure, and we looked ahead to a gap in Trip Shakespeare's schedule when we might be able to record a cheaply made album. A pair of jumper cables had thus been fastened to my lifeless career.

Meanwhile, Trip Shakespeare's voyage through the music business was not going well. They had signed their record deal just as Nirvana and Pearl Jam were changing the rock-and-roll landscape with the massive success of the grungy Seattle sound. Trip Shakespeare's sound, by contrast, was built on three-part vocal harmonies sung with operatic fervor, quirky instrumental arrangements (employing sleigh bells, bongos, and xylophones), and lyrics written in elevated speech ("In the honey time of youth / When the wind had sweet breath / When the rent was way down / I would haul for no man"). Though they sold out large clubs, they were ignored by radio, and the band members complained of a lack of support from their label, A&M Records. Trip Shakespeare's albums were often missing from record stores in the towns where they performed. As the three of us recorded in my basement, Dan and John began to tell of Trip Shakespeare's tangled negotiations with their label concerning the band's most recent recordings. Then came a devastating shock: A&M dropped Trip Shakespeare from their record contract. A few days later, under growing stress, the band members decided to take some time off, and soon it was clear that Trip Shakespeare had broken up.

Now our side project became Dan and John's main focus, as it already was for me. Dan laid out a musical manifesto. Whereas Trip Shakespeare had intentionally cordoned itself off from other music of the day, Dan wanted to make music that was a part of what was happening now. For the past year, Nirvana had been blasting everyone away with the force and fury of their sound. The radio was filling up with imitators, but Dan saw that no one would be able to sound bigger or angrier. Instead, he wanted to anticipate a post-Nirvana world with music less centered on rage, though undoubtedly inspired by the scale of Nirvana's sound. He was inspired by the melodic and lyric-based songwriting of indie bands like R.E.M., the Replacements, and Teenage Fanclub. Both he and John enjoyed the brilliant recording experimentations of other bands such as My Bloody Valentine, the Flaming Lips, and Swervedriver. All of us were interested in using sampling technology and computers to create cool instrumental loops, as hiphop artists like Public Enemy, De La Soul, and the Beastie Boys had done for years. We wanted to write some great songs, get our hands on some samplers and distortion boxes, and marry these elements of the do-it-yourself traditions of indie rock and hip-hop to the high-production values, the wider grooves, and the vocal emphasis of pop. The result, we hoped, would be fresh and big.

In the daytime, Dan applied himself exclusively to songwriting, and every night when we gathered in my basement, he brought in more songs. Before long, we had a list of twenty. John took the controls of my home studio and applied his superior studio know-how. *Using distortion on the vocal—why didn't I think of that?* It wasn't unusual for John to uncover some piece of gear that I had thrown in a closet and hook it up, even as I told him of its uselessness. Then I'd watch in frustrated amazement as John turned its knobs as if he were tickling a cat on the chin and within seconds produce a warm, rich sound. As needed, my new bandmates passed their knowledge on to me, and as I learned, even the ever-relaxed John was a taskmaster when it came to rehearsing and recording. "Try to match Dan's vowel on *mind*. You're singing *mahy-eend*. Make it more like *mahnd*."

We made mixes and went upstairs and out to Dan's mildewed Chevy Corsica, where we listened. (We had quickly determined that the acoustics of my basement underrepresented the low end, so the mildewed Corsica became our listening room.) Before long, we had a great four-song demo—up-tempo melodic songs with smart lyrics rendered by the wry optimism of Dan's tenor, the sour skronk of his guitar, and a fat bass and drum groove below.

Thanks to the fact that record companies regularly fire and hire from the same pool of executives, Dan and John had an impressive network of connections, including former A&M employees who had moved on to other labels. After rehearsing and recording in my basement, we'd retire to the living room, where Dan and John would compare notes on their discussions with Anna at Interscope, Geoff at Warner, Jim at Geffen, Steve at

Elektra, and others. It was a crash course in how to get a record deal.

"I spoke with Anna at Interscope. She doesn't think Jimmy Iovine is going to like us." I had no idea who Jimmy Iovine was, why he was so important, and why his not liking our tape would be a deal-breaker. Nor was I aware that a possible downside to signing with Warner Brothers was the number of bands clogging its roster, or that signing at smaller but super-successful Geffen might also be a risk, since the other bands on Geffen's roster were louder than us, and the executives might therefore give Pleasure little of their attention. Signing any sort of record deal had previously seemed so unfathomably appealing to me, I had never thought to distinguish among labels.

As our four-song tapes went out in the mail, Dave Ness, the business manager for Trip Shakespeare and a former booking agent, booked us a show at the 400 Bar, the same small club where we had played for Heather's graduation party. We rehearsed intensely, and I encountered the work ethic and demanding standards of my far more experienced bandmates. I swallowed hard as Dan broke me of my drumming habits—still rooted in soul and funk, the music I had grown up playing on the drums—and encouraged me to develop a style more appropriate to rock. "It's too relaxed. Hit the high hat more insistently, more like the Replacements than the Spinners." Funk drumming had skewed my focus toward playing groovy drumbeats, something many rock drummers neglect in favor of dramatic drum fills, those moments when the drumbeat stops and the drummer punctuates the end of a phrase with a roll around the snare and tom-toms. John pushed me on the issue of fills and loaned me his Led Zeppelin collection as a bit of assigned listening.

Business manager Dave continued to help by preparing press packets and sending them to local journalists—a tape, a press release, and a picture that a friend of ours took in front of an old brick warehouse. Dan designed some postcards to mail to the Trip Shakespeare fan mailing list, and Dave gathered us at a coffee shop for two hours of labeling and stamping. Then we drove around town, taping posters to streetlights, telephone poles, and kiosks. This homemade publicity campaign was an inconvenient step backward for Dan and John and an exciting leap forward for me.

The night of the show came. I arrived at the 400 Bar an hour before we were scheduled to play. The word was out about Dan and John's new band, and the place was packed. After wading through the crowd and down the stairs to the basement dressing room, I waited as the weight of 200 pairs of shuffling feet made the floorboards creak and my adrenaline surge. I had been recently diagnosed with Type I diabetes, and my preshow nerves sent me into insulin shock, so I loaded up on cranberry juice and paced around until Dan and John arrived. In the ten years since college, I had played a total of ten shows. Most of those were open-mike night performances in near-empty bars.

At ten o'clock, we took the stage, greeted by a smattering of shouts and whoops. I sat down behind the drums and looked out at a roomful of staring faces. Dan said "Hello," and 200 voices spoke back in unison: "HELLO."

Dan turned up his guitar and said, "Thanks for coming. We're Pleasure." Then he started the riff of our first song. I smacked out my drum entrance and Dan turned to me with a scowl and mouthed "Shhhhhhh!," correcting the horribly misjudged volume of my drumming. I backed off and peeked at the crowd, wondering if they noticed my drumming retreat. Then I turned back to Dan, then John, to see if I was too loud, soft, fast, or slow. I looked back at the crowd, only to hear one of my bandmates yelling "Softer!" We hit the final chord of the first song and the crowd shouted their approval. Dan said, "Thank you," and we continued.

My attention pulled in different directions. Was I rushing? Singing in tune? Were Dan and John mad? How did I look? *What are those two women whispering?* In contrast to watching a rock show, time passes quickly when you're playing one, and before I knew it the three of us were walking off stage to a huge ovation and shouts of "More!" I watched Dan and John acknowledge the applause. I gave only a slight nod, figuring the shouts and clapping were meant for the two stars of the show. Half an hour later, I packed up my drums and a couple of friends stopped by the stage to say "nice job" on their way out.

In the following weeks, we returned to the creaking wooden floors of the 400 Bar and then moved on to other Minneapolis clubs—the Seventh Street Entry, a small dark cement enclosure where I could feel years of duct tape residue sticking to my shoes; and the Uptown Bar, a diner with a terrible sound system and booth seating that required half of the audience to sit facing away from the stage, watching us with twisted necks. The buzz on the band was good, largely owing to Dan and John's local celebrity, but also because of the songs and how well we played them. More and more people predicted that we would be the next big band out of Minneapolis. On show nights I entered the club and waded through the crowd, lowering my eyes and feeling my face go warm. I was being noticed. Strangers brushed by and said, "Hi, Jake." Musicians I had admired but whom I barely knew smiled at me from across the room and raised their beers. When we took the stage, people shouted out the names of our songs. Some even yelled my name. On at least one occasion, as I took a swig of sports drink from a clear bottle, a fan whooped his approval, perhaps mistaking my bottle of Ultra Fuel for liquor. But on the periphery of my attention lurked something besides the glory of performing.

Panic.

My first episode of stage panic happened in the sixth grade.

Standing in front of a packed auditorium of students and parents, I froze halfway through the recitation of a Christmas poem, said, "Wait a minute," and walked off stage. Since then, in various school plays and later playing drums in high school and college bands, I had feared another, more complete meltdown, losing my mind and perhaps even vomiting in front of a crowd. Now, on stage with Dan and John, my fear of panic made me all the more vulnerable to it. If, during the first few songs, I dwelled on it for too long, it closed in and threw a black sheet over my brain. My mouth dried up, my skin went cold, I gulped for air, and nausea spun me about. Only intense focus on a particular drum or cymbal could pull me out of the near-blindness of these downward spirals. A thirty-second attack was more exhausting than a seventy-minute show. Once I recovered, I'd look for something to feel good about. *She's smiling. Wasn't she at the 400 Bar show?*

As our reputation grew, so did the pressure. Dave booked us a short midwestern tour. We got in the van with our engineer, Brad Kern, and drove south. I was the oldest in the van but by far the least experienced. Dan, John, and Brad had learned the routine of the road through their years of touring, a routine that reflected the utter lack of privacy that the road inflicts. After our first hour of driving, we stopped for lunch at a McDonald's near the Iowa border. I was last in line, and when I brought my tray into the dining area, I was surprised to see Dan, John, and Brad sitting at three separate tables, eating in silence. I sat at a fourth table, watching the three others and wondering what other alienating customs awaited my acquaintance.

We left behind the flannel-shirted Minneapolitans and played in new cities for new crowds: the beer-soaked screamers at the Hurricane in Kansas City, the frat boys in Lawrence, the aloofly glamorous at Lounge Ax in Chicago, and the bashful kids at Shank Hall in Milwaukee. The entirety of each day on the road was spent with my three travel companions, cooped up in the van, in dressing rooms, in coffee shops, and in motel rooms. It was hard to say which agitated me more, Dan's ceaseless journal scribbling, shuffling of CDs in and out of his portable disc player, and vigorous page turning in the back seat; the wisps of smoke from John's cigarettes and his custom of propping up his leg and blocking Brad's driver's-seat view of the passenger-side mirror; or Brad's cursing of other drivers on the road. Though desperately lonely, I learned to avoid incursions into anyone else's space, even as I wondered how long I could endure my feelings of alienation. At a Milwaukee restaurant, I sat across from Dan as he read a book and slurped his soup.

"Dan, do you find the road to be an emotionally cold place?"

"Yes."

"What do you do about that?"

Without lifting his eyes from the page, he spoke. "Eventually, you'll grow to enjoy that coldness and learn to crave it."

Crave it? Until touring with Dan and John, I had spent little time in rock clubs. These dark caverns of stale beer and cigarette smoke were now home to my afternoon routine of loading equipment from the van to the stage and setting up my drums. The club staff and house techs, covered in gothic tattoos and 666 shirts, blasted frighteningly aggressive rock over the house sound system while I assembled my kit, insecurity furrowing in my brow. Dan and John were familiar faces to the club employees. For now I was known as "new guy," a moniker given to me by Conrad Sverkerson, the legendary stage manager at First Avenue.

The settings I found myself in gave little comfort to my strained nerves. The typical dressing room was a corner of the cracked concrete floor of the club's basement, where a ripped-up couch with at least one broken leg sat surrounded by empty beer kegs and crumbling plaster walls covered with scatological poetry and Magic Marker penis art. At the Hurricane, I hung my bags from the pipes to keep the roaches out. John cautioned me that this very practice had ruptured a ceiling pipe at the Seventh Street Entry, covering the musicians with shit and piss. The house managers told stories, like one about the singer of some band who "shoved one of the microphones up his butt last week." *And which mike was that?* I was embarrassed by my sensitivity to the crudeness of it all. I felt like one of the children in the singing Family von Trapp. At thirty-two, I imagined I was the oldest tenderfoot in the history of rock and roll.

I skipped dinner before shows. My nerves had more than they could handle. Down in the dressing rooms, I would hear the rumble of the gathering crowd on the floor above us as Dan and John slipped into their clothes—big-cuffed shirts, droopy slacks, and sneakers—and I rummaged through my suitcase for my hopelessly square attire—fitted jeans, lace-up shoes, and shirts that Dan said made me "look like a doctor." As we took the stage, the fans, many of them drunk, pressed to the front, fighting for a spot at the feet of their idols: Dan—with his wiry frame, handsome Norwegian features, and mop of ash-brown hair—and John—six-four and big-boned, with a hood of thick dark hair, a broad face, and sly eyes that, depending on the light, would shift from hazel to steel gray. I got a few curious looks and wondered if anyone could detect the fear leaking out of my smile.

Even in these small clubs, the energy created by both band and crowd was unnerving. The fans whooped and pumped their fists, and I was ashamed to see how very much at home they were in a setting that I found so overwhelming. Once we got rocking, the speakers on stage were deafening. Earplugs were absolutely required, especially on the drums. The stage volume and the stares of the crowd produced more fear, and I responded by clenching my sticks and hitting too hard. Dan and John would turn around and shout, "I CAN'T TAKE THE CYMBALS," but drowning in a sea of noise, all I'd hear was "I C**T *AK* **E ***BAL*!"

After the shows, I'd feel grateful for having made it through yet another night without throwing up or passing out. As Dan and John were mobbed by fans, I'd calculate how many times I could walk through the crowd in search of flattery without looking like a guy walking through the crowd in search of flattery. I'd take a few laps with minimal results. No need for the unlisted number.

On the road between cities, Dan and John gave updates on their phone calls with label people. There was a buzz on our tape. Soon the suits would come to see us perform. They had the power to change our lives. That meant I had the power to fuck things up if I had a meltdown on the drums. *I guess now is not the time to ask Dan or John if they've ever had panic attacks on stage.* At one point, my traveling companions mused about another Minneapolis band that wouldn't travel because the drummer was petrified of the road. "Scared of the road? Those guys are so fragile!" I kept silent.

The long drives were a chance to reflect upon the beginnings of my rock-and-roll dreams, which stretched all the way back to junior high school. I would step off the school bus in front of my house in Champaign, Illinois, carrying my cello and schoolbooks under my left arm and lugging my tuba and lunch bag with my right. I was grateful to be home from school, where even girls shoved me around. I'd set down my books and instruments and run upstairs to the room above our garage, where my drum set, a stereo, and some headphones waited inside a large closet. I had played drums since the fifth grade, when I bought a set for $25 from a kid who rode my school bus. I'd spend the rest of the afternoon drumming along to my collection of records and songs that I'd taped off the radio. I could spend the whole afternoon playing the same song again and again. The euphoria of a great pop song—"Day After Day" by Badfinger, perhaps—was unavailable anywhere else, and it inspired visions of me on large stages, playing drums for a famous band. An afternoon under the spell of that euphoria was sweetly sickening, as if I had run upstairs to hyperventilate out of a bag of lilac blossoms. Adrenaline seized control of me, and the dizzy high would follow me into the night, making it impossible to focus on schoolwork.

My mother, who had a Ph.D. in history, and my father, an experimental solid-state physicist and professor at the University of Illinois, supported my wide-ranging musical pursuits as well as the musical and artistic endeavors of my siblings. I took drum lessons from various teachers, though the best lessons, as I found, were informal affairs—such as my very first drum lesson, when my brother Bill drove me to the house of his friend Tom, who showed me the basics of the drum set. "Usually, you kick the bass drum whenever you crash a cymbal. It sounds better that way."

I dreamed of playing in a real band, but as long as I was confined to a drum set in a closet above our garage, my euphoria was an oversupply of hormones looking for a real-life object of affection. I found that object in Instant Kool, a black funk band in which my friend Gary Slates played saxophone. I first saw them play at a school assembly—nine musicians dressed in reflective polyester shirts, flared slacks, platform shoes, and wide-brimmed hats. As the drummer laid down his funky groove, the other eight musicians stepped from side to side with the beat, bending down and swooping their instruments over the floor. The singer stood center-stage, defiant in his dark glasses and applejack hat cocked to the side, grabbing the mike to sing and then pulling back and grinning between lines. The horn section punched out their parts, lifting the bells of their horns above their heads. As the bleachers shook beneath me, I sat with my elbows propped on my knees, holding my chin in my hands, light-headed from the melting desperation of love at first sight.

Two years later, Instant Kool fired their old drummer and Gary asked me to audition. Largely on account of having my own drum set, I got the job. Within a matter of weeks, I became one of the coolest kids in my high school. The white drummer for a black funk band was a unique role, and with it came the undeserved designation of badass. I walked the halls in my new platform shoes, slacks, shiny polyester shirts in loud colorful patterns ("Hollywoods"), and large-brimmed hats. Few dared to criticize my new wardrobe. After school, the kids who rode my school bus back to the subdivisions on the south side of town saw me ride off with my bandmates toward the north end in Electra 225s and Pontiacs outfitted with gangster whitewalls, curb finders, and zodiac stickers. Less than a year after I had last been pushed around with my cello and tuba—both of which I abandoned—I signed autographs for friends in the school cafeteria.

Even my social rebirth, however, could not compare to the thrill of playing shows—at bars, frat parties, and weddings in Springfield, Bloomington, and Peoria; at a VFW in Oskaloosa, Iowa; and best of all, in front of my friends at school dances—literally shaking rooms full of people across the floor with my drumming. It didn't take long for me to realize that this was what I wanted to do with my life. I wanted to live inside the excitement of performing, to rock people with my drumming, to shine at the center of their attention, to make records, to write hit songs and become the object of worldwide euphoria.

But now, as I rode in the van with Dan, John, and Brad, I wondered if I would ever surpass those high school memories. Did I have the emotional reserves to endure what looked to be a long and alienating journey? My musical pursuits since high school now looked like a stroll through the shelter of a naive daydream. I mulled over the tragic news—recently relayed by my mother— that Gary had drowned in a lake outside of our hometown. My career was accelerating toward something that felt overwhelming—the world of label executives, managers, record deals, MTV, huge crowds, nationwide tours—and I was terrified.

The upper Midwest was flooded by rains that had joined the Missouri and Mississippi Rivers twenty miles north of their normal meeting point. Dan and John, and even Brad, were anxious for things to go even faster, but as I looked out the van windows at the flooded fields, I wondered if my lifelong dream of being a rock star had been a terrible mistake. I put in panicked long-distance calls to friends. I woke up my bandmates in motel rooms as I screamed my way out of nightmares. When we returned to Minneapolis to play an opening slot for Chris Isaak at the State Theater, I had to calm myself down the day before the show by walking the three-mile loop around Lake of the Isles while chewing up half a pack of Rolaids.

Before long I was sobbing in front of a therapist, scared that either I would give up on the dream I had pursued for all those years, or that the dream would devour me.

SEVEN RECORDS FOR A PENNY

entered into my first contract with a record company at the age of thirteen, when I signed up for the Columbia House Record Club. Their ad, which showed pictures of popular albums, ran something like this: "Send us a penny, and we'll send you seven of the records shown here. Then you buy seven more over the next two years."

I filled out the forms, dropped a penny in the envelope, and mailed it. Soon, I received a flat package containing the seven LPs I had ordered: Barry White, Carly Simon, Gladys Knight and the Pips, Jim Croce, Edgar Winter, and the Love Unlimited Orchestra. Along with the records came a note reminding me that I had agreed to purchase seven additional records at full price. *Oops.*

Over the next few months, I received a series of notices from Columbia House promoting the featured record of the month, some piece of crap they were trying to unload.

> If you want this record, DO NOTHING. We'll send it to you automatically. If you'd like a different record or no record at all, check the appropriate box and return this form.

Somewhere between playing my drums and watching reruns of *Hogan's Heroes*, I forgot to send those notices back with the "No, I don't want the record of the month" box checked. Packages of unwanted LPs began to pile up, and soon my debt to the record club exceeded twenty dollars.

Columbia House sent payment-due reminders and finally a threatening collection notice. I appealed to my mother for help. She wrote a long letter, scolding Columbia for having entered into contracts with minors and declaring their agreement with me void. She concluded with the words "And in the future, conduct yourselves more appropriately!" I thus cut short my obligations and scammed ten records for one cent.

After that episode, I would go on to hear more sinister tales of the music business: record execs hyping musicians on their future ("Fasten your seat belt and get ready for the fucking ride!"), bands having their records taken away ("The label locked the record in a vault and wouldn't release it, sell it back to the band, or let the band out of the deal"), fraud, embezzlement, extortion, mob associations, the Witness Protection Program, and cocaine, cocaine, cocaine. "He had a mirror with a map of the United States on it. I'd say, 'Okay, you snort a line from San Francisco to Denver,' then he'd tell me to snort one from Denver to Kansas City. We'd fucking snort coast to coast!"

These images—people with powdery noses slamming doors, throwing chairs, and screaming into phones—had dominated my visions of the music business for years. No wonder I had stayed in my basement. Now Dan and John were going to lead me into this world, and I would see for myself who and what was waiting there.

Dan and John had made contact with people from a number of labels: Epic, Elektra, Capitol, Interscope, Geffen, MCA, Virgin, Arista, Zoo, and Atlantic. I was learning to keep track of these entities, the names of our contacts at each label, the personalities who ran the companies, and the sprawling structures of the media conglomerates that owned them. And now it was time to start meeting with and playing for executives from these various companies, the A&R people.

An A&R person is a talent scout who signs bands to record deals. (A&R stands for artist and repertoire.) I knew as much, but never in my life had I actually met one. The picture of the quintessential A&R person is easy to sketch: a middle-aged man trying to recapture his youth with a ponytail that sticks out of his baseball cap and hangs down over his untucked shirt. At rock clubs he makes cell-phone calls as he leans on the bar and sips the beer he just charged to his American Express card. His most ardent hope is to persuade the band he's come to see perform that, unlike the nasty people who run the music business, he's cool. Thus, he takes the band out for dinner, makes conversation about the hip music of the day, buys the band members some records and maybe some clothes, and might even get them high, if that's their MO.

Dan and John knew this routine, having met with and played for numerous A&R people back when Trip Shakespeare was in the hunt for a label. I met my first A&R person in Chicago when a young guy from Warner Brothers flew out from Los Angeles to see us perform.

Warner Brothers, I learned, was a huge label with a long list of artists, including Madonna, the Red Hot Chili Peppers, R.E.M., and Green Day. This impressive roster was both a plus and a minus from the perspective of an unsigned band. Warner Brothers clearly had muscle by virtue of its stable of artists, but with so many stars absorbing the attention of the executives, a new band might easily be ignored.

We swung by Warner Guy's hotel to pick him up for dinner. He shuffled out to the sidewalk, nodded toward the van with his floppy head of hair and slacker's detachment, and eased inside when we opened the door. "Hey, guys. So where's a good sushi place?" Up close, his age, mid-twenties, and his deference to Dan and John suggested that his clout at Warner was minimal. He was a junior A&R guy searching for a band to sign, perhaps his very first—something that would impress his bosses and give him credibility. Or maybe he had landed this job through his college-radio connections and was merely enjoying life on an expense account for as long as he could.

At dinner, he gabbed up a storm, dishing industry gossip and complaining about the major labels' unresponsiveness to cool new music—the "I'm on your side" approach. I nodded and laughed in concert with John and Dan. He ordered more food, more sake. I wondered if Warner Guy was picking up the tab. I nodded blankly at the mention of various bands, familiar to Dan and John but not to me. When the check came, I reached for my wallet, slowly.

"No, Jake, I'll pick this up."

An hour later, we took the stage at one of Chicago's biggest clubs, the Metro, to play an opening slot for the Catherine Wheel, a big English band, as hundreds of their fans and a handful of ours looked on. The room was dark, and so was the vibe. Our connection to the crowd was uncertain. Stage fright toyed with me, and at certain moments in our set, Dan and John turned around as if to ask me, "Everything all right back there?" After the show, Warner Guy moseyed backstage. "Yeah, I think you should keep playing shows, but . . . um . . . yeah." Translation: No way in hell can I sign you, but it was really fun to get out of L.A. for the weekend.

Another of Dan and John's A&R connections worked for Interscope, which everyone acknowledged was the hot new label. The band I associated most with Interscope was Nine Inch Nails, whose music I knew because every morning my new roommate, our soundman Brad, dropped his Nine Inch Nails CD into the stereo and Trent Reznor's demonic voice came shrieking out of the speakers.

GOD IS DEAD
AND NO ONE CARES
IF THERE IS A HELL
I'LL SEE YOU THERE

The walls shook, the plates and glasses rattled, and if our landlord was home upstairs, the phone rang. Brad, who wears socks embroidered with the word *Satan*, loved it, but Nine Inch Nails scared the shit out of me, and so did their label. Interscope was started by Ted Field, the heir to the Marshall Field's fortune, and famed music producer Jimmy Iovine. Nine Inch Nails was originally signed to another label, TVT Records, but Iovine was evidently so taken with Reznor's music that he paid handsomely to bring Nine Inch Nails over to Interscope. Though I could not deny the sonic and theatrical genius behind Nine Inch Nails, it was hard to imagine the kind of person who could listen to music of such rage and alienation and then light up and declare, "I must have this band!" Having digested this story, I knew Jimmy Iovine was not someone I wanted to meet.

Anna, our Interscope A&R contact, flew to Minneapolis and took us to lunch. She loved our tape, she told us, but given the relative lack of rage in our music, "I just don't think Jimmy's gonna go for it." If she lobbied hard, she said, she might get some kind of offer, but if Iovine didn't like us, what would be the point of that? I couldn't decide whether to be disappointed at being turned down by the hottest new label or to be relieved at the thought that I wouldn't have to face Jimmy Iovine.

Next up was Geffen, perhaps the dominant label of the day. Its roster—which included Guns N' Roses, Aerosmith, the Counting Crows, and Sonic Youth—was an impressive list of either massively successful or super-cool bands, especially in the case of its best-known band, Nirvana.

Nothing triggered my panicked feelings of inadequacy as much as Nirvana and Dave Grohl's monstrous drumming. Grohl pounded a permanent change into the radio; in the wake of Nirvana's success, the airwaves were crammed with bands whose drummers tried to play the larger-than-life fills that thundered around his drums. None, however, could match his huge sound and hypnotic groove. Grohl, eight years younger than me, set the impossible standard by which all drummers were now judged. To hear Nirvana blasting out of Brad's speakers at ten in the morning—it sounded like the soundtrack to a nightmare. And what was that nightmare?

Dan: You're quitting?

John: Now? Just as our record has debuted at number one and we're going on a nationwide tour of stadiums in front of millions of fans?

Me: I can't take it anymore, guys. I'm scared.

Jimmy Iovine: Scared? I'll show you scared. We just sank a million bucks into your band. If you don't get out there and rock, I'll make sure you—

Satan: NEVER WORK IN THIS BUSINESS AGAIN.

Dave Grohl: Yeah, you wuss.

Nirvana ruled, and so did their label. As Dan and John informed me, to have someone from Geffen walk your single into a radio station and say, "We're going all the way on this one"—that was as close to a guarantee of success as a new band could get. It was the kind of label that could rocket you to overnight fame, ready or not.

Jim, our Geffen contact, was pleasant but evasive in his meetings with us. He liked our tape and even heard commercial appeal in it, but he stopped short of talking about signing us. Perhaps he thought, like Anna at Interscope, that the culture at his label favored more aggressive music and that if he signed us, we would languish as a low priority. I could never tell how interested he was in us, or even whether he had actually flown out to see *us* or some other band playing later that night in the same city.

We met more A&R people with similar results. It was 1993, and everyone was looking for the next Nirvana, something loud and aggressive, exactly what we had set out not to be. A few months into our label-courting, Steve Ralbovsky, the senior vice president for A&R at Elektra, entered the picture. Elektra was a well-respected label with a diverse roster that included heavy-metal giant Metallica, but also the Breeders, Tracy Chapman, 10,000 Maniacs, and They Might Be Giants, and the melodic, song-based music of these artists suggested that Elektra was a place where we could fit in musically. It was also known as being an "artist-friendly label," meaning it embraced the philosophy of artist development, the process of nurturing a band's success over time instead of demanding instant results. Most important, Steve had signed Trip Shakespeare when he ran the A&R department at A&M. (In that role he had also signed Soundgarden, Blues Traveler, the Neville Brothers, Soul Asylum, and Matthew Sweet, among others.) He was therefore predisposed to liking the new music that Dan and John were making. He saw us play in Milwaukee and then a month later in Chicago. During their phone conversations, Dan sensed that Steve was warming to the band. "Keep sending tapes. I want to hear a few more songs that sound like singles."

Soon, another A&R person took notice, Hans Haedelt. Hans had just taken a job at MCA, having left Interscope. While at Interscope, Dan and John's contact, Anna, had given him our tape and Hans had loved it. Now that he had left the company, he sought Anna's blessing to pursue us, and Anna, knowing that her Interscope bosses would never go for our band, gladly gave it. He came to see us in Nashville, one of three people in the audience that night. Afterward, he was ecstatic. "Send me some more songs."

Dan ran up hundreds of dollars in phone calls with Steve and Hans. We recorded new songs and sent them off. Steve was pleased. Hans told his boss about us. Steve called to say he was coming to our upcoming show in Minneapolis. Hans called to say he, too, was coming and that he was bringing his boss.

The day of the show, Steve called Dan from the airport. "I'm getting in too late for dinner, but I need to see you guys before the show. Stop by my hotel." An hour before the show, the three of us rode in Dan's car to the Whitney Hotel, the highest-priced rooms in town. No sooner had we walked into Steve's room and said hello than he took on a businesslike tone and said, "I'm in." Dan and John nodded, and after a few seconds of chatting—during which I looked at Steve, Dan, and John, hoping to understand the precise meaning of the phrase "I'm in"—we shook his hand and left. As the door shut behind us, I was sure Steve had just said he was going to make us an offer, but just to make sure, I turned to John in the hallway and said, "So . . ."

John confirmed: "He's going to offer us a deal." I followed my bandmates out of the hotel, adopting their confident gait while wondering why we weren't celebrating.

An hour later, we took the stage at the Seventh Street Entry, a small room into which 250 fans had packed themselves. Steve lurked in the shadows. Hans and his boss, Ron Oberman, stood ten feet from the stage, unusually close for A&R people and thus revealing their strong interest. During high points in the set, a guitar solo or a loud chorus, I could see Ron's eyes light up as he leaned over to nudge Hans. The surrounding crowd of head-rocking twenty-year-olds further excited Ron, the only person with gray hair in the room. By the time we left the stage, he appeared to be possessed.

After the show, Steve ducked out. Hans brought Ron downstairs to the dressing room, and Ron raved: "You guys are fierce!" Hans invited us to breakfast the following morning, and ten hours later, we convened on the garden patio of the Whitney Hotel (apparently, the only Minneapolis hotel deluxe enough for the A&R world). As the waiters paraded in with croissants, eggs Benedict, espressos, and fresh-squeezed orange juice, Hans poured on the details of his postshow conversation with Ron. "He fucking freaked! He told me to sign you, whatever it takes." In just over twelve hours, we had been told of two impending offers from major labels.

I shook hands with Hans, again mimicking my bandmates' restraint. But as I sped home afterward with my windows rolled down, serenaded by the splash of tires through puddles of melting snow, the first gusts of spring air rushed into my hyperventilating lungs and the sputtering carburetor of my rusty Toyota. Need I say how vindicated I felt after all those years spent in the winter of day-job misery and basement anonymity? Need I say how thrilled I was to call my parents and tell them the news? Need I list the ex-girlfriends I wanted to call?

Now we faced a choice: Did we want to sign with Elektra or MCA? Neither of those labels was a powerhouse on the level of Geffen or Interscope. Elektra was respectable, and MCA . . .

In the sixties and seventies, MCA's roster included such colossal acts as The Who, Elton John, Steely Dan, and Tom Petty, but by the early nineties, it was the butt of an industry-wide joke: "What does M-C-A stand for? The Music Cemetery of America." Only its monstrous R&B successes (including Bobby Brown, Mary J. Blige, Bell Biv DeVoe, and Jodeci, a group subsequently re-formed as K-Ci and JoJo) and an impressive catalogue of older records kept MCA afloat. The rock department was the worst in the business. Geffen had juice with radio, having delivered radio program directors a long string of hits—Nirvana, Weezer, Hole, and Counting Crows. What bands did MCA have? The Best Kissers in the World.

Our industry connections were unanimous. As one of them said, "Run screaming from MCA!" To counter MCA's horrible reputation, Hans's boss, Ron Oberman, offered to fly us to L.A. for a meeting: "Come on out so you can see how we're turning things around."

A week later, we followed Ron and Hans through the mazelike

hallways of MCA's headquarters, my first visit to a record-company office. Music blasted through closed office doors and rock videos played on television sets. The walls were covered with posters and rare photos of famous artists in the MCA catalogue: Tom Petty, Howlin' Wolf, Curtis Mayfield, John Coltrane, and The Who. MCA had an impressive past.

Ron led us into the office of the radio promotion staff, and a gaggle of laughing twenty-somethings turned and smirked like children whose father had just walked in on a dirty joke. Ron gave a blushing smile and made introductions, calling Dan "Danny," oblivious to polite corrections from Dan and Hans. The radio folks shook our hands and welcomed us while continuing to chuckle under their breath. We walked around the corner to the publicity office, an empty room in which a lone woman sat behind a desk. Ron introduced us. "Hi. I just wanted you to meet Pleasure. They're a band from Minneapolis. John, the bass player, Jake, the drummer, and Danny, the singer and guitar player." We shook her hand, and then she shook Hans's hand and asked, "And what instrument do you play?" Ron informed her that Hans was on the A&R staff (Hans was based in New York), and she joined Ron in an embarrassed giggle. To recover from this gaffe, she invited us to help ourselves to current MCA CDs from the closet behind her desk. We looked inside but found nothing worth taking. Such was the pathetic state of MCA's roster.

Ron then took us to meet the person in charge of MCA's new multimedia division. "You gotta meet her. She's helping us get out in front of the whole Internet/computer thing." The three of us used computers a lot, so we were amazed when, in spite of our protests, she spent five minutes instructing us on how to use a computer mouse. "Notice how, when you move it across the pad, the little arrow on the screen moves too. Now see, if you press that button there, that's called 'clicking.' Good!"

The sleepy ineptitude that informed these encounters put me

at ease. These people were nothing to be scared of. Now, however, we were led to a far corner of the building, escorted by a secretary through a large door, and presented to a large, middle-aged man with dark hair swooped back over his head. It was Al Teller, the chairman of the MCA Music and Entertainment Group. As chairman, Teller presided over several different record labels, a worldwide distribution network, and a music-publishing company. Earlier in his career, he had been president of Columbia Records and CBS Records, and now he commanded MCA's music empire, and although his was the smallest of the six major music conglomerates, he wielded enormous power. He focused his dark eyes and flicked a smile through his well-groomed beard and mustache. How many careers has he launched? Crushed? I steeled myself to meet MCA's alpha wolf. *Try to look like a rock star. Whatever you do, don't smile.* I smiled.

Ron made the introductions. "Danny is the guitar player . . ." Al nodded at Ron and Hans, and they excused themselves, closing the thick door behind them. There we were, alone with Al Teller in his big quiet office, quiet enough for us to hear Al's lips smack as he spoke. "So I've heard your tape. Who writes the songs?"

Dan nodded calmly. "I do."

Teller nodded back. "Great stuff." Then he looked at John. "Are you the bass player?"

John, too, looked composed. "Yeah."

Teller leaned back. "I thought the bass playing was great, too." He glanced at me and then turned back to Dan. "So I think we have an exciting opportunity here." As he continued, he searched into our eyes. I looked around his office, taking note of the picture of him posing next to Meat Loaf. My anxiety soon gave rise to fidgeting, distraction, and involuntary deep breathing. I became preoccupied with Teller's lip-smacking. Was that real hair on his head? What if I had a freakout right here in his office?

He ran down his résumé. ". . . Graduated from business

school . . . out to Hollywood . . . and then over to CBS, where I ran the Columbia House Record Club." The Columbia House Record Club! I looked away as scenes from my irresponsible adolescence—the record-of-the-month notices, the pile of albums I never paid for or returned, my mother's angry letter extracting me from the agreement—flashed briefly in my mind.

Teller's secretary buzzed. "Lew on line one." Teller picked up the phone for a brief inaudible exchange. "Lew" was Lew Wasserman, the chairman and CEO of MCA, Inc., the man who ruled the greater MCA corporate world, including Universal Studios, and one of the most powerful men in Hollywood. Teller hung up and smiled. "That was my boss." He continued, pressing his fingers together under his beard, leaning back in his chair, and restating in polished tones the pitch we had been hearing from Hans and Ron. "MCA has a great history and is going to have a great future. What we need is an exciting new band—you perhaps," he said with the understated tone that bespeaks authority. "As I'm sure you know, our resources are considerable, and we're committed to using them."

Oh to hear such promises from the smacking powerful lips of Al Teller! Wouldn't it be great to be the band that turned things around—heroes of the label that sold millions of records? Wouldn't it be great to wave at the receptionist, stroll through the halls trailed by excited whispers of "Jake Slichter's here!," shake the trembling hands of some unsigned band stopping in for a tour of their own, wink at Al's secretary, walk into Teller's office, and see him put Lew on hold so he could stretch out his arms and say, "Jake! Baby! How was Bora Bora?"

He concluded, "So take a look around, enjoy your visit with us, and think about what I've said. I look forward to working together." He opened the door and shook our hands. I ducked back in to retrieve the soda can I had left on his table and smiled awkwardly on my way out.

That night, Hans took us out for sushi. (With the A&R folks it was always sushi, even in Nashville.) Al Teller's sales pitch aside, Hans knew that our tour of the MCA headquarters had reflected badly on his label. In the absence of his boss, he spoke freely, as was his style. "Look, I know MCA sucks, and I don't know how any of those people still have their jobs. But look at it this way: With all the shit bands on the label, you guys will stand out." We liked Hans, and not only for his honesty. In the 1980s, he had spent months on the road with the underground metal band Merciful Fate (and later with the solo act of lead singer King Diamond), serving as everything from back-line roadie and guitar tech to tour manager. These experiences distinguished him from his record-business peers. He also told us that underneath his clothes was $30,000 worth of tattoos. "But you can't see them unless you sign with MCA."

We flew back to Minneapolis wishing that the other people at MCA had Hans's enthusiasm and savvy. Two days later, some Curtis Mayfield and Steely Dan boxed sets showed up in my mailbox with a note from Ron: "Happy Birthday! Keep in touch."

Elektra's man, Steve Ralbovsky, remained unfazed by MCA's full-court press. He knew we didn't have many options. While Hans was desperate enough to lavish us with expensive meals and CDs, Steve kept a tighter fist. In fact, on a couple of occasions he had invited us out for breakfast and lunch and then excused himself before the check arrived. Steve also knew that we liked and trusted him, based on his history with Dan and John. And the bottom line was that Elektra was well respected and MCA stank. Why else would the all-powerful Al Teller have deigned to meet with little old us? Everyone we knew in the business agreed. Only under unfortunate circumstances would we sign with MCA.

Recording contracts are complex legal documents, and with an offer looming from Elektra and possibly another from MCA, we needed a lawyer to represent us. In his hundreds of hours on the phone, Dan had cultivated a relationship with Jonathan Ehrlich, a partner at the prestigious New York City entertainment firm headed by Allen Grubman. Ehrlich liked our tape, and his insight into the motivations of various A&R people and his uncanny ability to reduce a tangled mess of contingencies into clear propositions became indispensable. Dan asked him to represent us.

We had to find a manager, too, someone to respect our vision and navigate the maze of recording- and publishing-deal negotiations that lay in our immediate future, and the world that lay beyond: booking agents, producers, the frightening world of radio, and much more.

Dan and John's contacts directed us to several candidates, and Dan arranged meetings with them. The first of them was pleasant enough. During our dinner with him, he made repeated eye contact with me, and though by now I was less afraid of being devoured by the music business, I nevertheless appreciated his assuring smiles and soft-spoken manner. Later, however, we heard of his reputation as a practitioner of the "Record companies all like me because I take it easy on them" school of management.

We met a second candidate in Minneapolis. He was late for a plane and our meeting was a three-minute encounter in a hotel lobby. He kept looking at his watch, and I wondered about his leather pants, the patch of hair under his lower lip, and the fact that he wouldn't remove his sunglasses. The conversation didn't go far before he excused himself to catch his flight. "Cool. We should talk. I'll get back to you." After this meeting, Dan and John speculated that Mr. Leather Pants probably had an assistant who did most of the managing for him. Leather Pants himself might show up when it was time to sign contracts, pose for photos at an awards show, or troll for starlets at the Sundance Film Festival.

After Mssrs. Easygoing and Leather Pants, we met Jim Grant, who came off as smart, friendly, and refreshingly neurotic. He grasped the indie-rock musical tastes that lay beneath our pop-band sound. His conversational style, an endless series of nested statements, allowed him and us to cover vast ranges of subjects in one sitting. "I went to school at Michigan—sidebar: I used to promote concerts there, a lot of jazz, speaking of which, John, you're a big Mingus fan, aren't you?"

"Yeah."

"I thought so. Anyway, where were we?"

He had an eclectic musical taste to match ours and was intrigued by Dan's ideas about how to make records and present ourselves. Dan wanted to embrace the do-it-yourself methods of indie rock—the lo-fi experimentations of our crude basement recordings, for example—but did not want to eschew the high gloss of pop, in contrast to the Minneapolis indie-rock tradition, which frowned on anything aspiring to mass popularity. Dan's vision resonated with Jim, even as he laid out the possible difficulties we might face in pursuing it. He had managed Living Colour, a black hard-rock group that had fought through racism, music-industry doubt, and cultural stereotypes to become a big hit in the 1980s. With that experience, he knew the world of record labels, radio programmers, and MTV. He was thoroughly skeptical of the music business and rightly suspicious of my claims to having been a Chicago Bulls fan before the messianic arrival of Michael Jordan. In his face one could fathom the depth of Jim's passion for the music he loved, much of which was not commercially successful, his political beliefs, most of which had been voted down by the electorate, and an enduring devotion to the New York Knicks, whose basketball fortunes had suffered greatly at Michael Jordan's hand. Impressed by this loyalty, his tastes, and perhaps also by the fact that he was a conspiracy buff—the perfect mind-set for anyone who has to deal with record companies on a regular basis—we hired him.

Thus armed with an attorney and a manager, we began our

negotiations with Elektra. Dan would relay the developments of those negotiations after our evening rehearsals, when we went out for drinks. I leaned back in my chair, sipped merlot, and listened as Dan and John tutored me in the basics of record contracts.

Elektra would lend us money, called an *advance,* so we could pay for the recording costs of making an album. As I already knew, those costs would be high—studio rental could run $2,000 per day and recording could take months. Producers' and engineers' fees might add another $100,000, not to mention mastering, flights, hotels, rental cars—we could easily spend $250,000. If there were anything left over, we'd get to keep it, but it wouldn't amount to much.

In return, we would grant Elektra the exclusive rights to our recordings. As money from the sales of our records came in, we would be allotted a percentage of the proceeds, known as *points.* In a typical deal, the band gets thirteen or fourteen percentage points. We'd have to give a few of our own points (four perhaps) to the producer of our record (producers typically get a fee *and* points). Then we'd be down to ten points. Before calculating the value of those ten points, however, Elektra would subtract a large percentage of the gross sales to account for *free goods,* records given away for promotional and other purposes. Thus, the amount on which our 10 percent was calculated would be reduced by 20 to 25 percent. So we'd be down even further, perhaps 10 percent on 75 percent of the wholesale album revenue. If our CD was sold in stores for fifteen dollars, the band's share of the revenue might be something between fifty cents and a dollar per CD. Would we get to keep it? No! Elektra would add up all of the expenses of recording and promoting our album—rock videos, radio promotion, touring costs, and so on. The total of those costs, which could run into the millions, would be our *recoupable debt* to the record company. Our share of each CD sold would be swallowed up by that debt. In other words, we wouldn't see one penny in sales revenue until we sold so many CDs that our slim percentage earned enough to pay off the entire recoupable debt. When it came time to record and release future albums, any unpaid debt from our past albums would carry forward. In fact, even if we sold millions of records (in which case the size of our share would increase), we might never recoup. As one friend of mine joked, we'd be rock-and-roll sharecroppers.

How long would the deal last? It was mostly up to Elektra. If our first record flopped, we'd pray for the chance to make a second. On the other hand, if we made four records, sold millions of copies, and felt that Elektra was treating us like shit, too bad. A label can drop a band at any point, but the band is bound to the record company for the number of records specified in the contract, perhaps as many as six or seven. Recording and touring through seven records might take twenty years. We'd be lucky if our career lasted five.

If Elektra dropped us, there were clauses that would cover a variety of contingencies, including a "rerecording clause." Even after dropping us, Elektra would retain the rights to any recordings we had made for them and could prevent us from rerecording those songs for a period of several years. Sometimes bands get dropped before their album is released. If that happened to us, the specifics in our rerecording clause would be crucial, because we'd want to rerecord those unreleased songs for another label and an unfavorable rerecord clause would make that difficult. Jonathan reported that Elektra's opening offer included a five-year rerecording prohibition. Dan insisted he would never agree to let our songs be held hostage for that long, and his stubbornness on this point later proved to be prescient.

In addition to our negotiations with Elektra, Dan had also been talking to agents for music-publishing companies who were interested in buying a portion of the publishing royalties earned by the songs we wrote. These royalties are not only potentially lucrative, they are not subject to the band's recoupable debt to the record company. Here's how it would work: As mentioned earlier, our points on the record deal would earn us a small share of each CD sold, and that share would be swallowed by our huge recoupable debt to the label. But separate from those points and the recoupable debt, each CD sold would also yield a *mechanical royalty*, a few pennies for each song on the album. The record company would have to pay this money to the publisher (or publishers) of the songs, who would divide it with the songwriters. (We'll get to that part soon.) Additionally, every time one of our songs got played on the radio it would earn a *performance royalty*, also divided between writer and publisher. Performing-rights organizations such as BMI and ASCAP monitor airplay, collect fees from the radio stations, and pass them along to the writers and publishers. Under BMI's system, a song played on the radio earns from as little as six cents to upwards of fifty cents per performance, based on the song's success and the size of the station playing it. (ASCAP uses a different method to calculate the earnings, but the results are roughly equivalent.) We could also make money off our songs if they were put into films or played on television. The list went on.

As it stood, we (mainly Dan) were both the writers and publishers (because we had not assigned the copyrights) of our songs and would thus collect all of these various royalties, both the writer's half and the publisher's half. Various publishing companies, however, were offering to pay us a cash advance in return for half of the publisher's share. Under this arrangement, every dollar earned by a song would be divided thus: 50 cents would go to the writer as "songwriter," 25 additional cents would go to the writer as "publisher" (owner of the song's copyright), and the remaining 25 cents would go to whatever publishing company signed us to a copublishing deal. The publishing company would keep all of the various royalties (except for the writer's half of the performance royalties) until its advance to us had been paid back. Unlike record contracts, however, a band has a decent chance of recouping its publishing advance, and thus a publishing deal is a much more attractive arrangement than a record deal is.

Dan had suggested that the three band members split everything evenly, including songwriting royalties. This was a boldly generous move on his part, since he wrote the vast majority of the songs. He was surrendering two-thirds of his songwriting income in order to put the band on equal footing, provided that John and I accept and support his artistic leadership. John and I agreed to this arrangement, but not before I silently promised myself that I'd make it up to Dan by writing a hit.

I listened to all of this and was unable to keep the byzantine structure of the agreements clear in my mind. I did grasp the basic principle—that the record company gets to charge all of our costs against our points and that it would require sales of a huge number of records before our recoupable debt could be cleared. Until then, we'd get by on songwriting royalties. But the fantasy that had fueled my pursuit of rock stardom did not allow that we were like most other bands. The typical band might never reach the point of recoupment, but certainly we would. Right? And the tingling excitement of discussing our pending deal with Elektra Records while sipping merlot in Minneapolis's fashionably bohemian Loring Bar—this didn't facilitate sober assessments of our future, especially when other patrons stared at us and walked over to our table.

"Are you Dan and John from Trip Shakespeare?"

As the negotiations stretched over weeks, I would eat dinner with Dan and Diane and then lie on the carpet while Dan played me music by new bands I hadn't heard and told me more about Jonathan's conversations with Elektra. The final issues pertained to creative control. For example, if the label wanted us to work with a producer we didn't like, would we be able to veto the choice? If we hated the label's concept for album artwork, could we say no? Would we have a voice in choosing a single? As I lay on the floor and listened to Dan's reports, I felt myself becoming comfortable with all of this record-deal stuff. I liked Steve. And I liked the fact that Elektra, as far as I could tell, was not dominated by high-voltage personalities.

Finally, after weeks of negotiating, Jonathan called Dan to say that Elektra had submitted a *deal memo*, a document summarizing the crucial points. Dan called John, then called me at my day job to tell me the particulars of the deal and convey Jonathan's opinion that it was a strong offer for a new band.

That afternoon, we gathered at Dan's house to call Steve and accept Elektra's offer. I walked in the door and Dan said, "Did you hear about Kurt Cobain?" Hours earlier, the world had learned of his suicide. That news threw a shadow on things and retriggered my nightmarish visions of the high-pressure world of megastardom. It was a strange day to be accepting a record deal.

We called Steve, who was happy to be working with Dan and John again and eager to get rolling. Later, Dan called Hans, who was disappointed but understanding: "Thanks for the call. I can't wait to hear your record."

The finished contracts arrived weeks later, and the three of us sat around Dan's dining-room table signing our names. Page after page, section after section, the contracts addressed everything: our recordings, our likenesses, and so on. Our business manager, Dave, stood over us, directing me to the adhesive "sign here" stickers pointing to blank lines with the words "Jacob Slichter—Artist" underneath.

At the time, I didn't reflect upon the ironic similarities between the Columbia House Record Club and the record contracts waiting for my signature. The record club concept is known as a loss leader, meaning the customer is offered a bunch of goodies up front in order to lure him into a deal where he ends up paying for those goodies and more at the back end of the deal. In this case, the goodies were the advances we'd receive. In the end, however, our share of the seven records we might end up making for Elektra would be limited to whatever advances we received. Furthermore, an irate note from my mom would not get me out of the contract.

I signed and signed, following the "sign here" stickers and skipping over the pages and pages of legal text, which probably outlined all of the ways Elektra could screw us if they so desired. I told myself that our attorney, Jonathan, our manager, Jim, and my bandmates knew what they were doing. Also in the pile of contracts was a copublishing deal with Warner Chappell. The legalese was intimidating, but I knew that signing these contracts was a moment of great triumph.

And an even greater triumph came a few weeks later, when our publishing advance came through and I quit my day job.

Chapter III

A MILLION-DOLLAR ELECTRONIC PLAYGROUND

hadn't always been so musically backward. As the drummer for Instant Kool in high school, my taste in music lay on the cutting edge of funk, if one accounts for geography—Champaign, Illinois—and my age—sixteen. I may have been the first kid in my high school to buy the 45 for "Rigor Mortis" by Cameo, and I was among the first to own the Bootsy Collins album *Ahh…The Name Is Bootsy, Baby!* By the time I graduated from college, however, funk was in decline and my listening was at a dead end. Dan and other friends had spent their college years listening to the Clash, Echo and the Bunnymen, Joy Division, Gang of Four, and R.E.M. They tried to turn me on to these and similar bands, and while I recognized a certain vitality in this music, I could never identify with it. The smart lyrics and melodies could not atone for the frenetic and clunky rhythms, which offended my funk drummer's ears. It sounded as if this music was being played by people whose glasses were slipping off their noses.

By the mid-1980s, I was certifiably uncool, well behind the times. My clothes were an embarrassment—a stonewashed denim jacket and pointy shoes in the age of ratty flannel shirts and Doc Martens. Musically, I lagged even further behind. U2? I didn't buy any of their records until *The Joshua Tree*, seven years after most of my friends had worn out *Boy*. When I got into Bruce Springsteen, everyone else had moved on to the Smiths, the Replacements, and Sonic Youth.

I was largely ignorant of the music that inspired much of Dan and John's vision for our band. Dan gave me a mix tape of songs by R.E.M., My Bloody Valentine, the Flaming Lips, Teenage Fanclub, and others to bring me up to speed on the past five years of what was called "alternative rock." But a sixty-minute tape could not fill the gaping holes in my rock-and-roll literacy.

So, as I sat in my living room and leafed through a dozen faxes listing various producers and the records they had produced, the gaps in my musical knowledge remained a hindrance. *So this guy produced Killing Joke? I know I've heard of them. Aren't they kind of punky?*

It was time to make a record, and Steve, our A&R guy, and Jim, our manager, had sent us these discographies to inform our search for the right producer. In music, a producer functions much like a film director, overseeing both the technical and artistic aspects of a record's creation. Just as some film directors are known for their cinematic vision and others for eliciting great acting performances, some record producers are known for innovative recording techniques and others for capturing spirited singing and playing. We wanted both.

What I cared about most was each producer's personality, which could influence our record as much as anything. Some producers, for instance, are control freaks. A band we know worked with a producer who erected a tent over the mixing console—the center of the action in a studio—to keep the musicians away. A few weeks into the recording, he heard a mysterious problem with the bass sound, inaudible to everyone else. Figuring that the producer was an expert, with ears more sensitive than theirs, the band stood back as the producer halted the recording and spent days investigating this mysterious problem, testing the amplifiers, guitars, cables, microphones, compressors, every possibility. After a week of investigations, at a cost of $3,000 a day in studio time, he concluded that the problem lay in a faulty power line from the studio to the street. So, at the producer's insistence, the band packed up their gear and moved to another studio, unsure if the producer had lost his mind or was merely asserting his authority. ("You may not hear the problem, but I can, because I've got better ears. That's why my fee is so high.")

Other tales portrayed producers as outright monsters. A singer we know reported that his producer had yelled, "Take one is shit. Take two is shit. They're all shit. WHEN ARE YOU GONNA SING A FUCKING VOCAL?!" And then there are the devious ones, such as the producer of an unsigned band who sent the band members home, one by one, until he personally had replaced the performances of each band member with his own guitar playing, bass playing, and drumming. Only the original singing remained.

My biggest fear concerned the stories of producers bringing in outsiders to play the drum parts. This is a common industry practice. (Recall that before Ringo, there was Pete Best.) Producers are finicky about drummers, because, more than any other instrumental element, great drumming brings a song to life and bad drumming ruins it. A&R people sign bands based largely on singing and songwriting, but the issue of drumming is often ignored until the producer shows up to make a record. Then, if the drummer proves to be a bad chauffeur for the band—accelerating, braking, and swerving from side to side, making it impossible for the rest of the band to play and sing with conviction—the producer has a big problem.

Two bands from Minneapolis had already been through drummer firings in the studio, and in both instances, the producer had initiated the drummer's removal and replacement by a big-name studio pro. One drummer I know had to listen to his friends compliment the finished album—"You're drumming better than ever!"—when in fact he had barely played a note of it.

I spent a lot of time worrying about such a scenario. The threat of being fired resurrected high-school memories of my first days as the drummer for Instant Kool. I had stumbled through the audition, playing so badly that the singer refused to sing over my desecration of the groove. Amazingly, the musicians asked me to come to the next rehearsal, and another, and another. I was so bad that the band continued to audition other drummers *on my drums* as I watched from the sidelines. Each rehearsal, I wondered if that would be the night that they'd dump me for someone else.

After a few weeks, however, Instant Kool resigned itself to the fact that, as bad as I was, all other options were worse and they needed someone to play drums for their upcoming shows. Then they set out to make me into the drummer I had to be, warning that I had better improve quickly. I was in boot camp for funk drumming, a private with eight drill sergeants.

"Stop rushing!"

"Jacob! You're playing flat-footed on your bass drum. Lift your heel up and kick that motherfucker!"

"DAMN, Jacob, stop dragging!"

I took their direction, but only after months of hard practice did talk of my imminent firing cease. Eventually, I became one of the better musicians in the band.

Dan and John assured me that they loved my drumming and that if a producer tried to fire me, they'd fire the producer. But wouldn't such an episode linger in the memories of the band, Jim, Steve, and anyone who heard about it? Wouldn't I then be publicly marked as an impediment to the band's best chances? I found out which producers had reputations for firing drummers and subtly steered the conversation away from them.

Having scanned the discographies, Dan and John called Jim and Steve with their top picks.

"What about_____?"

"Too expensive."

"So then what about_____?"

"He only records bands that have already gone platinum."

"Fuck. Well, then let's get_____?"

"He's booked for the next six months."

We culled through the list of available people, narrowed it down, and Dan called our favorites to get a sense of their personalities and methods. If he felt good about the phone conversation, Jim and Steve arranged a face-to-face meeting between producer and band.

One of the finalists was a young producer who seemed expert at recording rich-sounding guitars, though his records lacked the spark of inspiration. Maybe it was the bands he worked with that lacked spark. He was coming to Minneapolis on other business, so Steve and Jim arranged for us to meet him for drinks. It was the first of several blind dates.

"I'm pretty easy to get along with," he told us. "I like everyone to have a good time. In fact, I'm kind of a practical joker." Dan's I-hate-practical-jokers sensor started to blink, unbeknownst to the young producer, who waded into further trouble. "I've been listening to your tape, and I've got some suggestions for lyric changes."

Dan took a sip of Scotch. "What changes did you have in mind?"

"Well, that line 'Fascinating new thing, you delight me'—I don't like the word *delight*. It sounds kind of . . . twee. What about saying 'You're *stunning*' or something like that?"

Had we been characters in a James Bond film, Dan would have set down his glass and pressed the button that opened the floor and dropped the young producer into a pool of hungry piranhas. With no such button at his disposal, Dan affected a smile. "*Stunning?* Well, let me think about that." John and I forced smiles, too. *No fucking way.*

We met with more producers, including some heavy hitters.

Even if the chemistry between band and producer seemed off, one could only be impressed by what these producers had to offer. Ed Stasium concluded our meeting with him by saying, "Well, I recorded 'Midnight Train to Georgia' by Gladys Knight and the Pips and 'I Wanna Be Sedated' by the Ramones. Not many guys can say that." *Damn straight.*

After two months of meetings and phone calls, we chose Paul Fox, a Los Angeles producer. His credits included *Oranges & Lemons* by XTC, *Our Time in Eden* by 10,000 Maniacs, and our favorite on the list, *Loose* by Victoria Williams, a record of inspired performances and inventive arrangements. I was especially won over by his easygoing vibe.

A few weeks later, we flew to L.A. to begin recording. We settled into our Hollywood hotel, a short walk from two record stores and a coffee shop where, an hour after our arrival, Dan asked a woman in dark glasses for directions to the nearest health-food store and discovered that he was talking to Jodie Foster. It was the first of many star sightings (we spotted Brad Pitt and Leonardo DiCaprio over the next two days) and a tantalizing reminder that in Los Angeles fame might be waiting around the corner.

The next morning, we began our production rehearsals in a windowless rehearsal room in North Hollywood. There we spent the next two weeks playing our songs over and over for Paul, as he made various suggestions concerning the arrangements. Such preproduction rehearsals allow the band and producer to address problems before the expensive studio clock—$1,000 a day and higher—begins to run. As I feared, the drum parts received a large share of the attention. "Play a fill in the same rhythm as the guitar and then switch over to the ride cymbal instead of the high hat."

I took direction, tried new things, mopped my sweaty face and hands, and suppressed the accompanying swells of paranoia.

"Jake, can you hit them any harder?" That was a direct challenge to my drummer's self-esteem. I pounded and smashed through our eight-hour rehearsals as the lactic acid built up in my arms and legs and my back began to stiffen. If during a break Paul, Dan, and John mused glowingly on the drumming of Dave Grohl or Led Zeppelin's John Bonham, I strapped on a smile and waited for my next chance to take out my revenge on the drums. After nightfall, we'd drive back over the hills and I'd collapse in my hotel room, too physically and psychically drained to explore the Los Angeles night.

After thirteen exhausting days of rehearsal and a badly needed day at the beach, we moved into American Studios, tucked into a canyon near the Malibu coast. It was a studio preferred by Paul and his engineer, Ed Thacker, both of whom had made several records there.

I was acquainted with recording studios and the general mechanics of recording: the control room, with its mixing console lined with faders, buttons, and switches; the racks of black boxes housing compressors, preamps, echo, and reverb effects; the patch bay of wires that routed audio signals from here to there; the mammoth tape deck with its large aluminum reels spooling a two-inch-wide ribbon of tape between them; the hundreds of indicator lights that blinked and the needles inside the VU meters that flipped up and fell back down with each blast of sound. These sights did not amaze me as they had when, as a teenager, I visited my first professional studio to record a demo tape of funk covers with Instant Kool. Still, it took me a few days to absorb the reality that this million-dollar electronic playground was at our disposal for weeks and maybe months.

Our first two days were entirely devoted to setting up the equipment, selecting from a variety of guitars, amplifiers, and drums, and choosing the right microphones and tweaking their placement. Paul had already deemed my drum set unacceptable and had rented a variety of vintage drums, no doubt the best drums I had ever played. One of the snare drums was said to be the very one used on Steppenwolf's hit "Magic Carpet Ride." And carefully positioned around my drums were microphones worth thousands of dollars mounted on a jungle gym of stands. Through my headphones I could hear Ed, who sat on the other side of the control-room glass and instructed me to keep hitting the drums as he adjusted the sound. It took hours of drum-smacking to get the sounds just right.

Smack. Smack. Smack. *I wonder how much these mikes cost.* Smack. Smack. Smack. *I wonder how much Paul's house cost.* Smack. Smack. Smack. *A two-bedroom in Laurel Canyon with a nice garden.* Smack. Smack. Smack. *Half a million bucks?* Smack. Smack. Smack. *Maybe we'll blow through our songs and be done really fast.* Smack. Smack. Smack. *Stone Temple Pilots made their record in two weeks.* Smack. Smack. *Paul said Joni Mitchell used to live on his street.* Smack. Smack. *The Beastie Boys live a few houses down from him.* Smack. Smack. Smack. Smack. *Hey, where did Ed go?*

"Jake, can you keep going, please?"

My mind continued to wander. Sometimes, looking through the control-room window, it appeared that Ed or Paul was telling Dan and John a joke, in which case I'd stop to rest my arm, only to see Ed lean forward and switch on the control-room mike. "Just keep hitting the snare until I tell you to stop."

Once the drums were dialed in, I lay on the control-room couch in a daze and listened as Ed tweaked guitar sounds, twiddling knobs on the mixing console and speaking into his mike. "Turn down the bridge pickup. Try driving the gain a little harder." Occasionally, Ed would silence everyone as he stared at the speakers in horror. "Shhhh. What's that?"

"What's what?"

"That!"

"I don't hear anything."

"That! That fucking buzz. What the hell is it?"

I leaned closer to the speakers and heard the faintest buzz imaginable. The assistant engineer sprinted from room to room checking the connections, replacing cables, and slamming the heel of his hand on various pieces of electronics until the buzz disappeared. Then Ed's scowl eased back into a smile, as if he had just been cured of a migraine. Such drama reminded me that my studio ears and experience lagged far behind everyone else's, including those of the assistant engineer, whose band had recorded an album in that very studio months earlier.

On the third day, we got down to recording. We chose "Falling," an easygoing song with a simple arrangement that was not on the list of potential singles. The band could get off on the right foot, and Ed could have more time to dial in the sounds before we took on the marquee songs. Paul, seated in the control room next to Ed, leaned over the control-room mike. "Okay, let's try one," to which Ed added, "Rolling."

To my great relief, we got through the first take just fine. Paul was pleased, and over the course of the next hour, we played three more takes, pausing between to allow Ed and his assistant to make more adjustments. I focused on perfect execution of the parts that I had rehearsed, though Dan soon urged me to loosen up. As he later observed, many musicians view the mission of recording an album as documenting perfect versions of the songs, failing to recognize that many classic recordings are full of accidents, improvisations, and even mistakes, all of which give the recording character. I nodded along with Dan's advice, though inwardly I remained determined to play the parts perfectly, not wanting my flaws to be the character marks on our album.

We proceeded at an easy work pace—several takes of a song followed by a walk to the control room to assess what we had done. I listened to the drumming, the beginning and end of my attention. Everyone else, however, listened to the performance of the entire band. Alas, the drum takes with the fewest mistakes were often attached to the blandest performances by the band at large. (As I later learned, this was no coincidence; the blandness of my focus on avoiding mistakes stiffened everyone else's playing.) When we identified a standout take of the song, we'd listen several times in a row. I'd lie on the couch in the back of the control room, looking up at the ceiling and zoning out in a state of physical, mental, and psychic fatigue. Was it good? Great? Magical? Listening over and over dulled my senses in the same way that repeating the word *surgeon* a hundred times leaves one wondering if it's a real word.

"Jake, what do you think?"

"Yes. I agree."

Often, the solution to producing the best take was for Paul to take out a razor blade and slash the tape, splicing together the beginning of take one, the middle of take five, and the end of take two. As violent as this procedure looked, I couldn't hear the edits. Still, I felt better when a single take sufficed. It's a drummer's point of pride for the drum take to shine from beginning to end, and since the attention in this early phase of tracking was focused mainly on the drum tracks, which are crucial to the foundation of each song and thus must be as good as possible before other elements are added, I assumed that the various pluses and minuses of each take reflected on my inconsistency. Soon I got over it and adapted to the routine: takes, edits, and on to the next song and a new drum sound.

Smack. Smack. Smack. *When are we gonna use that "Magic Carpet Ride" snare drum?* Smack. Smack. Smack. *Whatever we use it on, I hope it's a single.* Smack. Smack. Smack. *That'd be cool.* Smack. Smack. Smack. *I wonder what time Jodie Foster goes for coffee.*

"Keep hitting, please."

We continued to record the basic instrumental tracks, averaging a song every day and a half. The reward for finishing a basic was lying on the control-room couch and listening to the sound of the band as rendered through a million dollars of studio gear. At the end of each day, Ed made rough mixes for us to listen to in our rental car. We'd drive back to the hotel with the car stereo cranked, rocking out to what we had just recorded. These nighttime rides down the freeway, listening to rough mixes of our evolving album, were positively dreamy.

As the weeks rolled by, I accepted the reality that I had never been in danger of being fired. My drum performances, in fact, were well received though never extolled in the superlative terms reserved for Grohl, Bonham, or other legends. With the drumming finished, I overdubbed some piano and keyboard parts, and shook a few tambourines and shakers. Then I sat next to the recording console as Ed recorded Dan and John, and I discovered that in the fog of my anxieties, I had missed the fact that my bandmates were frustrated by the direction of the record. Paul and Ed preferred a naturalistic approach to recording: capture everything at once, as the band might play it at a show, with few overdubs and little or no processing. Dan and John, however, had envisioned a studio album full of overdubs and effects wizardry. Dan pointed around the studio at various audio processors—"Come on, let's use that to distort the bass!"—only to be rebuffed by Paul—"But if we distort it now, we can't change our minds later." The substance and language of these debates were beyond me. I knew what a 57 was (a microphone) but had no idea what an 1176 was (a compressor). If someone invoked the likely effects of radio broadcast compression on the bass sound, who was I to comment? Fearing that my uninformed attempts to support my bandmates would only undercut their positions, I kept silent. The first month of recording had been psychologically fatiguing enough. Better to watch instead of engage in these clashes. In fact, part of me found them a welcome diversion; if there was tension in the studio, at least it didn't revolve around me.

As the recording of guitars and then vocals proceeded, I retreated to the control-room couch, to the pinball machine in the hallway, and then to the television lounge. With the drumming behind me and feeling incapable of adding meaningful commentary to the rest of the process, I grew bored. If the day's agenda included no tambourine parts to play or background vocals for me to sing, I snagged the keys to the rental car and escaped for long drives through the canyons, up and down to the coast, and looping back over the freeways to the studio, rewinding the rough mixes over and over. Back at the hotel, I took nightly walks to the record stores and bookstores on Sunset Boulevard, soon learning every twist and turn. I followed the sidewalk underneath a billboard of a giant Marlboro man and past a Calvin Klein billboard in which, as Dan had pointed out, the pose of a female model combined with the "CK" logo to suggest the word *fuck*. Farther along were overpriced restaurants peopled by a clientele of aspiring models and the international leisure class. Down the hill to my left was the city, stretched across the horizon in a giant grid of lights. Up to my right was a dark hillside of trees—the south side of Laurel Canyon—from which a warm intoxicating breeze would descend on me with a familiar rush, lulling me with thoughts of living on that hill and assurances that what I wanted from the band's success was better than the scenes of corruption I had walked past. Then I rounded the bend and saw Tower Records and the giant reproductions of top-selling album covers painted on its outside wall.

After six weeks of recording, we relocated to A&M Studios in Hollywood for the mixing sessions. The building contained a number of separate studios. Each morning we walked by the room in which Melissa Etheridge was recording her new album, past a cigarette machine said to have been brought in at Joni Mitchell's request when she recorded her masterpiece *Blue*, around the corner past the recording hall where a gallery of stars once recorded "We Are the World," and down the back hall to our mix studio, where the Carpenters once recorded a long string of hits.

The general idea of mixing is to combine the many discrete tracks that have been recorded—bass, guitar, vocal, snare drum, bass drum, and so on—into a properly balanced stereo recording. That right balance can prove elusive, and the bulk of the time is spent agonizing over tweaks that are so minute, most nonmusicians would be unable to hear their effect. Once again, I was the least opinionated person in the room. Ed would nudge a fader on the mixing console, or dial the controls on some black box, and turn to ask, "What do you think of *that?*" Dan and John responded with resolve. Not to respond felt embarrassing, but I was reluctant to speak up unless I really discerned the differences made by Ed's fiddling, for sometimes I wondered if he was pulling the old engineer's trick of flicking switches that make no effect at all, a ruse designed to elicit a response from a meddling musician—"Yeah, that's better"—when nothing has changed, thus enabling the engineer to expose the bothersome musician as an unreliable listener.

I didn't need ears, however, to realize that these were the final versions of the songs, and therefore this was my last chance to push myself into the spotlight. I wanted the drums nice and loud, but asking the mix engineer to turn up your instrument is one of the oldest clichés of the rock musician. Not only that, by asking that your instrument be turned up, you invite the others in the band to make similar requests. The resulting tit-for-tat inching up of all tracks is known as "fader creep." Instead, I learned to take an oblique approach. I'd begin by scowling.

"Jake, what's up?"

"Something about the chorus . . ."

"What about it?"

"I don't know, we need to announce those choruses with a little more oomph."

"You mean 'Here comes the chorus'—that kind of thing?"

"Yeah."

"Hmm. Let's hear it again." At which point Ed would rewind and roll the tape.

After listening, if the plan worked right, someone other than me would say, "You know what? I think we have to push up that drum fill. That's the thing that really says 'Chorus.'"

At which point I could tilt my head—"Hmm. You think?"— thus setting the trap.

"Yes, turn up the drum fill." Checkmate.

Entire instrumental parts were eliminated, so another tug-of-war determined which parts would stay and which had to go. Should I admit that the twelve-string guitar part that I had proposed now be scrapped because it competed for frequencies better occupied by a six-string? Should I fight to preserve the weird helicopter sound that I came up with? After all, I let John keep his synth idea.

Similarly, we had finished fourteen songs for the album and wanted to cut that number to twelve. Dan had written most of the songs on his own, but I had cowriting credit on several of them. Being a songwriter continued to be my highest aspiration. To outsiders, the songwriter is always more interesting than the drummer. Therefore, it was quite a loss for me to see "Wishing Well," the song to which I had made my most significant songwriting contributions, dropped from the album. As I had feared since recording it, the tempo was too slow; the performance, too brittle.

One by one the mixes were finished, and each completed mix yielded another cassette, audio fuel for another two hours of driving around Los Angeles. After fourteen days of mixing, we were done. Handshakes and farewell hugs to Paul and Ed, and we were off to our hotel to pack our bags. Dan and I shared a room, and after packing we stretched out and listened to a tape of our newly mixed album. After the last chord of the final song died, Dan mused, "What if it's a big hit?" Was there any question? *It's gonna be a smash.*

Chapter IV

THE CORPORATE JUNGLE

I remember watching a television documentary about lions. One factoid stood out: When a new adult male takes over a territory, he kills all of the existing cubs so he can sire his own. The accompanying footage was gruesome. A few flickers of moral outrage gathered into a full-blown wince as I slowed the spooning of ice cream into my mouth and witnessed the cubs' demise. Only years later did I discover the relevance of this animal behavior to my life as a rock drummer: Simply replace the word *lion* with *record company president.*

Let us rewind the tape to the first month of our recording sessions. As we were busy in the studio, an executive war broke out at Time Warner, the media conglomerate that owned the Warner Music Group, which in turn owned Elektra. One of the casualties of that war was Elektra's president, Bob Krasnow, who left as a new president strode through the door. Run, lion cubs, run!

Jim, our manager, called us with the news as we were in the studio. Rumor had it that Elektra's new president, Sylvia Rhone, was likely to fire many of the current executives and replace them with people of her own choosing. Our A&R man, Steve, was in danger of losing his job. What would we do if he got the ax? We didn't have to wonder long. Within the first weeks of Sylvia Rhone's reign, Steve was fired. So were most of the coworkers

Steve had introduced to us a few months earlier. By now we had returned to Minneapolis, only half of our album had been recorded, and the rest of the recording and all of the mixing was put on indefinite hold.

Elektra, which had always felt so safe to me, was now a dangerous environment for a new band, especially one with an unfinished record. What would happen to us? We might be assigned to a new A&R person, someone with little investment in our success, since if we did succeed, the new A&R person could not be credited for signing us. When we returned to the studio to continue recording, the new A&R person would likely have little to contribute, since Steve had been the one to suggest and approve of the producer choice. And once completed and released, if our record did poorly, our new A&R person would be quick to say, "Don't blame me for this lousy band left over from the old regime."

We might be dropped. What would happen then? The regime change occurred after we had already recorded six songs with Paul, so Elektra now owned those six recordings. The rerecording clause in our contract prohibited us from making new recordings of those songs until a period of eighteen months had elapsed, so we faced the prospect of waiting a year and a half before rerecording those six songs again, a depressing thought, especially since most of the potential singles were in that batch.

I had heard of worse scenarios: the label burying a record and not letting the band out of the contract. Why would a record company do such a thing? Because, if the band finds a new label and the record becomes a hit, the executives at the old label look stupid for having released the band from its contract. Thus, bands have been kept under contract while their tapes gathered dust in the darkness of the tape vaults, never to be heard.

Jim got on the phone and persuaded Sylvia Rhone, Elektra's new president, to meet with him to discuss the band's future. She understood our plight—we were orphans at the label—but of course she had her own dilemma to consider. "If your band is an asset to Elektra," she told Jim, "I want to keep it on my label." What, after all, would she tell her bosses at Time Warner if she released us from our contract and we became the next Nirvana?

So she and Jim made arrangements for one of her new A&R people to see us perform and assess our potential value to Elektra. If this new A&R guy thought we were nothing special, Sylvia would let us go. If new A&R guy thought we were great, we'd be stuck at Elektra.

Jim made arrangements for new A&R guy to see us play in Kansas City. We now faced a dilemma, put succinctly in a question from our soundman, Brad, as we drove down Interstate 35 from Minneapolis. "So, guys, should I turn up the 'suck' knob on the mixing board tonight?" This has to be one of the few cases ever where a band wanted to turn off an A&R person. Should we play a bad show? No. Should we load up the set with slow songs and covers? No. What would we do? New A&R guy was in a tough spot, too, for he knew we wanted out of our contract, but he had to do his job.

Just before we took the stage, new A&R guy tapped Dan on the shoulder and introduced himself. "Look, I'm feeling sick. I'm not sure if I'll be able to see much of the show." He thus provided an artful solution to both sides of the dilemma; by leaving after one or two songs, he let himself and us off the hook. We could have a great show without fearing that we had impressed him, and he could truthfully report to his bosses that he left the show with no great love for the band. A few days later, Sylvia Rhone told Jim, "I don't want to hang you up on this," and agreed to let us go. Jonathan, our attorney, negotiated a deal wherein Elektra agreed to sell our recordings to another label for the recording costs incurred thus far and a percentage of the album sales.

Jim had meanwhile been looking around for interested labels, but ultimately, there was only one choice. Good-bye Elektra, hello Music Cemetery of America.

Hans was elated. He was desperate for a good band to sign, and he had kept in touch even after we had signed with Elektra, going so far as to fly to Minneapolis to see us play. MCA's president, Richard Palmese, gave quick approval to offer a deal. Jonathan, our attorney, having finished the termination agreement with Elektra, got on the phone with MCA's legal department and brokered the transfer of the existing recordings from Elektra to MCA. Thus, we were free to use the recordings we had already made. Because the Elektra shakeup happened halfway through the recording of our album, we had endured five months of contractual limbo. Now that we had a new contract, Jim scheduled our return to the studio with Paul, who had been busy producing other bands.

Our business manager, Dave, drove us to the Minneapolis airport. He had the final versions of the MCA contracts with him, and Dan, John, and I signed them in the back seat. Dave weaved his way through traffic and once again directed us to the "sign here" stickers, handing us our plane tickets, our per diems for the next month, and our hotel and rental-car information.

So we returned to Los Angeles and finished the record. Hans flew out for the mixes, and as he had once promised, showed us the $30,000 worth of dazzling tattoos that covered his torso and legs. After a few days of listening on the control-room couch, he pulled me aside. "Congratulations, Jake, your drumming has finally arrived."

Then, when we were nearly finished with the record, Jim reported that Jonathan had done a trademark search on the name Pleasure and found that it was already registered to another band. After calling the attorneys representing that band and learning that they were unwilling to part with the rights to the name, he called us to say that we had to name ourselves something else.

Dan had another word in his head, one coined by a fellow musician in Minneapolis, who once complained to Dan, "Why does all the music on the radio these days have to be this semisonic bullshit?" *Semisonic?* Dan liked that word and how it suggested something modern while remaining inscrutable. At his suggestion, we adopted it as our name, a fun choice although one that frequently defies apprehension.

"What's the name of your band?"

"Semisonic."

"Supersonic?"

Thus, we had begun recording our album as Elektra recording artists Pleasure and finished it as MCA recording artists Semisonic. We had been signed twice, dropped once, had changed our name, and our record wasn't even out yet. I was beginning to feel like an old pro. Then there was another corporate earthquake, this time at MCA. Seagram, the liquor manufacturer, bought Universal, MCA's parent company. More lions were on the loose. Resignations and firings cascaded down from the top of yet another corporate empire. The body count was high. Al Teller, gone. MCA president Richard Palmese, gone. Hans's boss, Ron, gone. And Hans? Hans kept his job. The new president of MCA Records, Jay Boberg, didn't know us, but Hans sent our finished record to Jay, and Jay liked what he heard. For the moment, we were safe.

To introduce ourselves to some of the new people at the label, we flew to MCA's New York offices to perform on acoustic instruments for a conference room full of executives, an awkward proposition. The idea of playing an acoustic guitar, a bass with a tiny amplifier, and a pair of bongos for a bunch of suits seated around a table sounded vaguely like having sex in front of one's parents.

We filed into a conference room with our instruments, and a few minutes later the executives trickled in and took their seats.

The last one closed the door, sealing the room with a high-powered claustrophobia and setting the band on edge. As Dan and John tuned up, I gave everyone a start when, for some unknown reason, I opened my bongo case and pretended to pull out a machine gun and fire it at the executives seated around the table. "PA-PA-PA-PA-PA-PA-POW!" This was met with a few nervous execulaughs. John and Dan chuckled under their breath—"Jesus fucking Christ, Jake!"—although it was unclear if their chuckles reflected horror at or edgy admiration of my stunt. Soon, Hans stepped forward and introduced us and the suits gave us a light helping of applause.

We started with the title song of our newly named album, *Great Divide*. Halfway through the first verse, Dan developed a prolific nosebleed. We played on as the blood streamed down his face and splattered onto his guitar. Because we and our music—especially when stripped down to acoustic instruments and Dan's boyish tenor—reeked of civility, the sight of dripping blood only enhanced the rock experience of the executives seated around the conference table. As we ended the first song, they burst into a loud ovation while Dan attended to his nose and bloodied guitar. We resumed. At the end of our three-song performance, Hans looked around the room at a dozen enthusiastic MCA executives, who all shook his hand as they left, congratulating him on his latest signing.

hree months before the release of our record, we returned to New York. As we stepped off the plane at La Guardia, I spotted a man in a dark suit and cap holding a sign that read "Jake Schlighter." Jim had arranged our pickup, and his protective instincts told him to choose me as the limousine driver's contact. My name was least likely to attract attention from the other Minneapolitans on our flight. Unfortunately, my name was also the hardest to spell. I held in my hand a plane ticket for Jacob Flichter.

The driver collected our bags and led us outside to the limousine, and we climbed in. It was our first limo ride as a band. The driver closed the door behind us, and as he walked around to the driver's seat, I pressed a few of the buttons on the panel above my head, raising and lowering the glass and wooden dividers between the driver and passenger compartments. Dan looked up at me from his book. I stopped and turned my attention to the minibar, where I found a Coke. Then I plucked a cell phone from its holder. Who might enjoy a call from me as I rode into Manhattan in the back of a limo? John yawned. I put the cell phone back. We pulled into traffic, and I reclined, popped open the Coke, and looked through the window at the other cars on the expressway.

We had flown to New York for our album photo shoot. Two weeks earlier, we had gathered at Dan's house to look through the portfolios of several photographers suggested to us by MCA's publicity and art departments. We each had brought a few of our favorite album cover shots to show each other: Bruce Springsteen's grin on the cover of *Born to Run*, the Beatles walking across the street on the cover of *Abbey Road*, The Who taking turns pissing on the cover of *Who's Next*, John Coltrane's stonelike profile on the cover of *A Love Supreme*. We wanted to emerge from our photo shoot with a similarly iconic image of our band.

After passing around these album covers, we flipped through the laminated pages of the heavy lap-sized portfolios of the photographers MCA had suggested, turning the pages from pictures of R.E.M. to those of Beck, and from Dr. Dre to Natalie Merchant. Soon, one of these photographers specializing in rock stars would be taking pictures of us.

I preferred clear shots to blurry ones where smeared light obscured the faces of the band members. That eliminated two of the five photographers from my list. Dan and John, less averse to blurry, found other reasons to remove those photographers from contention. One of the portfolios was almost exclusively devoted to fashion models, a bit too superficial, even for the ambitious members of Semisonic. The two remaining contenders had strong portfolios, and one of them seemed certain to capture what we were after: vibe. The opening shot of her portfolio showed Snoop Doggy Dogg pointing a large gun at the lens, a terrifying but undeniable rendering of a star persona. Other shots inside the same portfolio had an eeriness about them that we found compelling. Dan called Jim and informed him of our choice.

Now, as we glided over highways and bridges toward the approaching New York skyline, I took casual glances out of the window. Previous cab rides into Manhattan had resembled a spring-launched skittering through the world's largest pinball machine, but the limousine suggested an eight ball that had been kissed across the felt.

That afternoon, we met at MCA's midtown offices with the publicity and art department people supervising the photo shoot and the stylist in charge of dressing us in the right clothes. The publicity department needed a variety of photos—black-and-white and color, band shots and solo portraits of each band member, expansive shots full of lots of texture and small simple portraits—to supplement all the upcoming press coverage. The art department had an additional list of the photos it required for the CD booklet and posters.

We arrived to a meeting in progress. Christine Wolff, of MCA's publicity department, and Shari Simonsen, the clothing stylist, were thumbing through fashion magazines as Kevin Reagan, the art department director, looked on. Our manager, Jim, was also present to ensure that the band's vision and taste were respected but perhaps kept under control as well.

The question of how to dress us had implications beyond the realm of photos. Our music was not easily placed in any particular category. It lived somewhere between the grinding textures of alternative rock and the catchy lyrics and melodies of top-40 pop. We faced a cultural fork in the road. What if we dressed down in jeans, gas station shirts, and work boots? The upside would be we'd get a head start with the alternative-rock crowd. The downside would be that other listeners might see our picture and write us off as too loud. And if we dressed up in Helmut Lang suits? That was the riskier but potentially more rewarding choice. Alternative listeners might look upon us as too slick. On the other hand, if our music connected with them, dressing up might set us apart from the grungier bands at that end of the radio dial, and the top-40 listeners would feel more encouraged to check us out. As a band and as individual dressers, we were not squarely in either camp. We wouldn't look right in ripped jeans, and any suits we wore would have to be matched with funkier shoes and shirts. So the stylist, Shari, was charged with finding us a workable midpoint between the plaid flannel shirts of Minneapolis and the silk suits of Milan.

The conversation first centered on Dan, the front man and focal point for listeners and viewers alike. Shari had plenty of ideas, some funky but most of them glamorous. "I think you'd look great in this suit here."

Christine approved. "Great! Or maybe that black one a few pages earlier." Dan nodded his head and flipped through the pages and pointed to a few suits that had caught his eye, bringing affirming oohs and aahs from Shari and Christine. Then it was on to leather coats, velvet pants, glam shoes, shirts (with clerical collars, wide collars, no collars, ruffled sleeves, and cuff links), sweaters, sunglasses, and scarves.

Pretty soon, the three of them, with a little help from Kevin, had identified a dozen possible looks for Dan, from rock-club funky to fashion-show glamorous. John had spoken up, and by the time the conversation turned to him, a few suits, shirts, and pants to his liking had already been noted. Dan and John had adventurous taste in clothes.

Finally, my turn came. "I really like those suits, too."

Shari folded up a list of our sizes and gathered the magazines. "Maybe. I could also see you in something tougher. What about that leather jacket you're wearing now? That with some cool boots." Christine and Kevin looked at their watches and pushed back from the table. Dan and John stood up to grab their coats. "Yeah, Jake. Tough." Even Jim, closing his briefcase and looking the other way, nodded in agreement. I have to admit that I, too, was prepared to cast myself in the role of the tough guy, even if the phrase "Let's take the subway" could put me on edge. Tough. Good. On the other hand, what about those suits?

Two days later, we took an early-morning limousine ride to a brick warehouse in Tribeca and walked up several flights of stairs to a huge white room with tall ceilings. Annalisa, the photographer, introduced herself and her assistant, who waved from a ladder, where he adjusted lights mounted on aluminum stands. Open briefcases of cameras and film covered the floor. "We're just getting set up, so help yourselves to some food and then you can get made up."

Against one of the walls was a table piled with fresh croissants, bagels, cream cheese, kiwis, bananas, berries, mineral water, fresh-squeezed orange juice, French roast coffee, tea, and several tins of Altoid mints. I had already begun to tally our escalating recoupable debt, starting with our recording sessions, hotel bills, and flights, to which I now added our flight to New York, the limo rides from the airport and around the city (!), and our single rooms at the hotel. Fresh-squeezed orange juice couldn't cost that much, but the overabundance of luxury snacks added another line to my imaginary ledger of our accounts with the label. Perhaps, as everyone speculated, we'd never recoup, in which case I ought to enjoy the fact that the label was willing to spend a little extra to make us feel like stars.

The makeup artist sipped coffee and waved to us from her station. Dan walked over. John and I gravitated to the corner, where Shari and her assistant stood among several racks of clothes, enough to fill a shop. She pulled shirts out of large shopping bags and handed them to her assistant, who steamed out the wrinkles. They had spent the day before running around to department stores, designer shops, vintage clothing stores, shoe stores, and sunglasses boutiques. Versace, Armani, Dior, Calvin Klein, Helmut Lang, Hugo Boss, and a flock of designer names unfamiliar to me—we were looking at tens of thousands of dollars of clothes. The makeup artist waved John and then me over to her station for a little foundation, some eyebrow darkening, and soothing small talk.

By the time I pressed my lips together to spread out the lip gloss, Dan and John were already trying on clothes. There was no dressing room. They walked from rack to rack in their socks and underwear in full view of Shari, her assistant, Christine, and Kevin, while holding up shirts and pants and asking for opinions. I found a cool pair of suede pants, took them off the hanger, and slipped out of my jeans and quickly into the suede. Then I took a black Calvin Klein dress shirt off its hanger, unbuttoned it, draped it over the rack, sucked in my belly, took off my own long-sleeve T-shirt, and shot my arms into the Calvin Klein.

I turned to Shari. I've always been wary of dressing myself, partly because I'm color-blind. I wasn't aware of the effect of this handicap until, one day in high school, I walked into chemistry class and a girl in the back row said, "Hey, he matches today," upon which the classroom burst into laughter. Since then, I've relied on outside opinions.

Dan and John, both stylish dressers, had made occasional suggestions, but I learned to accept them with caution. During our recording, we visited a Los Angeles shoe store, and Dan persuaded me to buy a pair of white Doc Marten boots. "Your Stacy Adamses are too old-fashioned. Try these." I put them on, looked in the mirror, and blanched. Dan insisted they were cool. Figuring I would have to make myself uncomfortable if I was going to dress hipper, I plunked down eighty bucks and wore them out of the store. I tromped down the sidewalk feeling as if loudspeakers had been attached to my feet. Dan was ecstatic. "Awesome. It's kind of a gay punk look."

That my new boots were marching in the opposite direction of my heterosexual inclinations was not the sales pitch I wanted to hear. Nevertheless, I soldiered on, lacing up those boots every morning. I tried to convince myself of the new look, but the confused stares of passersby got the better of me, and upon our return to Minneapolis I threw the white Doc Martens in the back of my closet and slipped back into my black Stacy Adamses—an ankle-high fashion statement from the jazz age.

John, too, had recommended various items, many of them orange. He once gave me a pair of sunglasses he had purchased at a truck stop. "Try these on. . . . You look like a total badass!" Or perhaps a welder.

Every band needs a sex symbol, and every sex symbol needs a weird-looking guy to stand next to. Now, at the photo shoot, I had to factor this into my bandmates' recommendations. A picture taken today might become an enduring image of us, one that millions of people might see. Was I fated to be the weird-looking guy? I thought about that as I watched Dan and John button up in Versace shirts and slip into Helmut Lang pants. I walked over to Shari wearing a blue shirt with hidden buttons. "What do you think?"

"I like it. Here, try it with these pants." I tried them on. Very nice. I found a mirror and stared into it. *I look good. Do I? Maybe. Yes. Mysterious. Especially when I give my eye a half-squint, like that. Are those guys looking? Good. Or maybe raise my eyebrows slightly. Yes. That looks very sensitive, misunderstood. How about tough?* I intensified my stare. *Like that. Yeah. I'll be the sensitive, mysterious, misunderstood tough guy.*

Shari looked at each of us, making sure the various ensembles went together. Annalisa called us over to the camera and pointed to a spot on the floor. Dan stood with the toes of his thick, bulbous shoes touching that very spot. John and I stood on either side of him and looked up at the camera.

Click.

"Dan, would you step forward, please." Click. *Should I hold my hands behind my back?* Click. *No. How about in my pockets?* Click. *I know, I'll put them on my hips.* Click. *Yeah.*

"I'm sorry—what's your name?"

"Jake."

"Jake, could you take your hands off of your hips? Thanks. Anybody feel like smiling?"

Smile? Click. Like this? Click. Shit. Click—I'll bet that looked like I was saying, "Let's ride bikes!" Click. Fuck that. I want people to see me as being just out of reach—click—*so when I walk by them in a restaurant*—click—*their hearts beat faster. "Hey, isn't that..."* Click.

"Okay, let's try a different look." We changed into different clothes. I put on my leather coat and stepped in front of the mirror. Shari peered over my shoulder. "Yeah. Tough. I like that on you." I checked my left and right profiles and tended to a small cowlick with a dab of hair gel.

Shari tied a piece of leather around Dan's neck. *Should I say something? Isn't it in my interest that the star of our band not wear pieces of leather around his neck? Won't people think we're too frou-frou?* I gave Dan a "Not so sure about that" look, but Dan brushed it off. Christine spoke up: "I'm not sure about the leather thingy." *Thank you. Now, someone has to say something to him about those ridiculous bulbous shoes, and it can't be the guy who wimped out on wearing white boots. Why is John wearing orange pants?*

"Great, guys. Let's go on the roof for some shots." We walked up some stairs to the rooftop and stood in front of a brick wall.

Click. *OK, tough-guy intensified stare. Like this.* Click. *You're under arrest, motherfucker.* Click. *These shoes feel good.* Click. *Wonder if I'll get to keep them?* Click. *I'll bet they cost $250.* Click. *If I keep them, it means we have to sell 250 more records before*—click—*recouping. Plus all the other clothes, lights, photographer's fee, flights, limo.* Click. *And all of that fresh-squeezed orange juice.* Click. *Fuck.*

"Okay, guys, back downstairs." The morning proceeded. Christine wanted some simpler clothes that would look good in black-and-white. Click. Headshots. Click. Kevin wanted some colorful full-length poster shots. Click. Annalisa's assistant loaded film while she snapped away with various cameras and at various angles. Dan and John flirted with the lens. I stuck with tough.

"Great, guys. Let's break for lunch." A delivery person dropped off several shopping bags full of gourmet sandwiches and bottled juices. I munched down turkey and avocado on baguette, staring at the table along the wall. The fresh-squeezed orange juice was warm by now. The unconsumed croissants, fruit, and Altoid tins would all be thrown out at the end of the day. After Jim's commission, I owned a third of those fucking croissants.

"Okay, guys, brush your teeth. Let's get you in some of those suits." *Yes.* I love wearing a suit. A really expensive suit. I've always felt like a millionaire trapped in the body of someone with a lot less money, so I relished the opportunity to dress in a higher tax bracket. Shari had separated the suits according to whom they would fit. She handed me a velvet suit. Was it green? Gold? Brown? I put a bluish-gray shirt on underneath and looked in the mirror. Does he match today? Was I looking at a rock star or the keynote speaker at the annual meeting of the American Association of the Color Blind? I turned to Shari. "Is this suit orange?"

"No."

"The shirt?"

"It looks great."

The others chimed in. "Yeah, Jake. You look great."

Christine spoke up. "Let me see. Oh, Jake, that's awesome."

Annalisa grabbed my arm. "Here. I want to get a solo shot of you in that suit."

Click.

"Jake, you look worried."

Click.

"That's better."

Click.

Dan and John put on their suits and stepped into the frame. I backed up.

Click.

Dear Jake, I just bought your album, and my friends and I all wonder why you stand in the background when you are so…

Click.

On the cover, the mercurial Jake Slichter of Semisonic. He tells Rolling Stone *about life with Gwyneth and the long road from the copy machine to the stage and screen.*

Click.

And the Oscar goes to… Jacob Slichter in Tough.

"Okay, guys. Let's get some solo shots. Dan, you first."

Christine needed a lot of Dan shots to go with all of the interviews he would soon be conducting. I walked back over to the clothing racks where John was standing, shirtless, negotiating with Shari about what clothing items he could keep.

"What about these pants?"

"If you take the gray pants, then you might have to give up either the red Armani shirt or the shoes. If you want the blue DKNY shirt, I could let you have all three."

I joined in, wearing a shirt, underwear, and socks. "So what about that shirt, those pants, that jacket, and those shoes?"

"The jacket's a rental from a vintage house, so you can't have that. If you want those shoes, you won't be able to take anything else. You could take the Versace short-sleeve and the Calvin Klein long-sleeve, and the pants."

The shoes were killer—ankle-high slip-on boots that would be an elegant step forward from my Stacy Adamses. On the other hand, I needed shirts. "I'll think about it." I got dressed for my solo shot, knowing that I wanted to leave with more than just a pair of nice boots. There was obviously some system at work whereby Shari borrowed or rented clothes from trusting store owners and returned almost all of them two days later, buying the items that the band kept with whatever was left in her budget.

Jim stopped in to see how things were going. Dan stood under the lights, working his masterful half-smile. Jim stood next to me and leaned over.

"Dan looks great."

"Yup."

Jim turned around. "Whoa, John looks great, too."

"Uh-huh."

Then he gave me a friendly pat on the back. "All you guys look great. I'm gonna make some calls."

Half an hour later, I was sitting on a wooden box.

"Look up, please."

Click.

Half-squint.

Click.

Mystery.

Click.

Eyebrows up.

Click.

Sensitivity.

Click.

I'm sorry, were you talking to me? Why, yes, I am Jake Slichter. And to whom do I have the pleasure of speaking?

Click.

Annalisa asked, "Jake, is something wrong?"

Kevin asked for some shots of the band in more casual dress. Shari scanned the clothing racks, pulling likely items. I ended up in a gray vintage jacket, dark pants, a blue shirt, and a red knit applejack hat. Annalisa sat us on a window ledge and looked through her lens. Dan looked straight up at the ceiling.

Click.

Looking straight up. Shit, why didn't I think of that?

Click.

Now he's got his eyes closed.

Click.

I'll try looking away.

Click.

"Jake, back at the camera, please." Click, click, click until the end of the afternoon.

Two weeks later, on tour in Detroit, we opened a box of proof sheets that had been sent to us at our hotel. Each sheet had twelve miniature prints on it. Black-and-white, color, solo, group, dressed up, dressed down. It was a thick stack, more than fifty rolls of film. Christine and Kevin had initialed the shots they liked. Now we had to do the same.

Before we started, Dan said, "Guys. Try to find a vibey shot. Don't veto something just because you don't think you look good in it." Then he took the contact sheets and spent the next twenty minutes squinting through a loupe at the hundreds of shots, initialing those he liked with a wax pencil. John went next. Then it was my turn.

I slid the loupe over the contact sheets from shot to shot. *John and Dan actually like this shot?* Next. *That's my tough-guy stare? I look like someone just stepped on my toe.* Next. *Why do I look so tired?* Next. *Raised eyebrows? I look like a substitute teacher.* Next. *Dan and John look like fucking gunfighters, and I look like a kid ringing a fire-engine bell.* Next. *Why does everyone want to use these shots?* Next. *But I look good in this shot. Why did John say no?* Next. *Why does Dan blink every time I get the right look on my face?*

One shot that everyone had noted with exclamation marks was truly alarming. The three of us looked into the lens, in soft focus—Dan and John with distant confidence, me looking as if I was in the middle of mouthing the word *esophageal.* Dan pointed it out. "What do you think of this shot?"

"That one?"

John peeked over at it. "Yeah. I love that one. Jake?"

"Hmmm." *Don't veto vibey shots.*

"Don't you like it, Jake?"

"I'm not sure about how I look."

"Here, let me see." Dan squinted through the loupe. John did, too.

"You look good."

"Very . . . human."

Great. I'm the human-looking guy in the band.

"Hmmm."

"It's really definitive. It could be a great album shot."

"Hmmm." *Album shot?! What if our record sold millions?*

"What don't you like?"

"My face is kind of . . ." *Imagine that shot on posters in record stores nationwide.*

"What?"

"My mouth, it's . . ." *That face, on magazine covers, billboards, and a giant video display in Times Square.*

"What?"

"I LOOK LIKE A FUCKING FROG!"

"Really? I don't think so." Dan squinted down through the loupe again. "I mean, it's kind of a different look, but I wouldn't say 'frog.' "

Oh yes, I was the human frog about to be sacrificed on the altar of vibe.

"I mean, if you really don't like it, we can find another."

"What about this windowsill shot?"

I peered through the loupe at the three of us—Dan leaning back, John leaning forward, and me sitting with my hands on my knees. I might have fallen short of rock star, but I came as close as I was going to get. I could accept the idea of millions of people looking at that version of me. In fact, that seemed exciting.

"Yeah."

What a relief. I might have to explain the hat I was wearing in the shot to Mimi, the Minneapolis hairdresser who cuts our hair, but I'd have plenty of time to think about that on the flight home from Detroit. Seat 11C, an exit-row aisle, my legs stretched out. Passenger Flichter, finishing off the last of his five tins of Altoids.

Chapter VI

DOWN IN FLAMES

In the seventh grade, my parents gave me a small tape recorder for Christmas. I set the plastic microphone next to the radio and taped songs off of WLS, the big AM station in Chicago, 130 miles north of us. It wasn't long before I had several tapes of my favorite hits. I knew that if I had just missed recording "Benny and the Jets," it was only a matter of time before I'd get another chance, for the songs rotated through a cycle. In fact, somewhere in my mind I had the idea that WLS was a big building with a lot of stages where bands waited to play in turn, so that as Abba reeled through the last bars of "Waterloo," Carl Douglass was in another room, awaiting the cue for "Kung Fu Fighting."

Decades later, my ideas about radio were a bit more informed, and one thing was certain: Radio is king. There is no better guarantor of a band's success than a hit single on the radio luring listeners into record stores to buy the album. With a hit song on the radio, we'd sell lots of CDs, lots of tickets, and enjoy an abundance of press coverage. Thus, the first step to launching our album was to decide which one of the twelve songs would be our single.

Stylistically, Semisonic was not easy to pin down. The songs on the record were not easily lumped into a preexisting subgenre, and that was a problem because the stations on the dial are separated musically into niches known as formats. The names of the formats were new to me. I understood what an alternative-rock station was, but what were AAA, rock, adult top 40, and CHR? The labels were cryptic, but they represented familiar cultural spaces.

Alternative stations, as I already knew, play mostly aggressive loud guitar-rock by new bands. In the early 1990s, that meant Nirvana and Pearl Jam, and now, in early 1996, Green Day, Smashing Pumpkins, and the Beastie Boys. The listeners were Mountain Dew–guzzling skateboarders and their more ironic older siblings——the crowd that might line up to see a movie where Keanu Reeves leads an army of tattooed rebels on snowmobiles to overthrow an oppressive arctic government of the future.

AAA, or "triple A" (adult album alternative), stations are aimed at listeners in their late twenties and thirties who want to hear new music of a less aggressive variety. In the mid-1990s, this meant Counting Crows, R.E.M., Sarah McLachlan, Chris Isaak, Phish, Indigo Girls, and John Hiatt. Some of the less commercial AAA stations play so-called album tracks, songs that have not been released as singles. As for the listeners, picture the customers at the Starbucks café situated inside the Barnes & Noble.

Rock (or active rock) stations play a mix of old and new music by bands like Van Halen, AC/DC, and Def Leppard. Think monster-truck show.

Adult top-40 stations play new music that is less aggressive than alternative and more mainstream than AAA; in 1996, this meant Alanis Morissette, Goo Goo Dolls, and Barenaked Ladies. AAA listeners have graduated from sitting alone at Starbucks to holding hands with their spouses at Blockbuster, where they stand in line to rent the movie where Adam Sandler plays a pizza-delivery guy who gets appointed Chief Justice of the Supreme Court.

CHR (contemporary hit radio) stations play the songs that are hits at all the other formats. This is where you'll hear Shania Twain and Britney Spears. If you have a hit song on CHR, you are on your way to mainstream success. Your music is being heard by the people who watch *Survivor*, read *People*, and do a lot of instant messaging.

Which of these formats would Semisonic fit into? The consensus hung somewhere between alternative and AAA. The new president of MCA, Jay Boberg, favored alternative, and with that in mind, he nominated as our single a dark and angry song called "Down in Flames." This song selection surprised everyone—no one else considered it to be among the four or five single contenders—but the politics of opposing the new label president were risky. We accepted Jay's selection, and as one executive told Jim, "I don't know if it's the right decision for the band, but it's the right decision for your future with Jay." That, however, did little to cheer Jim.

MCA's goal was to get "Down in Flames" on the radio six weeks or more before the release date of our album—standard procedure. This allows time for listeners to hear a song enough times to get excited about it so that they rush out to buy the album during the important opening weeks of sales. Our album's release date was scheduled for early April, so MCA's target "add-date" of "Down in Flames" was mid-February. (In the world of radio, "add" can be used as both a verb and a noun referring to a song's addition to a station's playlist—for example, "They're adding the song," or "We got the add." The add-date is the day on which the label hopes stations will begin to play a single.)

Two weeks before the add-date for "Down in Flames," we flew to Boston and began a cross-country campaign of station visits, hoping to line up support for our single. Our chaperones for these visits were the MCA promotion staff, the *locals*. Each of the locals was based in a big city and covered a several-hundred-mile radius of territory. His or her job was to get MCA's singles added to the stations in that region. The Boston local was an old pro who covered every station in New England. The San Francisco local was a former DJ who covered a huge swath of terrain all the way to Vegas. As far as I could tell, being a local was miserable work, where most of the day was spent behind the steering wheel, driving to stations, handing off new CDs from MCA's bands, schmoozing with the station bigwigs, and then driving to the next station while answering cell-phone calls from the impatient bosses in Los Angeles.

We met most of these locals at five in the morning. They would pick us up at our motel to drive us to the first station of the day for an interview and an on-air acoustic performance. As we opened our eyes to the predawn light, we'd ride down the vacant highways of some big city and toward a distant radio tower, sipping coffee and eating donuts thoughtfully provided by the local. The local, always one cup of coffee ahead of us, would give us a sketch of what awaited us. "This first station's the big alternative station in town. They haven't added 'Down in Flames' yet, but I'm working on them. This interview is gonna help."

At 5:30 A.M., we'd pull into the station lot and park, often next to a Humvee painted with the station's call letters. Then we'd yawn one last time before following the local through the station doors, past the receptionist, who knew the local by name, and down the hallways. Dan carried his acoustic guitar, and John lugged his electric bass and a small practice amp. I would scan the hallways for an empty water-cooler jug or a wastebasket that I could turn upside down and convert into a makeshift drum for our on-air acoustic performance. After snaking through the hallways to the back of the station, the local held open the door to the broadcast studio and we'd walk in, greeted by a wave from the DJ who was introducing the next song, shuffling CDs, and punching buttons to play and eject them in proper order. Within a couple of minutes, we were on the air.

"We've got some special guests with us this morning, Semisonic from Minneapolis. Dan Wilson on guitar, John Munson on bass, and Jake . . ."

"Slichter."

We had been on the radio in Minneapolis a few times, and having seen Dan and John handle interviewers' questions, I had learned a lot. Being so well acquainted with my bandmates, I gleaned beyond their easy manner a certain delicacy in their answers. For instance, when asked to list our influences, Dan and John never mentioned the Beatles. Though we, like a majority of the musicians we knew, were intimately familiar with everything the Beatles had ever recorded, for interview purposes it was apparently better to name artists less likely to pigeonhole us—Elvis Costello and the Clash, for example. During the next interview, answering the same question, Dan and John might list other influences—Joni Mitchell and the Jam, perhaps—so we wouldn't be too strongly associated with a particular artist, I gathered. Only years later did I discover the truth: What looked to me like carefully managed answers were usually nothing more than random workings of my bandmates' brains.

The interview proceeded. "So, Dan, you guys are up awfully early this morning."

"We're on a whirlwind schedule right now, so we aren't getting much sleep." *Whirlwind schedule* was good. In reality, we were an unknown band who had actually come to the studio at this awful hour in hopes of ingratiating ourselves to the program director.

"How would you describe your music for our listeners?"

Dan had this answer, too. "Take all the best records in your collection and melt them down into one record."

"Cool. Who are some bands that you like?"

John leaned toward the mike. "My Bloody Valentine." *A nod to the hipsters.*

Dan went next. "Björk." *Aha! A smart trumpeting of our popstar aspirations with an off-center (Icelandic) choice.*

"Jake, how about you?"

"Marvin Gaye." *A bit conservative, but unassailable. My Bloody Valentine, Björk, and Marvin Gaye—that ought to keep people guessing.*

"So you brought your instruments with you. What are you going to play for us?"

The MCA local, knowing the station's musical leanings, had usually suggested a song to us in advance. "This is a song from our album called 'f.n.t.' One, two, three, four . . ."

We strummed, plucked, whacked, and sang as best we could, given the hour and the quality of the coffee we had just sipped. We were quite good at these on-air performances, something the locals could take advantage of in arranging other station visits. I trained my eyes on Dan, who was notorious for taking early-morning detours around entire verses and choruses, sometimes absentmindedly and other times in the interest of saving his voice. His scowls and smiles were good indicators of how well I had judged the volume of the overturned water jug I was using as a hand drum. Upon strumming the final chord, he would hold his hand in the air to suspend the silence and then lower it to mute the strings, at which point the DJ and the local would applaud—joined by the band members, of course. After all, no one could see us engaging in self-applause.

"Great. That was called 'f.n.t.,' and that's off your new album, *Great Divide*. When is it coming out?"

The answer was Tuesday, April ninth, but I knew better than to betray such uncool attention to the realm of commerce. "I don't know. Dan? John? In a few weeks maybe?"

"Sounds good. The band is Semisonic, and here's their new single, 'Down in Flames.' Thanks for coming in, guys."

"Thank you."

The DJ would punch a button and our first single would play on tens of thousands of radios across town. We packed up our instruments, shook hands with the DJ, and followed the local out of the studio and down the hall, past boxes and cabinets overflowing with station swag—posters, T-shirts, and hats, all covered with the station's logo—to the corner office of the program director.

The program director, or PD, is the most powerful person at a station. He or she decides what songs the station will play and how frequently it will play them. Unlike the old days of rock radio, the DJs have no say in the matter; they play songs only as dictated by the playlist. Requests are largely a fiction. If a DJ says, "Here's a request from Bob in Long Beach," chances are Bob in Long Beach requested a song that, according to the printed-out playlist, was already slotted for imminent airplay.

As far as the airwaves were concerned, the PDs held absolute power. Each station's PD would decide whether or not to play our single, whether to put it into light rotation (ten spins a week) or moderate or perhaps power rotation (thirty spins a week or more). The right PD could "break" us, turning thousands of listeners on to us and thereby launching our album and career. Or, even in the face of building momentum, an influential PD could kill our single by dropping it from the station's playlist, sending our stock plummeting. No wonder that when introducing us to a program director, the MCA locals typically bounced on their toes, smiled too much, and laughed too readily.

Some of the PDs were most welcoming, inviting us on a tour of their stations, embarking on discussions of new music that they found inspiring, and sometimes handing us CDs of bands they thought we would like. Dan and John were a great asset in these cases, for this subgroup of PDs, the music addicts, knew of Trip Shakespeare and enjoyed engaging with two musicians with superior musical literacy and taste. These PDs had a mission: turning the world on to interesting new music, a cause that usually doomed them to program obscure stations with weak broadcast signals and a listening audience that was loyal but small. A commitment to variety meant that their playlists accommodated a greater number of songs, giving fewer spins to each song, and thus they were excited to add Semisonic. They hinted that we should return sometime to play a longer set on the air, and such happy encounters would conclude with the MCA local snapping some pictures of the band and PD, photos that would then be sent off to the radio trade magazines—"Semisonic with WXYZ program director John Doe."

Another subset of PDs shook our hands limply. Just as they had sprinkled us into their playlists, they were equally hesitant to embrace us in person, but they left open the possibility of warmer relations in the future, depending on our success. One undecided PD in Wichita, after hearing our on-air interview—entirely devoted to hockey—said of us, "Kinda cerebral, but I like you." He disappeared before we could pose for pictures.

Most of the PDs, however, were egomaniacs for whom it seemed music was nothing more than the ammunition in the all-important ratings war with rival stations. Their connection to our music had been reduced to gauging the effect of "Down in Flames" on listeners. Their playlists were short—lots of spins for the proven hits and no room for anything else. Their bulletin boards were covered with updates on the on-air sports car giveaways and in-person appearances by the DJs at the local shopping mall. How depressingly predictable it was that these stations enjoyed the highest ratings.

The PDs who ran these stations had not added "Down in Flames." Nor would they grant us on-air interviews. One morning in Houston, the MCA local took us to visit two stations, neither of which was playing our single. At the first station, we had been refused an interview, but the PD allowed us to perform three songs for him and his staff in a conference room. The applause was restrained; no employee dared applaud too heartily and undermine the verdict of the glowering PD. After an icy good-bye, we drove to a second station, where again the PD refused to let us be interviewed on air. Furthermore, he refused to let us play for the station staff. The local pleaded with him and negotiated a compromise: We took our instruments into a coffee-break room and played for three secretaries as they ate pizza.

The PDs who liked us always invited us to record a few station IDs for future use. An engineer led us to a small studio and handed us a printout from which we read.

"Hi, I'm Dan."

"I'm John."

"And I'm Jake."

"We're Semisonic, and you're listening to Mary Lucia on Rev One-O-Five."

In addition to call letters and a frequency, most stations have a moniker such as "The River" or "Drive 105" and perhaps a slogan: "Where the music never stops." I noticed that some stations in different cities used the same nickname—"The Edge," for example. The locals informed me that this was because those far-flung stations used a common programming consultant, someone who advised the various program directors on song selection and station image. The number of people who decided whether or not our song would be played was frightfully small.

After recording the IDs, we'd wait on the couch in the lobby as the local finished business with the PD, perhaps talking about other MCA records. I'd sift through the magazines on the coffee table and pick a copy of *Hits,* a tip sheet for industry insiders full of columns promoting various songs and bands, and advertisements taken out by record companies to tout a particular single's early successes—"Most added at alternative last week." By contrast, the full-page ad MCA had taken out for "Down in Flames" included a picture of the band and a short list of stations playing the song.

Sometimes I'd get up to look at the gold and platinum records hanging on the wall of the lobby. These giant thank-you cards from record labels consisted of a framed picture of an album cover and a gold or platinum LP or CD. (Multi-platinum award plaques often display several platinum CDs, one for each multiple of one million records sold.) "Presented to WXYZ in recognition of sales of over 2,000,000 copies of 'Siamese Dream.' " Finally, the local and the PD would emerge, the PD with station shirts draped over his arm: "Here, guys."

"Thanks." I didn't dare refuse a station shirt, no matter how cheesy it looked. We'd hit two coffee shops and three stations before lunch. When the second and third DJs asked us the same questions, we'd twist the old answers into new ones. Our favorite locals would reward a good morning's work with lunch at a nice restaurant. "What do you guys feel like? French? Italian?" I always thanked the locals for lunch, and then one day it occurred to me . . .

"Dwayne, that's a corporate Amex, right?"

"Yeah."

"And you write 'Semisonic' on the credit-card slip, and that gets billed to our recoupable account, right?"

"Yeah."

"So really, shouldn't you be thanking us for lunch?"

That was met with an appreciative laugh. "Yes, Jake. Thanks for lunch." Actually, several locals confided that they billed many of our meals to the accounts of more successful artists who were notorious pains in the ass.

After lunch, we'd get back in the car and ride to the next station while sitting on a pile of station T-shirts and sipping carryout coffee. The local's cell phone rang constantly. The highway speed of the car varied by as much as thirty miles per hour, depending on the tenor of the conversation that the local was having with the label bosses in Los Angeles. Occasionally, we'd shout as the local, still on the phone, absentmindedly veered into the path of another car.

After a few days of radio promotion, it was clear: The little stations loved us, and the big stations ignored us or perhaps even disdained us. Our Chicago local brought us to perform at a private party for radio insiders thrown by Q101. The program director got up on stage and welcomed everyone and then gestured to the MCA local. "Tom from MCA gets the label suck-up award for bringing a band." Then she laughed, rolled her eyes, and waved us on stage. The next day, Jim called us to say that it was wise of us not to have told this PD to fuck off.

Soon the various locals began to say, "The phones are slow," which meant that "Down in Flames" wasn't producing a rush of telephone calls from listeners. An accumulation of listener calls can make a decisive impact on a program director's playlist. It's the first indication that a song connects with the listeners. Alas, "Down in Flames" scored poorly in that department.

Couldn't MCA just stage a bunch of calls to the stations? No, the stations have too much at stake not to be wise to such tactics. One local told me, "A lot of these stations have caller ID and they take down the numbers. Twenty calls from the same house won't make a dent. I had my teenage daughter call one of the stations asking for a song from one of my bands. The DJ said, 'So you said your name is Lisa? You sound a lot like someone I talked to half an hour ago. What high school do you go to? Central? Tell me the name of the principal.' She didn't know. Busted." Because the identity of the callers is unknown, program directors are wary of phone requests, except when the station is flooded with them. "When it's real, it's insanity."

What program directors are most interested in are record sales. If one station plays a song and the listeners go out and buy the record, the locals have "a story" to relate to other program directors, hard evidence that a song is connecting with listeners.

Most songs do not produce floods of calls, and the sales information can be inconclusive or, if the record is not out yet, unavailable. So the stations hire researchers to call the listeners so that the ever-impatient PDs can measure the listeners' response to the songs. The researcher plays a series of song clips for a listener and asks which clips are familiar. Then the researcher asks the listener to grade the songs. The results determine how long a PD is willing to keep a song in rotation. "Research" favors songs with catchy repetitive hooks, and because listeners generally prefer the songs they've heard the most, research rewards songs already favored by the program director (although a song that listeners love in spite of its unfamiliarity may rocket up the playlist). Theoretically, song research is said to be valid only after a song has received a minimum of 200 spins on a station, but the PDs get impatient. Our locals complained that "Down in Flames" was being tested after only 100 spins at some stations. No surprise, the word came back that "the song isn't researching well."

Meanwhile, the locals concerned themselves with getting the PDs who had already added "Down in Flames" to increase the number of spins, to move us from light rotation into medium or power rotation (thirty to sixty spins a week, depending on the length of the station's playlist). With increased spins, "Down in Flames" would move up the radio charts (which are ranked according to total spins nationwide), thus creating momentum and giving the locals a better case to present to program directors.

In the past, each station submitted a weekly log of songs and spins to the publishers of the various radio charts. However, stations routinely accepted payola from record companies to falsify the reports, thus allowing the labels to purchase chart position and create the perception of a hit. The locals told us that such blatant cheating had ceased. For instance, *Billboard*'s charts rely on a nationwide network of computerized listening posts operated by *Billboard*'s sister company, BDS. The listening posts monitor the airwaves for the audio fingerprints of songs in a database. So, for example, if a listening post in Philadelphia tuned to WXPN detected something that matched the audio fingerprint of "Down in Flames," it would credit the song with a spin. City by city, station by station, the results are tallied and reported to *Billboard*. An impressive showing on the alternative-rock or AAA charts might have helped "Down in Flames," but it received so little airplay that it never made it onto either chart.

There was more working against us than phones, research, and our nonexistence on the charts. Most of the influential stations were ignoring us. When WBCN in Boston added us, and when we shook hands with WBCN's legendary program director, Oedipus (the professional pseudonym of Ed Hyson), I had no idea what a valuable endorsement we had received. Getting on WBCN's playlist would give us validation in the eyes of other program directors. Unfortunately, WBCN was the exception. As we hit more cities, I saw the billboards advertising other ruling powers of the radio dial—The End in Seattle, Live 105 in San Francisco, 99X in Atlanta, and of course the mighty KROQ in Los Angeles. None of those prized stations was on our schedule of visits. Their playlists were beyond our lowly reach, and, being ignored by the big stations, our stock fell even more. I couldn't help thinking we had made a mistake by accepting Jay Boberg's decision to make "Down in Flames" the single. "f.n.t." (which stands for Fascinating New Thing) had always been the obvious choice in my mind. In fact, one of the big alternative stations, WHFS in Washington, D.C., played "f.n.t." before MCA decided on a single, then abandoned it once MCA decided on "Down in Flames." I gnawed on that missed opportunity.

If getting played on the radio wasn't hard enough, the wars between the stations turned our few victories into potential disasters. In any given city, if we became too cozy with station A, we'd be punished by station B. For example, if station A played our song in exchange for the right to present our next local appearance ("Station A presents Semisonic live at the Springfield Bar") with on-air ticket giveaways and a visible presence at our show (a station banner hung near the stage and a station truck parked outside the club, staffed by DJs giving away station T-shirts), station B would drop us. That sounds acceptable if station A is the bigger station, but suppose station B is owned by a powerful media conglomerate (Clear Channel, Infinity Broadcasting, ABC Radio) with stations in many cities around the country. We might pay a severe price nationwide for our relationship with station A.

This cast our handshakes with program directors in a new light. The stations that were playing us were generally smaller, but they nevertheless expected our fealty. "We want to present your next show." The program director at a bigger station, however, might threaten us with lasting banishment if we accepted the small station's offer. Several times, before agreeing to play a show for a small station, the local had to first get clearance from the big station.

The war we knew the best involved two alternative stations from Minneapolis, The Rev and The Edge. When The Rev (short for "The Radio Revolution") went on the air in 1994, Minneapolis music fans rejoiced. They finally had an alternative station that honored Minneapolis's eclectic taste with a long and varied playlist—everything from Nirvana and Green Day to hip-hop to cool British bands that the bigger stations ignored. Unfortunately, The Rev had a feeble transmitter. Whole sections of Minneapolis were out of signal range. I'd drive down Hennepin Avenue rocking out to Liz Phair, and suddenly the music would vanish into a haze of static.

Crosstown rival The Edge, on the other hand, had a massive signal and a force-feed playlist that seemed exclusively reserved for multiplatinum bands, the proven winners. The Rev uncovered new delights every day; The Edge was the alternative radio equivalent of McDonald's. The Rev listeners despised The Edge and were painfully aware of the ratings war between the two stations. The Rev was owned by a local millionaire; The Edge, by a conglomerate, Disney's Capital Cities/ABC. With its stronger broadcast signal, The Edge enjoyed the higher ratings, but The Rev's program director, Kevin Cole, would not retreat from his programming maxim: "Just enough hits to stay on the air." The Rev's loyal listeners slapped bumper stickers on their cars: "Vote Rev 105."

For Dan, John, and me, there was more than listening preferences at stake. The Rev had embraced us from the start, making Semisonic a centerpiece of their playlist. By contrast, The Edge refused to play us, even though by now we were one of the bigger bands in town. The Edge's boycott of Semisonic damaged our credibility elsewhere. A program director in North Carolina might ask MCA, "If their hometown station won't play them, why should we?"

Finally, The Edge's PD grudgingly added us to his playlist in modest rotation, but he then acted as if he owned us. On a day when we had scheduled live interviews at both stations to promote our show that evening, we conducted the first interview at The Rev and then drove across town to The Edge. Having heard that we had visited the rival station first, The Edge's PD kept us waiting in the lobby for almost an hour and then canceled our on-air appearance as punishment.

Some of the PDs were known to have volatile personalities. One of them, a guy who called himself Super Frank, almost kicked us off his station festival because instead of showing up at 10:00 in the morning for our midafternoon set, we arrived at 10:10, having taken a wrong turn and thus been delayed. He was furious, and Jim, when informed of the situation via telephone, was exasperated to hear that we had ignored his warnings about Super Frank's fickle reputation. Jim made an emergency call to apologize to Super Frank, and Dan apologized in person, but Super Frank was unresponsive. Maybe we'd play the show, maybe we wouldn't. A half hour later, with the verdict still undecided, John walked up to Super Frank and offered his hand. "Listen, Frank, we're really sorry for—"

"It's *Super* Frank."

We waited an hour before learning that we would be allowed to play. After the show, we apologized again.

In spite of our cross-country efforts to promote "Down in Flames," it slowly expired. I asked myself how many more singles MCA would be able to afford promoting. I tallied our flights, meals, and hotels and reckoned that radio promotion had added $20,000 to our recoupable debt. I called Jim to confirm the price tag. The actual amount, he told me, was closer to half a million dollars.

"What?!"

Yes, having lived in fear of the vindictive PDs and their station wars, having spoken with such care during our interviews, having placed my vain hopes on the phones and research, I had been blind to the biggest player of all—money. I knew about payola, but whenever I asked the locals about it they said that the "illegal practices of the past" were no more. Little did I realize that the airwaves were being bought and sold all around us, and that it was all perfectly "legal."

What's illegal is payola, when a record company pays a station to play a particular song, and the station plays the song without disclosing the record company's payment to the listeners. There is, however, a way around this prohibition—independent radio promoters. Imagine an alternative rock station called WXYZ. Now imagine an independent radio promoter named Bob Tapeworm. Tapeworm goes to WXYZ and says, "Give me an exclusive peek at your playlist before you announce it each week over the next twelve months, and I'll pay you a hundred thousand dollars." Now Tapeworm has exclusive access to WXYZ and WXYZ has additional income—which is "legal," as we will see. Tapeworm calls up the record labels and says, "If you want your songs played on WXYZ, you have to hire me." MCA, like the other labels, says "Okay, Mr. Tapeworm, here's a thousand dollars. Help us get 'Down in Flames' added to WXYZ's playlist." The record company's accounting records will show "consulting fee" payments to Tapeworm, the radio station's records will show revenue from Tapeworm's "consultant's contract," and since there's no identifiable link between payments from the record companies to Tapeworm and the payments from Tapeworm to the station, none of it is "illegal."

The next Tuesday morning, when the program director for WXYZ is hours from declaring the upcoming week's playlist, Tapeworm meets with him or her. The PD knows that Tapeworm has paid for the right to meddle with the playlist, and also that Tapeworm is being paid by the various labels to have their singles added. So the two negotiate the changes. For his part, Tapeworm will know, for instance, that Interscope is paying him more money that week than MCA, so he'd better focus on Interscope's single. And for his part, the PD knows that Tapeworm may help get various bands to appear at WXYZ's spring festival or Christmas show. All of this factors into their negotiations with each other.

During Tapeworm's discussion with the PD, "Down in Flames" might be downplayed or even omitted, but Tapeworm can always tell MCA, "Hey, I tried." Even if MCA doubts his word, they know that if they don't pay him, they'll have a tough time getting other singles played on WXYZ. And if Tapeworm is a major promoter with scores of stations under exclusive contract, there's no way MCA can avoid hiring him.

In addition to paying the independent promoter, sometimes labels offer to sponsor a contest: "The tenth caller will be entered in WXYZ's drawing for a weekend trip to Hawaii to see Semisonic in concert." Or, what might begin as a legal means of promotion can turn into something else, such as when a label sends a station a widescreen television to "give away" over the air, but the television ends up in the program director's living room. Then there are blatant violations of law, such as when a label sends a PD an overnight envelope full of cash. Sometimes it's a lot of cash. I once heard of a PD whose backyard swimming pool was paid for by an appreciative label whose record he had added.

There are more than a hundred alternative stations nationwide, and even though some stations don't take money from independent promoters—megastations like K-ROCK and other stations like The Rev, whose playlists are not for sale—paying the network of independent promoters to launch "Down in Flames" on alternative radio was a several-hundred-thousand-dollar proposition, all of it charged back to Semisonic's recoupable account. If the song had connected at alternative radio and MCA had wanted to cross it over to the CHR format, it would have cost an additional million in independent promotion. Thanks to the stranglehold that the radio promoters have on labels, some of them make millions a year. One of these independent promoters, I later learned, tried to double-dip on us: He billed MCA and then separately phoned Jim and hinted that an additional payment from the band was expected. Jim reminded the promoter that they had met previously, and the promoter, realizing that Jim was onto his attempt at double dipping, excused himself to take another call. Such extortion, however, is widespread. We heard of a promoter telling a band from overseas, "If you want to get on the radio in the US, you'll give me twenty-five percent of your US gross."

Back in Minneapolis, the battle between The Rev and The Edge raged on, until one morning when The Rev's staff was summoned to a meeting room and informed that The Rev had been bought by the company that owned The Edge, Capital Cities/ABC. The employees had two hours to clear out their desks and leave the building. A few loyalists stayed until the end, pulling out all of their favorite discs and playing them before the premises were seized. One of the last songs they played was "Down in Flames."

Chapter VII

THE BAND LOOKS STUNNING

In the early stages of the "Down in Flames" radio campaign, before the song's fate as a dud single had become apparent, MCA decided we should make a video. They offered us a $40,000 budget and Jim succeeded in raising the figure to $65,000, which was only a fraction of what the best-looking videos cost. MTV's tiny rotation is almost exclusively reserved for high-budget videos of hits by established artists, and the odds of us sneaking on the air with a cheap video for a little-known song were remote. Indeed, some labels were already reexamining the wisdom of dumping so much money into videos that had the barest chance of being seen. That, however, did not stop MCA from asking us to make a video, nor did it curb my hopeful belief that once completed, a Semisonic video would prove irresistible to those in charge at MTV.

Our first task was choosing a video director. We had a candidate in mind already: Doug Gayeton. Doug had made many videos, including one for Dan and John's prior band, Trip Shakespeare. Perhaps the most memorable video on his reel was for Matthew Sweet's song "Time Capsule," in which Sweet was tied to the ground à la Gulliver and cockroaches crawled over his body and face as he sang with an eerie deadpan. It was hilarious. It was also banned from MTV—according to Doug, because the executives complained that it was "too gross." (Ironically, a few months later, MTV released its first feature film, *Joe's Apartment*, about a man whose apartment is overrun with cockroaches.) Fed up with bands, labels, and MTV, Doug retired from making videos. He interrupted his retirement in 1995, when, as a favor to Dan and John, he made a home movie for Semisonic that became part of our promotional package. Now we wanted to hire him again.

MCA had other directors in mind. They sent us a box of director's reels that made its way from Dan's living room to John's and finally to mine. Each director's reel had five or more videos, so I sat down with a notebook for a full evening of screening. In our initial video discussions, I had listened on the sidelines as Dan and John made specific references to a host of videos I had never seen. Thus, as I watched, I paused the tape and took detailed notes so as to be better prepared for our discussions about the various candidates. The notes would have looked something like this:

Reel #1—Elliot Painsworth
First video—Meat locker is an interesting setting. Seeing the breath of the singer good way of showing temperature. Drummer partially hidden behind hanging side of beef. Longer shots more effective, especially meat saw . . .

Fifth video—Overhead shot of singer chained to bathroom pipes effectively claustrophobic. Girlfriend smearing him with shit drags on too long. Fast edits fatiguing, but OK during electrocution sequence . . .

Reel #2—Tim Fluffington
Third video—Nice slow-motion shot of singer as she watches cotton candy machine at work. Cool camera movement during bumper-car sequence with boyfriend. Crane shot of balloons released from Ferris wheel a nice ending . . .

By the end of reel two, I felt like writing a thank-you letter to the inventor of fast-forwarding. Between these philosophical extremes—Jeffrey Dahmer and the Brady Bunch—there were a few inspiring reels. We talked among ourselves and called Jim with our top choices.

"We really love the Jamie Thraves reel, especially the Radiohead video."

"We can't afford him."

"What about_____?"

"He doesn't make rock videos anymore."

"Okay, well then how about_____?"

"He's booked for the next six months."

Irritated by the fact that MCA sent reels of directors who were too expensive or otherwise unavailable, we nevertheless narrowed down the list. The remaining contenders sent in treatments— written descriptions of the videos they proposed to make for us.

Elliot Painsworth—

"Down in Flames" by Semisonic will be an unprecedented look at death, life, and possessiveness.

Dark interior of unlit morgue. A woman in a white lab coat rolls a sheet-covered body out of its refrigerated container. She pulls back the sheet to reveal a charred face. It's Dan. She lights a candle, illuminating the room. Dan's eyes open and he begins to sing and his badly burned corpse comes back to life. She rolls out two more sheet-covered bodies, and lighting two more candles brings back to life the burned corpses of John and Jacob. Suddenly the room is ablaze and the band members are playing their instruments. Flames fill the room, flickering in the woman's eyes. Dan thrusts his guitar as if to implore her to let them live as he sings with anger. John scowls, and Jacob pounds the drums with fury. The band looks stunning.

As the flames burn out and Dan sings the final words, they lay their own wilting bodies back onto the rolling trays. Our heroine pulls the sheets over their cold lifeless bodies and rolls them back into the refrigerated lockers. This will be one of the most talked about videos of the year.

Tim Fluffington—

"Down in Flames" by Semisonic will be a passionate exploration of our place in the natural world.

Night. Exterior. Close-up of roasting marshmallow. As the music starts, the camera pulls back to reveal Dan, John, and Jacob, sitting around a campfire. Dan starts to sing. John strums a guitar as he and Jacob listen. Jacob ducks into their tent and pulls out a bongo drum and joins in. The campfire embers glow in their eyes. The band looks angelic, serene, stunning.

Soon squirrels and rabbits come out of the surrounding woods to listen. A turtle pokes his head out of his shell to hear the band's message of peace. Just when we think we've seen everything, a deer emerges and lies down, resting its chin on Dan's knee. As the song ends, an owl hoots, scaring the band members until they realize it's just an owl. Fade out as they smile and Dan pets the deer. This will be the first video to make such extensive use of raw natural elements—live animals!—and is sure to be an impact video.

"Jesus, Jim, are you sure we can't get Jamie Thraves?" With no satisfactory alternative and time running out, Dan insisted that MCA hire Doug. Doug had prepared a good treatment: band performance intercut with a side narrative of a woman who mourns the death of her friend by going to the desert and making an altar from the friend's belongings and setting it all on fire. We trusted him to make a smart, good-looking video that wouldn't clash with the personality of the band or the song. MCA consented. Final revisions to the treatment were faxed back and forth and submitted for MCA's final approval.

Two days later, we were in L.A. trying on clothes with Shari, who had dressed us so well for the album photo shoot that she was asked to find clothes for the video, too. Her budget was minimal, so she relied on vintage clothes from a Hollywood rental house— slacks and vintage sweaters for Dan and John, and a beautiful white leather jacket for me.

"Shari, I hate to ask, but is there any way I can keep—"

"No."

It would be a two-day shoot—one day at a studio stage to film the band and the next day in the desert to film the side narrative. Central to all of it would be fire. Some of the band performance would be filmed through a burning picture frame; other shots would be filmed through a pane of glass that was smeared with a special-effects gel that could burn on the glass, creating a transparent flame effect. Doug wrote that into the treatment because, given our low budget, our video would rely heavily on the cost-effective entertainment value of flames. And mindful of the cockroach fiasco of years earlier, Doug made sure that MCA cleared the fiery content of the video with MTV *before* any film was shot.

The first day of shooting took place on an old Hollywood stage where some of the Keystone Kops movies had been filmed. By the time we arrived, twenty people were already at work, setting up cameras on booms, laying a small set of railroad tracks on the floor for the camera dolly, testing the audio playback system, adjusting and metering the lights, setting up the rented drums and amplifiers, and hanging a giant screen behind the instruments. One day of low-budget video making was as labor-intensive as months of recording. A wooden picture frame had been suspended in front of the set, and technicians stood around it, discussing how best to set it on fire and safely extinguish the flames. Then they turned their attention to the large pane of glass, soon to be smeared with gel and set on fire so the camera could capture us blazing in rock-and-roll glory.

The camera team asked me to set up the drums over two strips of tape marking an *X* on the floor and then stretched a tape measure from the camera lens across the stage to the tip of my nose. The pace was manic, and soon we were made up, dressed up, fully caffeinated, and shown to our places in front of the camera, guitars and drumsticks in hand, ready to begin shooting. My drums were fifteen feet behind Dan and John, all the more reason for me to make grander gestures when the time came. I took a few practice swings with my sticks. The drums themselves were deadened with foam, and the deadened cymbals were thicker and heavier, so in order to knock them around like real cymbals, I had to hit them twice as hard. I practiced lifting my arms above my head and swinging the sticks down hard on the cymbals—not my usual approach, but it would make for more exciting viewing. I thought through the drum performance on the CD, which my stick movements needed to match if I wanted to avoid looking like the drummer from the Partridge Family.

Doug clapped his hands and said, "Okay, let's get a few full performances here," and the bustle hushed to a murmur. The makeup person darted onto the set to give each of us a last-second powdering and hair adjustment. "You're beading up already."

Shari followed her. "Your collar is crooked. There."

The assistant director barked out commands. "Quiet, everyone. Roll camera. Roll playback."

Four beeps counted off the guitar intro. As the song played back through the speakers, Dan strummed his mute guitar and lip-synched the words. There were no drums for the first forty-five seconds of music. *What do I do? Look at the camera? No. Straight ahead? That'll look too spacey. Down?*

I played the opening tom-tom fill—boom boom boom, which on the deadened drums sounded like tap tap tap—and we were off. *Don't drop the sticks. I can barely move my arms in this jacket. Here comes the chorus, switch to high hat. Let it slosh like I'm*

really hitting it hard. I AM hitting it hard. Christ, I'm fucking ex-
hausted. How do those arms-above-the-head drummers do it? He's
panning the camera. Don't look into the lens. Fuck, I blew that fill.
Here comes the end. Think of something. Dan's looking at me. I'll
look at him.

The song ended and the film crew burst into applause. Doug
stepped forward. "Okay, guys. Good. Dan, can you angle in a bit?
Now move over to your right. A little more. A little more. Good."
Now I'm totally out of the shot. "John, great stuff. Let's do
another." Jim whispered something to Doug and Doug nodded in
response.

"Roll camera. Playback."

I'm just gonna stare straight ahead during this guitar intro. Look
steely. Rock and roll. Here come the drums. Boom boom boom.
John's looking at me. Give a confident stare back. There's Dan.
Damn, forgot the fill again. Dan's smiling at me. Where's the cam-
era? Pointed at Dan.

Again, applause. Either we were really good, or this room full
of seasoned video-makers knew the appetite of rock-and-roll
egos. Doug liked what he saw. "Great, guys. John, that's great
when you go over to Dan and rock out. And Dan, I love that thing
with your hips swaying back and forth. Really great rock energy
between you two."

After several more full-band takes and a lunch break, Doug
brought us back to the stage for some solo shots of Dan and John.
I played drums in the background, lest the camera find the drums
without a drummer. Then Doug stood us three abreast and had
the camera pan slowly from left to right as we stared into the lens.
Behind the camera crew, Hans and some of the MCA publicists
huddled in the corner. They nodded a hello in my direction and
then whispered among themselves. Finally, Doug excused Dan
and John and the camera crew set up in front of the drums.

"Roll camera. Roll playback."

Boom boom boom. *All right, MTV. Here I come. No guitar player in my way. I'm gonna do some damage with a big cymbal crash like THIS. Here comes the big fill. Nailed it! Keep those arm movements big. Ouch, my fucking knuckle. Here comes the end. Get a good facial expression ready. Don't flare those nostrils. Pick a point far away and stare after you give them a big two-armed... CRASH. You're one badass motherfucker.*

Hans and the MCA publicists joined in the applause, and Hans walked up and slapped my hand. "Great job." Then he pulled me aside. "Listen, I know everyone says Dan is the cutest, but a lot of us wonder if John isn't really the sex symbol of the band. What do you think?"

By late afternoon, it was time for flames. The crew positioned the camera to look through the picture frame that had been suspended from the ceiling by two thin wires. Two members of the crew set the frame on fire—"Action!"—and we performed until there was barely any frame left to burn. Then the pane of glass, smeared with the magical burning gel, was set ablaze. "Let's go, go, go, people. Action!" The band rocked, and the flames burned until the wires suspending the frame melted and the burning glass crashed to the floor. "That's a wrap."

In Minneapolis a week later, the three of us gathered to watch the first edit of our video. The screen started black and then faded up on a montage of flames that dissolved into a close-up of Dan singing the opening verse.

"Nice, Dan." *Always make the first compliment.*

Boom boom boom. The camera pulled back to reveal the entire band. There I was in the background, hunching over the drums and grimacing. An alarming patch of scalp showed on the top of my skull. *Eew.*

"You look really good, Jake."

While Dan and John were shown tossing their full heads of hair and staring coolly into the lens, I looked like a man strapped into a burning Tilt-a-Whirl. The camera cut to me for a cymbal crash, and instead of the satisfying downward arc of my arms I had imagined, my sticks flicked at the cymbals as if I were tapping wineglasses with a pair of spoons.

"The fire looks cool."

"Yeah. The fire looks awesome."

"Whoa, another cool shot of you, Jake." *Help!*

There was fire everywhere—flames superimposed behind Dan, flames burning around the picture frame, flames licking over shots of us standing side by side. We watched several times and made notes. Only after repeated viewings was I able to stomach the shots of me playing drums, of which there were too many.

"I think we need more shots of Dan."

"And maybe another shot of the burning picture frame."

"And the video shows me hitting the rack tom when I should be hitting the snare."

"No one's gonna worry about that."

We passed our editing comments along to MCA, who had to sign off on our suggestions before relaying them to Doug, who made the final tweaks. Two days later, he handed the finished video to MCA, and MCA delivered it to MTV. And what was their response?

"We can't show a video with all this fire!" Our timing could not have been worse. MTV had recently become embroiled in controversy because some teenagers, allegedly inspired by the cartoon characters of the MTV show *Beavis and Butthead*, had started a fire and a lawsuit was pending. MTV handed the video back to MCA, and MCA handed the video back to Doug. "Get rid of the flames."

Doug, who had been down this road before with cockroaches, asked if there was money available to shoot new footage. There wasn't. MCA instructed him to excise all shots of flames, a revision akin to removing the sinking ship from *Titanic*. Doug complained that this didn't leave enough footage to work with, and MCA made a list of the most egregious fire shots that had to be removed.

The final version, still flame-ridden, was redelivered to MTV, but it hardly mattered. By this point, the song had flopped at radio. Furthermore, MTV's executives were still freaked out by all of the fire footage. I saw its premiere on *120 Minutes*, a Sunday-night show featuring new videos by lesser-known bands. I waited patiently through the shots of Dan, John, and me hunched over the drums and looking concerned, and enjoyed my two seconds of glory—a slow pan across my face as I stood in that handsome white leather jacket, staring at the lens with iconic blankness.

After that, it was played a handful of times and then thrown onto the big pile of videos that never get seen, a very big pile. For $65,000 we had a video that made it no further than the next band's box of director's reels. Actually, it didn't even make it that far, because Doug pulled his reel out of circulation. After his second major fiasco with MTV, he quit making videos for good.

Chapter VIII

FASCINATING NEW THING

The major label offices in L.A. and New York must have looked like ghost towns. The entire music business, it seemed, was jammed into the lobby of the Four Seasons Hotel in Austin, Texas. Label executives, music publishers, program directors, radio promoters, booking agents, and managers—all of them shaking hands, laughing, exchanging private words, and then shouting across the room. Personal assistants stood on sofa cushions scanning the crowd for their bosses, and publicists led band members through the mob, searching for the journalists who would interview them. For the next seventy-two hours, this sea of schmooze was the temporary nerve center of the rock music industry—the South by Southwest Music and Media Conference and Festival (SXSW), a long weekend of rock shows, panel discussions, and buzz management.

In the weeks leading up to the release of our album, scenes like this were increasingly familiar. A month earlier, a slew of MCA's executives, including the new president, Jay Boberg, had crammed inside the upstairs lounge at the Roxy in L.A. to meet us after seeing us perform on the stage downstairs as openers for Aimee Mann. The Roxy show and the party afterward were our introduction to many of the new faces at the label, and I shook hands and posed for pictures with an endless train of executives and people who were "helping out at radio"—independent promoters. (I had yet to learn what their help entailed.)

"Jake, this is_____." Flash.

"And this is_____." Flash.

Each name and face was blotted out with the ensuing splotch of light, but keeping track of the names and faces didn't matter. We had taken the stage that night knowing that with all of the important MCA executives on hand, it would be the Most Important Show we had ever played, and we met that challenge. In fact, we destroyed. My stage confidence was growing along with the muscularity of my drumming and my self-assurance in the face of music business insiders who came backstage after our shows to say, "Un-fucking-believable!"

With my budding confidence, I was starting to get off on scenes like the one at the Roxy, and now in the lobby of the Austin Four Seasons. As we pushed through the throng, I saw Hans, who walked up and slapped our hands. "Ready to blow these fucks away tonight?" *Absolutely.*

Jim looked around. "We'll do okay. The band everyone wants to see is Girls Against Boys."

"Yeah baby!" Hans gushed. "You guys gotta see Girls Against Boys." My confidence dialed itself down a few notches as I dwelled on that familiar band name. While we had looked for a record deal after escaping from Elektra, all A&R eyes, it seemed, were fixed on Girls Against Boys, a punk band whose music was described to me as heavy, rhythmic, and ripe for massive success. Hans himself had taken part in the multilabel bidding war, following the band across the United States and all the way to Amsterdam before losing the signing, as he knew he would, to Geffen. Their shows were legendary, thanks in part to the monstrous low-end produced by two bass players, and by the fact that, as Hans put it, "Every guy in the band is hot!" The A&R man for Geffen who had passed on signing us stood off to the side of the lobby crowd, smiling.

Hans went off to find out what time Girls Against Boys were playing, and I realized that our show would be judged not only by how well we played but also by the attendance. When we took the stage at the Copper Tank at 8 P.M., at least ten other acts would be on stages at other clubs around town, all competing for a finite pool of listeners. By the end of the night, we could be the talk of the music business or MCA's latest flop.

Thus, at 7:55 P.M. I sat in the front seat of our van, sharing a pack of Rolaids with John as we watched the crowd file into the Copper Tank. Dan, lying across the seat behind us, changed his pants, put on his shoes, and the three of us walked into the club for another Most Important Show of our lives. I sat down at my drums, looked down at the setlist taped to the monitor wedge on the floor to my left, picked up my sticks, checked my mike with a "Tssst," and then looked at the crowd. Dan said hello, and as he began to strum his guitar and the chords rang out, hushing the crowd, my attention drifted down from the faces in the front row and onto my drums. I rolled around the tom-toms and crashed the largest of my cymbals, launching us into our fifty-minute set.

We swayed through our opening number, a cover of the Hollies song "The Air That I Breathe" that started as a lullaby and gradually progressed to a final chorus of loud chiming guitars, loping bass and drums, and clouds of three-part vocal harmonies. The applause that overtook the final note soon gave way to Dan's guitar as he started the next song, our own "f.n.t." The energy in the room lifted with the tempo of this song and the eight that followed. I had never drummed so well. I channeled fills from my drummer's imagination that caught even me by surprise, as if I were sitting down at the drums for the very first time and discovering instant mastery. On several occasions, John lifted the head of his bass and snarled back at me in approval, and Dan crashed toward John with his guitar, grinning as he surfed the groove with solos that bent at strange new angles. After fifty minutes of this insanity, we walked off the stage to the crowd's roaring approval and directly out of the club to our van, where we leaned against the back bumper. We said nothing, as if waking from a dream of the best show we had ever played. Hans walked out, giddy. "Un-fucking-believable! People were wetting themselves!"

We changed out of our stage clothes and walked into the Austin evening. Our job was done. The first few hundred yards had the feel of a victory lap, but soon we came upon fans screaming at a rousing outdoor performance by Ben Folds Five. Then we filed into Liberty Lunch to watch Fred Schneider, the singer of the B-52s, rock the capacity crowd of a thousand with songs from his new solo record. Before long I lost track of Dan and John, and I walked through the streets looking for the Girls Against Boys show. By the time I found the club, the line stretched around the block and I couldn't get in. I did more walking. Just after midnight, I bumped into Dan and the two of us walked down Sixth Street in search of a cab. Every ten yards, the sound of drums, cymbals, and guitars came crashing out of the clubs lining both sides of the street, and when we climbed into our taxi, the last shows of the night had not even begun. The next morning, I got a report from Hans on the Girls Against Boys show: "People were wetting themselves!"

Thus went the battle for attention in the weeks leading up to the release of our album. Our stellar performance at South by Southwest received scattered praise from the music press—mainly journalists for midwestern newspapers—but had largely gone unmentioned. Now all we could hope was that the release of our album would catch fire with the listeners the way our live performances did.

It was early April 1996. Our album had been finished the previous July, but its release had been delayed until spring to skip the dreaded fourth quarter of the calendar year, when labels flood record stores and radio playlists with new releases by popular artists, hoping to cash in on the holiday shopping season. We were on the road on the day of our album's release, so I had my first official sighting of our album in a record store in Detroit. I wasted a minute looking for the "Semisonic" section, then dug through the "Miscellaneous Rock—S" section, where I found two copies of *Great Divide* by Semisonic. I bought one for myself.

The album cover art was a painting of snails crawling among rocks and plants by Alexis Rockman, a favorite painter of Dan's. Other than the painting's beauty, the reasons for choosing that artwork elude me now, but at the time it seemed ingenious . . . at least to the band. When Jim first saw the cover design we had cooked up with MCA's art department, he reached for a bottle of aspirin. He had already questioned our choice of band name— "*Semisonic* sounds too mechanical"—and our album cover concept struck him as equally obtuse. He called each of us to express concern over the album artwork and was beat back with band logic about the distinctiveness of the painting and how great ideas always seem weird at first. The fact that MCA had approved the album design further frustrated him. Shouldn't record companies be counted on to correct a band's missteps in the areas of image and marketing? Not MCA. "Since when does the manager have to ask the record company to print the band's name in larger type?" Jim found himself sandwiched between rock-band impracticality and label carelessness.

Our snail-covered album was in stores, and all attention would now turn to sales. Record companies, radio stations, and music insiders depend on sales reports from a service called SoundScan to see which records are connecting and which ones are fizzling. SoundScan's subscribers receive weekly reports tabulating album sales, nationwide and city by city, and SoundScan's numbers are those used by sister company *Billboard* in compiling the weekly sales charts.

In the old days, the sales charts, like the radio charts, were subject to corruption. For example, record companies paid record-store managers to falsify the sales reports, crediting an album with phony sales and thus helping it attain a higher chart position than it had actually earned. SoundScan prevents that practice by down-loading most of its data directly from the cash registers. Another old method by which record companies overstated album sales was to buy huge quantities of records from the stores and then recycle them back through the system. SoundScan protects against this practice by discounting transactions that don't resemble the likely behavior of a consumer. For instance, if someone goes into a store and buys one hundred copies of the same CD, it looks suspicious and will therefore be kept out of SoundScan's reports. Thus, when talking about how many records an artist has sold, one talks about how many records that artist has "SoundScanned."

I had no conception of what our opening week's album sales figures might be. On the one hand, "Down in Flames" had done poorly on the radio. On the other, we had received some great press, and the crowds at our shows were bigger and more respon-sive than ever. By now, 7,000 people had signed up for our mailing list, in addition to the Trip Shakespeare fans and the hundreds of thousands of people who had heard us on the radio, some of whom had to have liked us. I rolled up all of those figures and es-timated that 20,000 people were eager to buy our record, and half of them would do so in the first week. Sales of 10,000, I later learned, would have been a respectable showing, though far short of the pace of a hit album, which can sell at many times that rate. I sat on my estimate, and then cut it to 5,000, just to be extra sure that I wasn't setting myself up for disappointment.

Great Divide sold 1,000 copies in the first week. I actually thought Jim had misspoken when he told me. According to the SoundScan report, hardly anyone outside of Minneapolis bought the album. The next week's SoundScan number fell below 900—a miserable showing. Hans said, "Give the record some time to grow on people," but I could hear the strain in his voice. We stayed on the road, and with each disappointing sales report from Jim and Hans I focused myself more intently on rocking every crowd and winning more fans.

We got an opening slot for The Verve Pipe, a band we knew from Michigan who quickly became our good friends. Their record had come out a few weeks prior to our own. Unlike us, however, they had a hit song, "Photograph," the opening key-board riff of which aroused cheers from the crowd that were louder than any our songs had generated. This was not the only point of comparison between us and them. After each show, while we drove to the nearest Super 8, The Verve Pipe and their crew stretched out on their luxurious tour bus and watched movies as they rolled down the highway to the next city on the tour. By the time they awoke in their bunks and stepped off the bus in front of the next venue at noon on the following day, we would have already been up for several hours, driving in our van to catch up to them. We would arrive in the late afternoon with sore legs and stiff backs.

Usually, the MCA local was waiting for us, ready to drive us off for a few radio visits before soundcheck. I was impatient for news.

"How's it going?"

"Good. My girlfriend and I just back from a great trip to Thailand."

"I mean at radio. How's that going?"

"Good. We're still working the Sublime song, and we've got Live's new single coming up." (Sublime and Live were two of MCA's recent successes.)

"I mean, how's it going at radio for *Semisonic?*"

"Oh . . . I mean, radio likes you guys, but it's tough right now."

We were now visiting some stations for the second and third time. The locals moved slowly and smiled stiffly as we unpacked our instruments in the broadcast booths. I, however, resolved to make things happen, hustling my bandmates along. "Here's your tuner. Anybody need water?" I dove into the interviews with newfound brazenness. How was our record doing? "Everywhere we go, people tell us how excited they are about it."

The DJ might say, "I won't take your CD out of my car stereo, and with all the press you're getting, you've gotta feel great."

And I'd affirm the fiction of our success. "Yeah. It's kind of amazing."

When it came time to play a song on the air, I smacked the overturned water jug with authority, as if my jug playing might somehow make a difference. I exercised the muscles of faked optimism all the way through our good-bye handshakes to the ever-more-distant program directors. Sometimes, as we shuffled out to the parking lot, we'd pass The Verve Pipe as they came striding in for a "drive time" interview, a prized segment of airtime during the evening commute, reserved for bands with heat. "Photograph" was a hit on alternative stations, and their album, *Villains*, was on its way to gold status. "Down in Flames," on the other hand, had all but expired, and our weekly SoundScan numbers remained submerged below 1,000. As *Great Divide* gasped for air, our friends inside the business voiced different theories.

"You guys handed MCA a great record and they're blowing it."

"It's a tough time for new bands."

"Why is MCA pushing you at alternative? Counting Crows broke through at triple-A."

But maybe it was us. Hans gathered the band for dinner in New York and said, "Guys, there's no nice way to say this, but you look old."

"How old?"

"Thirties."

"We *are* in our thirties."

"I know, but your audience is in their teens and twenties."

Jim sat next to Hans and looked on quietly, suggesting to me that Hans was speaking for both of them. John was particularly incensed by the tone of the conversation, and Hans, sensing the anger and agonizing over the duty of delivering unpleasant advice, tightened up and began to blurt. It didn't take long for things to deteriorate.

"Well, you . . . it's just that . . . I . . . You look like shit when you walk on stage!"

"Fuck you!"

Afterward, I called Hans and asked him for suggestions as to how I could improve my appearance, but he had nothing to say, which hinted at his regret at having raised the subject or perhaps the fact that his attention was focused on Dan and John.

At the clubs, I lugged my drums on and off stage, jealous of the drummers in the bands we played with. They were spared these chores, thanks to an extra crew member. Doing the lugging myself seriously undercut my rock-star aspirations. Our guitar tech, Toby Kutrieb, took care of Dan and John's equipment. I asked Jim when I would receive the same treatment. "Dan and John have been doing this for so long, I'm sure you'll agree we gotta take care of them first, but you're a trooper." Perhaps, but I hadn't worked years of day jobs so that I might someday become a trooper.

None of that, however, dulled the glory of our hour on stage every night. We were playing more strongly than ever, and even as we ventured far from our midwestern stomping grounds, the crowds were increasingly enthusiastic. In Seattle, Boston, Philadelphia, Portland, the Carolinas, and the Rockies, I recognized faces from our previous shows. And as we loaded our equipment back into the van at the end of the night, some of those fans walked down the alley to ask for autographs. Naturally, Dan and John received most of the attention, but I learned the art of pretending to load the van while making myself visible to autograph seekers.

"You're the drummer, right?"

"Me? Yeah."

"Would you sign my CD?"

I learned a lot by reading what Dan and John had inscribed. Including the person's name was customary. "To Joe. Best wishes, Jacob Slichter." Of course, you have to check on the spelling. Is it Joe or Jo? I ruined dozens of CDs for people named Kym, Sara, and Mandi. And what about the message? What if the words "Best Wishes Carol" feel too tame for someone with spiked hair, a pierced eyebrow, and glittery sneakers? What about her friends? *I better give each of them a different version.*

Cheers Teri

Rock on Tim!

4 Suzie

I experimented with more elaborate messages, sometimes scribbling fluff across the pages of the CD booklet while my mind searched for the elusive final flourish.

Dear Kristi, glad you like the music. Nice shirt. We'll come back to Kalamazoo. What a sweet town. I like your shoes too. Thanks for bringing your friends.

Jacob Slichter

P.S. Go Kristi!

Often I'd pause in the middle of an inscription, embarrassed to be standing in front of a fan with a Sharpie in my hand and a blank look on my face as I tried to remember the proper spelling of *occasion*. Once in a while, I even botched my signature, the ultimate autographing sin.

In the late spring and early summer, we played a string of radio festivals. These were outdoor concerts with names like EdgeFest,

The River Rave, and The Summer Splash, each drawing thousands of listeners to see a lineup of ten or more bands. These shows are often billed as charity fund-raisers, but as I learned, many of them are big moneymakers for the stations. Plus, by sponsoring a show featuring several of the listeners' favorite bands, a station enhances its image.

MCA had decided to release a second Semisonic single, "If I Run," and Jim told me that in return for playing a station's festival, we'd receive airplay that we otherwise would not. (I heard this referred to as "show-ola.") Sometimes we were returning a favor for the station's earlier support. Sometimes, too, the rival stations would drop Semisonic from their rotation, or at least keep us in low rotation until after our appearance at the crosstown rival's festival. Unlike the main attractions on the festival bill, big bands who received big money for their appearance, we received little or no money, though MCA usually covered our travel expenses, figuring that the airplay was worth it.

The concerts usually began in the afternoon, starting with the lesser-known acts like us and progressing to the main attractions who play under the lights after sundown. Typically, we walked on stage before most of the fans had even arrived. When we hit the stage for Planetfest at Pineknob outside of Detroit, the amphitheater was three-quarters empty. At The River Rave outside of Boston, the big acts performed for 7,000 while we played on a side stage for 300, and many of those fans ignored us, watching instead the acrobatic skateboarding exhibition taking place to our left. At 104 Fest in Massachusetts, while the big bands rocked tens of thousands of fans at a racetrack, we played in a nearby amusement park for a trickle of weary parents and toddlers. However small or uninterested the crowd, it made no difference. I hit the drums with the determination that we had to win over every listener.

On a few occasions, we took the stage in front of big crowds and the energy was fearsome—thousands of people pushing against each other, pinning the people up front against the stage barriers. Kids climbed up on top of their friends and grinned as they surfed across a sea of supporting hands. Often, the crowd surfers would taunt the concert security guards who pointed and shouted at them to stop, sometimes wading into the crowd to yank the surfers to the ground and haul them away with their arms twisted behind their backs. Women who crowd-surfed were sometimes groped from below. Shoving matches between fans sometimes escalated into fights, and a swarm of security guards would descend, sometimes inflicting more violence than they were trying to stop. Even in the absence of such disturbances, I had to play my drums while dodging Frisbees and beach balls and ducking under flying bottles. For some, hurling things at the stage was merely an expression of approval. In the autograph booth after a show, it wasn't unusual for a fan to smile and say, "Hey, I threw that bottle at you!" The festival crowds were manic and, if made impatient, capable of turning their unruliness against a new band, something Jim emphasized to me over the phone.

"Jake, tell Dan to stay away from the soft stuff and the slow stuff."

"Yup."

"Play 'If I Run' near the end of the set. That's the next single."

"Got it."

"No extended jams, okay?"

"Okay."

"Tell Dan it doesn't look cheesy to say, 'Hi, we're Semisonic and we've got a record out.' "

"Gotcha."

"And tell him 'no long stories,' okay?"

Dan's long stories were the subject of many calls from Jim. As the front man who did most of the talking from the stage, Dan had two personas, one of them to the point—"This is a song about seeing your ex walking around with someone new"—and the other, rambling—"I just read this really cool book called *Consciousness Explained* which talks about the brain, and, I know you didn't come here for an anatomy lesson, but anyway it turns out that . . ." When Rambling Dan got loose on stage, there was no telling what would happen. He perused the coffee table of his brain for minutes on end, sometimes forcing us to cut a song from our set. If his five-minute tribute to a building whose architecture he admired began to arouse scattered grumbles, John and I would look at our feet and point our thought waves in Dan's direction. *Abort! Abort!*

Some crowds, however, found these meandering stories enormously entertaining. So I'd relax, dose up on cranberry juice, and listen to a story that linked the biologist E. O. Wilson, the IDS tower in downtown Minneapolis, and the experience of being stuck at the top of a Ferris wheel on a first date. The fans were often charmed by Rambling Dan, though Jim, if he was on hand, would shake his head from the side of the stage.

Playing for tens of thousands of strangers at these festivals, our gestures, both musical and physical, became grander. I learned a lot by watching drummers for the headline acts and even taking cues from the air-drumming of some in the crowd. The finer subtleties that spiced up our club shows—small flourishes on the drums, a fast run on the guitar—had to be replaced with singular moves that made sense to people hundreds of rows from the stage—an arcing strum of a power chord, cavemanlike pounding of the tom-toms. The festival fans responded to some of these moves, but for the most part, it seemed we were merely supplying the background music to their moshing. Only the famous headline acts could command an audience of tens of thousands as Cracker's singer David Lowery did when he pointed his microphone at a crowd of 80,000 in Charleston, South Carolina, and they responded by screaming in unison, "EURO-TRASH GIRL!"

The add-date for our second single, "If I Run," was in June. The initial signs were good—Atlanta's 99X and a couple of other major stations added it—but these hopeful signs soon gave way to pessimistic reports from the locals about slow phones and weak research. This, in turn, gave way to more speculation from our friends in the business:

"There's a lot of singles hanging around radio right now."

"MCA should never have picked 'Down in Flames' as the first single. That fucked you guys."

"Radio is fucked."

"MCA is fucked."

In the months since we had met them, the MCA locals had gone from chipper to noncommittal and now to griping. "Don't tell anyone, but I'm looking for a new job."

Additional hundreds of thousands of dollars in independent promotion yielded nothing. According to the locals, the alternative stations said we were "too triple-A," the AAA stations said we were "too pop," and the pop stations wouldn't play us because no one else would. And, of course, MTV would never play the video we made (about a teenage boy who works at an ice-cream parlor and dreams of running away with a rock band to escape his oppressive boss and an endless train of customers).

MCA was at a loss. Our songs were catchy, but our sound didn't fit squarely into any particular niche on the radio. Perhaps we would have to try some other avenue. The worldwide staff of Universal Music International, the distribution company of MCA's parent company, was gathering in Dublin, and MCA convinced the executives in charge of that meeting to fly Semisonic over to perform. If they liked us, they might release our CD overseas.

We flew to Dublin, and after a morning of sightseeing, we set up in a pub rented for the occasion. At four in the afternoon, twenty-five executives from Universal International filed in and took their seats at the back of the club, far from the stage. Three young Dubliners snuck in off the street, and as soon as we started to play, these three took their beers onto the dance floor, spilling them as they shook their hips and whooped it up. The suits, meanwhile, applauded politely from their seats in the back. It was as if we were playing two very small shows at once. By the end of our set, the exuberance of the threesome in front had paved the way for a stronger reaction from the executives, and we walked off stage to a respectable ovation. A few of the suits stepped forward to shake our hands.

"Very nice. I'd love to release your record in Portugal. Perhaps we could bring you guys over."

"I work in the Norway office. You guys would do great in Scandinavia."

Before long, however, the main executive in charge elbowed his way into the conversation and quashed the offers made by his subordinates. "We don't release albums by American bands that haven't become hits in the States." We asked why, in that case, we had been flown over. "I'm just telling you our policy." He smiled, shrugged his shoulders, and wished us a happy Fourth of July. Our 1996 world tour lasted thirty-six hours.

Back home, nothing was changing. MCA's retail staff, those who manage the relationships with the various record stores, took us around to outlets of major chains and small independent shops to play short acoustic sets and meet the store personnel. We signed autographs for the handful of fans that came. It wasn't unusual to find our record displayed in the "store favorites" section.

On several occasions, in smaller independent stores, I saw the retail staff buy multiple copies of our album. I learned that this was a trick to circumvent a small vulnerability in the SoundScan system. The cash registers in independent record stores are not wired into its system, and rather than compile sales figures from hundreds of small shops, SoundScan identifies a select few independent stores, known as "weighted SoundScan stores," and multiplies their sales figures to calculate the cumulative sales of all the other independents. If the retail staff discovered that a particular store was one of these "weighted SoundScan stores," they could purchase ten records and create the illusion of citywide sales of 100.

I obsessed about the weekly sales figures, anguishing as they sank—751, 705, 611, 593—and clenching my fists as they rose again—834, 896, 949. By contrast, Dan and John shielded themselves from hearing these reports, all the more reason for me to be embarrassed by how easily my attention and vocabulary had been hijacked by SoundScan, research, and phones. *I'll bet the guys from Radiohead and R.E.M. don't call in for SoundScan numbers.*

I obsessed over even the smallest signs of hope—the sound of our music being played in a coffee shop in Philadelphia, "Semisonic" sections in record stores anywhere, the sight of our album in "recommended listening" displays, and reports from friends around the country who heard our album in various settings. A clothing designer in Los Angeles specializing in clothes for rock stars sent us a box of custom-made pants. And the MCA publicity department faxed us copies of our reviews, which continued to be positive:

> *"A touch of genius" (Steve Morse*, Boston Globe*)*
>
> *"One of the best bands to come out of Minneapolis in years" (Charles Cross,* Seattle Rocket*)*
>
> "Great Divide *is great music, and reason enough this summer to vote for Semisonic as the Best Pop in America." (Ken Richardson,* Stereo Review*)*

After months of opening for other bands, we embarked on our own headline tour of clubs, and the crowds continued to build. MCA even paid for a tour bus (though not as nice as The Verve

Pipe's, as our crew grumbled). I was relieved of my drum setup duties, free to saunter on and off stage with nothing but my sticks. Fans in Phoenix, Boston, Boulder, and Kalamazoo called us by name. The flirts in the front row winked, and their boyfriends in the second row were impressed enough to keep their hands planted firmly on their girlfriends' shoulders.

Some of the flirts persisted past the point of playfulness, sending obvious invitations to the possibility of postshow encounters with the drummer. That was a moment to turn away and make myself all the more unattainable, driving up my stock. Such blatant propositions were the first I had ever received from strangers, a testament to the magnetism of the stage and perhaps my growing confidence. The brazen nature of such an advance raised several possibilities in my mind: bad, a tease who toyed with the libidos of countless rock drummers; worse, a sex partner of countless rock drummers; and worst, a knife-wielding stalker of only one rock drummer—me! I directed my eyes elsewhere.

My back-and-forth with the crowd only made my drumming stronger and the sound of the band bigger. The crowds called us back for multiple encores. The growing response around the country excited my friends and family, some of whom outlined schemes for success.

"See, Jake, the people are looking for something different, and that's you guys. Print up the phone numbers of the radio stations and hand out flyers at your shows. Tell the people to call the stations and demand Semisonic, are you following me?"

"Uh-huh."

"And if the stations still refuse to play you, send out an e-mail to your fans telling them to picket the stations until they do. Start a goddamn listeners' revolt! Turn it into a contest with prizes and everything."

"Right. Thanks."

The SoundScan numbers continued to rise. When we hit 1,200,

Hans called. If we hit 2,500 in one week, he said, "Things can start to snowball."

Jim called with more good news. A Hollywood director wanted to use our song "f.n.t." in an upcoming action film, *The Long Kiss Goodnight,* starring Geena Davis and Samuel L. Jackson. The director evidently loved the song. MCA was releasing the soundtrack album and picked "f.n.t." to be the first single. New Line Cinemas, the studio producing the film, agreed to pay for the cost of the video since the video would include scenes from the movie and thus be a valuable promotional tool. Most important, New Line would advertise the film on MTV, and in turn MTV would likely show its appreciation for that advertising revenue by airing the video. Here was our chance to do an end run around MTV's usual prohibition against videos of songs that were not yet radio hits.

We shot the video in one night, and it looked great. The set was a giant replica of a camera. We stood in front of this replica and played as the enormous shutter eye opened, revealing the blinding glare from a floodlight, and then closed again. Two weeks later, the MTV executives reviewed the final edit—Semisonic inside a giant camera intercut with movie footage of Geena Davis and Samuel L. Jackson as they jumped through the air and ran around, punching, kicking, and shooting the bad guys. Movie stars, explosions, car chases, and even a bit of rock band dressed up in custom-made clothes—it looked like a big-budget video. After screening it, however, MTV handed the tape back to MCA. "We've had too many of these videos with film footage lately. Sorry."

MCA took "f.n.t." to radio, spending still more money on independent promotion but with little results. There was a new person in charge of radio promotion at MCA, and the department was in disarray. Some of the locals had quit or been fired, and their replacements were not short on excuses for why our song was getting shut out. "It's the fourth quarter. All the big records are coming out."

The music industry insiders offered their perspective. "No one at radio has faith in MCA to deliver on you guys."

"They should have focused more on triple-A."

"MCA's in the middle of changing their radio team."

"They should have focused more on alternative."

"The fourth quarter's fucked."

The SoundScan numbers inched up at Christmastime, as did our spins on rock radio, a format we had largely ignored in favor of alternative and AAA. Maybe that was the trick. Maybe, unbeknownst to us, our music was destined to entertain the spectators at monster-truck shows. And as I thumbed through *Rolling Stone*'s year-end issue in a bookstore, I was amazed to see that a senior editor had picked *Great Divide* as one of the best albums of the year.

> . . . Great Divide is that rare '96 beast, a record of simple but sparkling modern pop, rattling with power-trio vitality. The album's luminous guitar-vocal glaze bears the distinct imprint of singer/guitarist Dan Wilson and singer/bassist John Munson's former band, arch popsters Trip Shakespeare. But the subtle melodic torsion in songs like "Delicious," "f.n.t." and "Across the Great Divide," and the contagious vigor of the performances, are wholly Semisonic. By the way, "f.n.t." stands for fascinating new thing. Perfect.

I stood stunned, rereading the review for half an hour before buying the magazine. This was a major coup. Might it breathe life into our album?

Jim called. "Time to find a producer for the next record." What about the review? What about "f.n.t." at rock radio? "Jake, it's done. Time to move on."

Great Divide had sold just over 30,000 copies. It was a critical success and a commercial disaster. Our recoupable debt to MCA was well over a million dollars. After I hung up the phone, I looked over the floor of my apartment, which was littered with plane tickets, video treatments, tour itineraries, and lots and lots of reviews. Then I closed my eyes and envisioned the possibility of returning to my day job. This was not the way the year was supposed to end.

Chapter IX

A COLD YEAR AT HOME

The phone rang. It was Jim. "Everyone says The Verve Pipe's next single is gonna be a smash."

"Hooray."

"C'mon, be happy. They're your friends."

"I *am* happy . . . for them."

Jim urged me not to give up. Semisonic had impressed various people in the world of radio, he said, and a number of stations would be willing to play the first single off of our next record. "But the next single we bring to them has to be big. You know that, right?"

"But—"

After three failed singles on the last record, he said, we could count on only one more chance. "Gotta go. Stay positive."

A minute later, the phone rang again. It was Hans.

"Why doesn't Dan answer his phone?" Dan's aversion to the phone, especially when he had sequestered himself in his room to write songs, infuriated Hans, who then called me for reports on the progress of Dan's writing. When would Hans get to hear songs? What had Dan been saying about the direction of the material for the new album?

With nothing much to say, I made the mistake of offering the following tidbit. "He says he's been listening to some old Cat Stevens and Simon and Garfunkel albums."

"WELL, HE BETTER START LISTENING TO THE FUCK-ING RADIO!" I closed my eyes. Hans then launched into a rant about how our last record was too soft for alternative radio, and that with the alternative format getting louder, the last thing we needed to sound like was "Simon and fucking Garfunkel!"

Hans hated this part of his job, anguishing on our behalf and having to tell us to make our music louder and faster or to dress ourselves younger. As always, his furioso opening blast was followed by a quick decrescendo into a more reasoned explanation—"Remember how it sucked to be shut out by radio?"—a counterpoint of self-doubt—"I mean I'm no musician, why should anyone listen to me?"—a gradual diminuendo—"I guess I shouldn't worry . . . right?"—and then a grand pause, followed by his apology, pianissimo. I took a breath and softly reassured him that his point was a good one.

After hanging up the phone, I bundled up, scraped off my windshield, and drove over to Dan's. He met me at the door in his slippers and led me into his living room, where he sat cross-legged on the couch, holding his acoustic guitar. I plopped down into a chair and smiled. "So how's the writing?"

He strummed a little, humming to himself. A minute later, he answered: "Huh?"

"The writing. How's it going?" A drop of melting snow ran down my ankle.

"Good."

"Cool. So . . . what kind of sound are you thinking of for the new record?"

He brushed his fingers over the strings and hummed faintly. Then he stared into the gap between two books on his bookshelf. Time stopped, then started again. "Intimate."

I joined him in looking at the bookshelf. "Yeah. Intimate. That's cool." I waited for his eyes to look back in my direction. "What about intimate and loud?"

He tickled the strings and slowly swiveled his head back and forth, humming in a wispy falsetto. Then, fixing his eyes on a molecule of air inches above my head, he froze, and then spoke again. "Intimate."

Over the next few weeks, I made similar crosstown trips, relaying to Dan various opinions from Hans and Jim concerning the direction of our next album, but Dan rejected them. "This is our last chance to make the record we want to make. No one can predict where radio is going, so why worry about it?"

Meanwhile, Dan recruited an offbeat but inspiring producer for the album, Nick Launay, an Englishman whose discography ranged from punk (Public Image Ltd., featuring John Lydon, aka Johnny Rotten of the Sex Pistols; Gang of Four; and Birthday Party, led by Nick Cave) to pop (Midnight Oil), grunge (Silverchair), and the offbeat (Kate Bush and David Byrne). Nick eschewed standard production methods, something that excited Dan and unnerved Hans, who nevertheless gave his approval.

Dan then insisted to Hans that we be allowed to record in Minneapolis, a strategy to further insulate us from the Los Angeles way of doing things. "And I don't want to make demos. The demos always turn out better than the record, so let's wait until we're in the studio. Then the demos can *be* the record." A band with an unsuccessful first album going into an unknown studio in Minneapolis to record an artsy, intimate second album without making any demos—to Hans, this sounded like the story line of an A&R horror film, but given his reluctance to battle Dan's iron will, he yielded on every point.

For his part, John wondered why we should rush into making a new record so soon after our exhausting and disappointing year on the road. I, too, wanted to postpone things, hoping an extra month or two would give me a shot at completing one or two songs. Meanwhile, Dan had written sixty songs, all of them good and some of them great. He and his wife, Diane, were expecting a baby in June, and I wondered if Dan had gone on this songwriting binge to take advantage of his last days in a quiet house. Several of his new songs reflected his expectations of fatherhood.

With our time in the studio fast approaching, Dan sat John and me down and told us that there were problems with the pregnancy. Over the next few weeks, the situation worsened, and on the eve of Nick Launay's arrival an emergency forced the doctors to deliver the baby three months early. The baby girl, Coco, entered the world weighing eleven ounces—too small, it seemed, to survive. Dan told me that the span of her fully expanded hand, from pinky to thumb, was equal to the width of an adult fingernail.

The reports from the doctors and nurses were alternately hopeful and grim. Each hour that Coco prevailed over the odds was a victory, but a tenuous one. When Nick arrived (from Sydney, Australia), Dan gave him the news. Nick offered to postpone the recording if that's what Dan wanted. Jim and Hans assured Dan that canceling the sessions would be no problem, but Dan and Diane decided that recording would provide Dan a welcome relief from pacing the halls of the neonatal intensive care unit. The studio was a short drive from the hospital, and he could still visit several times a day.

So we started to record our second album, which had become both an art project and an emotional lifeboat. John and I had discovered a new studio planted in the shadows of downtown Minneapolis. The sidewalks and gutters in front of it were littered with empty bottles from the parade of customers stumbling out of the liquor store across the street. The larger building that housed the studio—an old brick structure whose rotting upper floors had been abandoned for years—was owned by the proprietor of a used-plumbing-supply store. Occasionally, his employees would knock on the door and disappear into the basement to retrieve a used toilet.

The studio itself was brand new, untested. The owner assured us it would be finished in time for us to make our record, and as we loaded in our equipment on the first day of recording, we held the door open for the painters, who emerged with their tarps, ladders, and paint buckets, leaving behind the fumes of the thick orange paint drying on the walls. Metal sculptures adorned various doorways and light fixtures. We walked through the control room, a treasure trove of vintage audio gear. Through the paint fumes and burning incense, the faint odor of what later turned out to be a leaky sewer line seeped up through the cracks of the creaking floorboards in the main recording space. The aging structure, the vintage audio gear in the control room, the orange walls and ceilings, and the funky artwork all conformed to the studio owner's bohemian aesthetic. He named his studio Seedy Underbelly, and we figured we were either going to make a vibey record there or perish in the building's fiery collapse.

Nick unpacked the gear he had shipped from Australia: several trunks of audio equipment, a toy X-ray gun, and a puppet of a boxing alien. I set up my drums in a small soundproof room, taking breaks to recover from the suffocating paint fumes. Nick positioned the microphones in configurations we had never seen, at times aiming them at extramusical elements—the creaking floorboards or an idle snare drum hissing in the corner.

As Dan had suggested, we had rehearsed only minimally for the record in order to keep the performances fresh. As a result, the music came forth with spontaneity and lots of mistakes as we fumbled our way through unfamiliar material. Nick, who wanted the album to sound as human and alive as possible, fought to preserve many of the mistakes captured on tape, overcoming the offending musician's objections.

"But I'm speeding up during that section."

"Trust me, mate, it's brilliant."

Nick loved the sound of messiness—the antique upright piano with its dicey tuning, the crackle of a guitar chord being unplugged from an amp and then plugged in again, the sounds made by an old synthesizer in the hands of someone fiddling with unfamiliar dials and switches. At the end of a take, he kept the tape rolling, as if to dare one of us to produce an unexpected guitar squeal or bass blast, or to crack a joke. Sometimes the boxing alien puppet appeared on the other side of the control-room glass, conducting us through the performance. During a percussion overdub, I laughed while shaking the tambourine, and, no question, we *had* to keep the laughter.

We rented an empty storefront two doors down from Seedy Underbelly and set up a second studio there, using our own recording equipment. There, led by John, we brewed up a lot of the sonic chaos (backward vocals, sampling and processing of existing guitar tracks, exploration with various synthesizers lying about) that we felt had been missing from the last record. Nick applauded these experiments, and at the end of every night, he took our overdubs back to the main studio and copied them onto the master tapes. Slowly, our album began to assume a bohemian aesthetic of its own.

The recordings, full of personality, moved me. As I listened, however, I kept in mind Jim's warning: "We get only one more chance." I heard the voices of music-business ghosts, past and future, telling me why our new songs might not get played on the radio.

It's too slow.

It takes too long to build.

It's not loud enough.

If the voices persuaded me, I spoke up, "Let's do a faster version," and often wondered if Dan and John had been hearing those same voices.

In the midst of all of this were the constant updates on Coco, who overcame various surgeries, fought off infections, and grew. After a few weeks, tiny as she was, she was big enough for Dan and Diane to hold, though even the best reports were shadowed by fear and anguish, and all of it seeped into the performances. The extreme fragility of Coco's existence revealed deeper dimensions to the songs Dan had written in anticipation of having a child.

Made to last awhile
And roll on
Made to move in style
And move along

Made to dream of flying
So high
Made to wake up crying
I don't know why

Beautiful one
Asleep in the sun
Secret, sweet & sublime
I hope you last a long, long time

Made to come alone
And pair up
Flash like a rolling stone
Seventy-one

One time love affair
With the earth
Waiting on the air
For some re-birth
(For what it's worth)

Wherever you are
Nearby or far
Black, white, lemon or lime
I hope you last a long, long time

We threw out several versions of that song, "Made to Last," before arriving at the final arrangement, slower and gentler than the rest. The prescriptions for radio success—faster, louder, and shorter—did not suit it, but as I sat in the control room listening to the playback of Dan's final vocal, I was overcome by sadness and awe.

In every regard, this second experience of recording an album was much more satisfying than my first had been two years earlier. Far from worrying about getting fired, I now felt confident about my drumming. In addition to a cowriting credit for "Never You Mind," Dan's song to which I added a bridge, I contributed one that was entirely mine, "This Will Be My Year." And in the final weeks of recording in July, I wrote some string arrangements for "Gone to the Movies" and "Secret Smile." We hired musicians from the local symphony, and as they read from my handwritten parts, I stood over them waving a drumstick. *A drummer who writes string arrangements—that ought to get me some press.*

We finished recording in August. Hans had promised he would find an "A-list mixer," and we got a call from Bob Clearmountain, the best-known mix engineer in the world. His discography is a parade of mega-smashes, including "Start Me Up" by the Rolling Stones, "Born in the USA" by Bruce Springsteen, "We Are Family" by Sister Sledge, "Rock the Casbah" by the Clash, and "Good Times" by Chic. By early September, we found ourselves in the lush hills west of Hollywood, reclining on the chairs around Bob Clearmountain's swimming pool and listening through the open sliding-glass doors as he mixed our album in his state-of-the-art home studio. Hans, who flew out from New York for the mix sessions, was feeling good about the record.

The personal nature of Nick's recordings suggested a black-and-white French film noir. By contrast, Bob Clearmountain's trademark sound resembled a wide-screen Technicolor blockbuster. Nick would have mixed our album differently, and Bob would have recorded it differently, but to the band's ears, the superimposition of their two approaches produced wonderful results—sort of a French film noir blockbuster. Bob himself delighted in uncovering some of the forgotten treasures that Nick had kept on tape. "Cool. There's someone laughing on the tambourine track!"

As we gathered in the mix studio to listen, Hans smiled from the couch in the back of the room and joked, "I knew it all along. I'm a fucking genius!" When the conversation turned to detail—the compression ratio on the Marshall—he left the room. At one point, I walked out to the pool and overheard him speaking into his cell phone. "They're talking with Clearmountain about something only a dog can hear, but it sounds great."

Enthused by the results, Hans invited MCA's new head of A&R, Gary Ashley, to hear the mixes and meet the band. (And, of course, to meet Bob Clearmountain, a name any music executive would love to drop into conversation.) Ashley strode into the studio, sat down, and enjoyed what he heard. The quality of the record put him at ease, and within minutes he turned the conversation to the palm tree that had fallen into his swimming pool the night before and the inconvenience of his wife's luxury car undergoing repair. We nodded our heads in sympathy for this upheaval. Then he pressed his hands into his thighs, stood up, and shook our hands good-bye, pleased with how our record was shaping up. After escorting his boss out the door, Hans returned and pulled me aside to shake my hand. "Jake, congratulations. Your drumming has finally arrived."

As mixing progressed, I resumed my old habit of driving up and down the coast and along the freeways while listening to our tapes. Sometimes I switched over to the radio to hear how our mixes stacked up to the fare on KROQ. Several of the bands we had toured with—The Verve Pipe and Tonic, among others—

were still riding out hit records that had been released at the same time as *Great Divide.*

A month later, back in Minneapolis, the weather was turning cold again, and we turned our attention to album artwork. No snails this time; everyone agreed that the album cover should feature a picture of the band. The photo shoot took place on the streets of Minneapolis in the middle of December, where it was ten degrees. *Why are we always getting our pictures taken in the cold?* As we stood outside, posing for the camera, I stuffed my hands into the pockets of my leather jacket and inhaled the frosty air through my reddened nose—"You look great, Jake"—and felt it nip my reddened ears—"Yeah, really great"—and blow through my freshly dyed platinum hair.

That's right, dyed hair. After months of encouragement from John, Dan, Jim, Hans, and my hairdresser, Mimi, I had walked into her salon and held my breath. An hour later, she pulled a plastic bag off of my head, and I saw my face imprisoned by a head of platinum-blond hair.

"Well, Jake, what do you think?" Did Mimi know what I was thinking?

"Jake?" That I had made a terrible mistake?

"Say something." That the face looking back at me from the mirror looked like a girl? A really weird girl?

"Okay, give yourself a few days to get used to it." Yes, she knew.

Resolving that I should try to like it, I walked into a local bookstore. Whom should I encounter there but John, the founding father of the Dye Jake's Hair movement. His response—"Whoa . . . shocker!"—was not the display of enthusiasm I had naively expected. Sensing my mortification at his response, he made a fumbled attempt to recover. "I mean, I'm sure you know it's really different."

For the next two days, I crept around town with a hat pulled over my head, lifting it up only in the presence of trusted friends. Their approval, however, was unanimous and unrestrained.

"You look like you have more hair!"

"You're really going to stand out behind those drums."

Eventually, I, too, was won over, staring at myself in mirrors and in the sidewalk windows of restaurants and shops in Uptown Minneapolis. Thus, by the day of our photo shoot, I felt confident under my platinum hair, more like a rocker than ever before. Two weeks later, we got the proof sheets. Once again, Dan and John picked a shot in which my mouth assumed a vaguely amphibian expression.

"What do you think, Jake?"

"You guys look good, but I like the way I look in the previous shot."

"Hmm."

"Can't they just clip my head from the first shot and paste it on the second?" Quite easily, as a matter of fact. Cut, paste, and voilà—our new album cover.

Dan proposed a title for the new album: *Feeling Strangely Fine,* a good description of our state of mind. Months after her birth, Coco was still in the hospital, but she had grown and gained strength. Now John and I could visit her, even rock her to sleep. She was still smaller than most newborns, innocently unaware of how over the past year she had absorbed so many of our thoughts and impressed herself into the mood of our new album. Even before the trials of her birth, she had inspired some of Dan's songs.

In late February 1998, after almost a year in the hospital, the doctors said Coco was strong enough to go home, where she would still require round-the-clock medical supervision. She left the hospital on the very day that our new single hit the airwaves. As Dan rode with Coco in the ambulance, the driver looked up into the rearview mirror.

"Hey, aren't you in Semisonic?"

"Yeah."

"Wow. I just heard your new song on the radio."

It was a song Dan had written in anticipation of fatherhood, a song about being sent forth from the womb as if by a bouncer clearing out a bar.

Closing time
Open all the doors and let you out into the world
Closing time
Turn all of the lights on over every boy and every girl
Closing time
One last call for alcohol so finish your whiskey or beer
Closing time
You don't have to go home but you can't stay here

I know who I want to take me home
I know who I want to take me home
I know who I want to take me home

Closing time
Time for you to go out to the places you will be from
Closing time
This room won't be open till your brothers or your sisters come
So gather up your jackets, move it to the exits
I hope you have found a friend
Closing time
Every new beginning comes from some other beginning's end

I know who I want to take me home
I know who I want to take me home
I know who I want to take me home
Take me home

Chapter X

CLOSING TIME

"**K-ROCK is adding** the single."

It was Jim, savoring my disbelief at such spectacular news. To be added to the playlist of Los Angeles–based KROQ ("K-ROCK") is to be anointed by the ruling superpower of alternative-rock radio. Not only was K-ROCK going to play "Closing Time," they were adding it to their rotation weeks before MCA's official add-date, before any other station had even heard the song. This was a resounding endorsement, one that would reverberate through the world of radio. Over the course of our previous album, K-ROCK had ignored us completely, but now they made a dramatic turnabout. As one of the K-ROCK executives said to an MCA higher-up, "We want to make Semisonic *our* band."

A month before this stunning development, MCA had not yet approved our album for release. Jim, Hans, and others reported that the president, Jay Boberg, and other senior executives wondered if the album we had handed in contained anything resembling a single. "There are good songs on here, but we don't hear any hits." Hans was exasperated. In his opinion, "Closing Time" and several of the other songs were obvious singles. And hadn't Jay chosen the wrong first single on our previous record? Alas, Hans lacked the clout to change the minds of those in charge.

Hans's boss, Gary Ashley, the head of A&R, called up Dan.

"Listen, why not go back to the studio and see if you can finish one or two more songs? It couldn't hurt." Dan reluctantly agreed. Jim, however, was adamant that we hold our ground. If we recorded new songs, he warned, MCA would choose one of the new songs and ignore "Closing Time," which he thought was a hit. Persuaded by Jim, Dan turned down MCA's request for more songs. Thus, Jim's resolve set the stage for the turning point in our career.

Jim and the label brass remained in a standoff, which was finally broken by MCA's new head of radio promotion, Nancy Levin. She knocked on Jay's door and offered her own opinion. " 'Closing Time' is a fucking smash!" Her conviction was enough to persuade Jay and his associates to release the record, and she committed herself and her staff to the job of delivering a hit while her superiors wondered.

The first issue was deciding on the right radio mix. By the time a song is played on the radio, it may have undergone several transformations from the album version. This is why radio listeners often have the confusing experience of buying a CD and thinking, "This sounds different from the radio." It *is* different— sometimes dramatically so. If the same song is played on a variety of radio formats, there may be several mixes: an alternative mix with louder guitars and drums, a pop mix with friendlier guitars and more vocals, an acoustic mix, a dance mix, and so on. The mix engineers all have distinct sounds. It's not unusual for the alternative-rock radio mix to be done by one engineer and the pop mix by someone else. Plus, the alternative-rock mix by engineer A may be scrapped, and engineer B may be called in to redo it. The competition is fierce, and mix engineers love to snatch a song away from one of their rivals and remix it. Sometimes they take their case directly to the band, as in the case of one mixer who cornered me and spoke with the overblown crassness of a used-car salesman. "Listen, _____ is a great mixer, a home-run hitter. And I heard the mix he did for you guys. It's okay. I'd say he hit a triple. No big deal, except that THIS SONG IS A HOME RUN! It's gotta have that oomph, that thing that makes you want to take some chick home, bend her over, and fuck her up the ass!"

Regarding "Closing Time," Hans wondered if Bob Clearmountain's mix was aggressive enough. We hired Jack Joseph Puig to remix it, hoping that his more guitar-heavy sound could wrap some sonic barbed-wire around the neighborliness that, for better or worse, lies at the heart of Semisonic's sound. In addition to being an A-list mixer, Puig is an unforgettable character. He sits at the mixing console under a tent of tapestries in darkness lit by dozens of candles that drip rainbows of colored wax onto the floor. His long black hair, beard, and mustache complement his black jacket, black shirt, black pants, and black boots. Occasionally, he listens to mixes in his car, a black Lexus.

Puig remixed "Closing Time," rendering it with more aggression but less groove than Clearmountain's mix. (Clearmountain, whose clean-shaven boyish face, tucked-in shirts, and shy manner suggest a man who has never set foot on a dance floor, is a master of groove. Though his name is often associated with eighties rock anthems by Bruce Springsteen and Bryan Adams, the world's discos are packed with dancers shaking their asses to Clearmountain mixes.) When the time came to choose which version of "Closing Time" to put on the album, we opted for Puig's; it was a close call, with Puig's louder guitars winning over Clearmountain's groovier drums.

In anticipation of "crossing over" the single to radio formats other than alternative rock, we did a pop mix (by Don Gehman with lighter portions of electric guitar) and an acoustic mix (by Puig, a soccer-mom version with no electric guitars and no drums until the second verse). Each mix had to be edited down to under four minutes, an important limit in the minds of radio programmers. (To submit a single with a track length of 4:01 is as foolish as pricing kitchen knives sold on television at $20.01.) We pestered Bob Ludwig, the mastering engineer, with a slew of editing adjustments. "Okay, shorten the intro to what it was two versions ago, cut eight bars off the end of the bridge, and undo the cuts we asked you to make to the final chorus." Each mix also had a "Clearmountain pause," an idea suggested to us by Karen Glauber, the senior vice president of *Hits* magazine and a friend of ours from Dan and John's Trip Shakespeare days. When she heard the original Clearmountain mix, she said, "Have him put in one of his famous pauses before the last chorus." We did, and the extra seconds of suspense worked so well that all subsequent mixes inserted similar pauses.

Mixing, remixing, editing, reediting, additional overdubs and more mixing, mastering and remastering—after all of that we had five versions of the song. Bob Ludwig, upon completing the final edits, needled Dan. "So have we reached 'closure' time?" MCA printed promotional CDs for radio. After all of the remixing, Nancy strongly preferred the original Clearmountain mix and insisted that it be listed first on the promotional CD sent to radio stations. (Program directors can listen to the various versions sent on a promo CD and use the mix that in their mind best fits their station. In the case of "Closing Time," the stations were divided in their preferences for the Clearmountain and Puig mixes.)

Finally, Nancy was ready to carry out her plan, winning over Kevin Weatherly, the program director of K-ROCK. Weatherly is thought by some to be the most influential person in the world of radio and one of the biggest names in the music business at large, but under Nancy's predecessors, he had largely ignored Semisonic. If Weatherly could be convinced about the band, many other programmers would follow suit. Hiring a promoter to buy airplay on K-ROCK was not an option, because the K-ROCK playlist is not for sale. (Evidently, this is the case with several of the biggest stations around the country. The massive ratings enjoyed by a megastation make it impossible to consider allowing an independent promoter to meddle with the playlist, which is the heart of a station's connection to its listeners.) In order to get played on K-ROCK, Kevin Weatherly has to think your song is a hit. Nancy drove across town and handed him our single and our album and asked him to give both a serious listen. In doing so, she wagered her credibility and the band's future on Weatherly's response. She drove back to her office, and later that day, K-ROCK began playing "Closing Time." In one day, Nancy accomplished more for us than her bosses and predecessors had in two years.

Soon, friends from Los Angeles called up, screaming about how often they were hearing "Closing Time." "Oh, my God! I'm in my car and the DJ on K-ROCK just said, 'Here's a band you're going to be hearing a lot of: Semisonic.' " That was a favorable horoscope indeed.

Other programmers, coming back from their Christmas vacation, now wanted to add "Closing Time," but Nancy instructed her staff to hold these other stations back until February 26, the official add-date. The independent promoters, armed with hundreds of thousands of dollars from MCA, made the rounds, buying up advance commitments from still more programmers. Then, when the add-date arrived, scores of stations nationwide added the song, making "Closing Time" the "most added" song at the alternative and rock formats. The song had huge momentum before most radio listeners had even heard it. It was a masterfully executed plan.

We were then whisked out west to play for various gatherings of music-business insiders. At the Gavin convention in San Diego, a radio-industry conference, we walked through more crowded hotel lobbies and received excited greetings from familiar faces—MCA locals (past and present), their L.A. bosses, promoters, and program directors. Among the CDs of new singles, strewn about the tables, couches, and floors like sample packs of chewing gum, were hundreds of promotional drink coasters advertising "Closing Time." And at our show that weekend, the notoriously unresponsive industry professionals gave "Closing Time" a tolerable ovation.

Next we flew to Las Vegas to perform for the national sales managers of MCA's retail distributor, Universal Music and Video Distribution. We checked into the Caesars Palace hotel after an early-morning flight and killed time by observing life among the civilians. For me that meant lying in bed and watching some of the hotel's televised course on basic gambling strategy, then walking along the cavernous hallways of the ground floor, past the casino, several bars and boutiques, and finally to an indoor plaza of restaurants set under a domed ceiling painted as a blue Mediterranean sky with white fluffy clouds. The three of us ate an early dinner as the artificial sky above us was dimmed to nighttime dark and then brightened back to high noon over twenty-minute cycles. An hour later, we played three songs for a small conference room full of sales managers who listened as they dined on filet mignon. As one of only three acts to perform at this private gathering, the managers were now to understand that Semisonic was a priority, and at the end of our short set, they put down their forks and wineglasses to applaud us with an ovation that called to mind a gallery of golf fans witnessing the sinking of a three-foot putt.

Messages from friends around the country reported on our newfound radio presence. After landing in Seattle for yet another promotional trip, I started up our rental car and heard "Closing Time" come blasting out of the speakers. A friend of mine in San Francisco told me that she started her car and heard my voice addressing her:

"Hi, I'm Jake."

"I'm John."

"And I'm Dan. We're Semisonic and you're listening to Radio Alice."

The MCA radio locals were excited to see us now that each of them had good news to report. Many of them were new, hand-picked by Nancy, and their sense of mission was a refreshing turn-about from the malaise and discontent of the *Great Divide* era.

On the air, DJs gave us the long-lost-friend treatment. "Guys, can you stay a while longer?" The program directors corralled us afterward and invited us to return soon for extended on-air performances. The buzz was unmistakable, but the question of whether or not "Closing Time" would catch on with listeners had not been answered. Two weeks after its impressive debut, those in the know were uneasy:

"The phones are slow."

"Obviously, it's not a reactive song."

"Let's keep our fingers crossed."

The ever-impatient programmers started researching the song too early, as they always do. The research firms called listeners, and the responses were disappointing. The PDs bit their lips, but Nancy pressed the locals not to let the PDs back off. Were it not for Nancy's resolve, the label brass might well have intervened at this point and shut down the song. Instead, they released more cash to buy off promoters and their stations. Semisonic's recoupable debt soared.

Nancy and her national directors worked the phones, calling stations around the country and urging patience. Cash sprayed in every direction and the song survived, but how many weeks of unfavorable research could "Closing Time" endure? Nancy called the research firms and encouraged them to use a different excerpt of the song for their listener tests. "Use the first verse with the piano hook."

And then the research began to come back favorably. "Closing Time" was a grower. The more people heard it, the more they liked it. The MCA brass came out from the safety of their offices. "Goddammit! We need a video, and we need it now!"

I opened a fresh box of video reels from L.A. and fast-forwarded through the usual fare—whips, chains, golden retriever puppies—realizing that what I despised the most were videos that showed a generic alternative-rock band styled in generic alt-rock clothes, playing a forgettable song and flashing ironic grins as disclaimers of their ambition. We narrowed the list of directors and received treatments, which seized upon the phrase "Closing Time" as an excuse to show the band dying in a car crash or some other surrogate form of execution-by-video-director. We threw those scripts away and picked Chris Applebaum, whose videos were quirky and whose conversations with Dan seemed promising. Weeks earlier it was unclear whether there would be such a video, thanks to MCA's initial hesitance. Now, as we flew to L.A. on the eve of the album's release, the video was dangerously overdue.

MCA reserved rooms for us at the Beverly Hills Sofitel, leaving me to conclude that the "Closing Time" video budget exceeded previous budgets in the same proportion that the Sofitel outclassed the Hyatt. I plopped down on the bed in my room. On the bedside table stood a small vase with a rose and a card that announced, "A French touch!" Bonjour Sofitel. Au revoir recoupment.

The first day of filming coincided with the release date of our record. MCA had neglected to send us advance copies of our album, so after breakfast at the hotel, I drove up to Tower Records on Sunset to buy a copy for myself. *It looks kind of vain, buying your own record, but who will recognize me?*

"Looking for the new Semisonic record?" The store's assistant manager spotted me instantly. I was too busy suppressing a blush to appreciate the fact that being recognized was a good omen. He led me to the new-releases display, where Semisonic was featured. I bought a copy and took it to a nearby coffee shop, where I spent an hour paging through the album booklet.

That afternoon, we drove downtown for day one of filming. It was an impressive scene. Truck drivers lowered hydraulic lifts; grips rolled trunks onto the pavement and down the street; production assistants ran in and out of trailers with clipboards; electricians started power generators and uncoiled thick black cables that stretched hundreds of yards; lighting technicians hovered in cherry pickers, affixing film lights to telephone poles; security people directed traffic as their walkie-talkies squawked; and a brain trust huddled around a cluster of video screens, sussing out problems and radioing instructions to far ends of the street. In the shadows of downtown Los Angeles, our video shoot had invaded an entire city block. While the crew members hauled, lifted, and shouted, I walked around, mingling quietly and finding my casual musings transformed into commands broadcasted over a network of walkie-talkies.

"Jake wants some hot chocolate."

"Copy that."

"Jake wants the *New York Times* crossword puzzle. Do we have a runner?"

"Ten-four. Tim's leaving right now."

Chris choreographed various shots with the cameraman, Marcis, and consulted with Danielle, the producer, Kim, the MCA video rep, and Dan as they ruminated over various questions. What if it rains tonight? What if it doesn't rain tonight but rains tomorrow? Should the street and sidewalks be sprayed down before every take, just for continuity?

During hours of waiting, John and I were in the trailer that was our dressing room, having consultations of our own.

"Okay, John: Swiss river, three letters, first letter *A?*"

"Aar. A-A-R. Where'd you get the hot chocolate?"

A week earlier, Chris and Dan had cooked up an unusual video concept: two continuous shots shown side by side on a split screen. The story line was simple: Dan and a fictional girlfriend—played by actress Denise Franco—are trying to meet up to go to a night-club but keep missing each other. Dan starts out on the right side of the screen rehearsing with the band, and Denise on the left at the restaurant where she works. As the video progresses, Dan leaves the rehearsal space on the right side of the screen just as Denise leaves the restaurant on the left, then they show up on opposite sides of the screen, still looking for each other. The cameras filming each side follow these two all the way to a nightclub, where the two characters enter seconds apart. They search the crowd for each other, but just as their eyes are about to meet, a waitress carrying a tray of drinks obscures their sight line and Dan leaves the club alone. No edits on either side of the screen. It would be one of those "How'd they do that?" videos, one that stood a chance of getting some attention.

Because the footage on each half of the screen would be uncut from beginning to end, the script demanded precise timing and lots of rehearsal for the two sides of the screen to dovetail properly. With "Closing Time" blasting from speakers everywhere, every action had to be performed in exact locations to coincide with specific musical cues. For example, at one point near the beginning of the video, Dan would sit on the rehearsal space couch to scribble down a phone message. As the camera panned away from him and around the walls of the rehearsal space, he would then slip on his guitar and take his place across the room in time for the downbeat of the first chorus, when the camera would pan back to the band. To guide us, the crew marked the floors and sidewalks with dozens of Xs made of thick white tape. The assistant director yelled "Go!" over the blaring music to signal those outside of the frame to run across the room or down the street to the next piece of tape where the camera would find them again. Thus, we would hit the X by the doorway at the end of the guitar solo, then stride quickly to the X beside our parked car in time for the "Clearmountain pause," and then sprint off camera to yet another X twenty yards away in time for the downbeat of the third chorus, and so on. A miscue in the final seconds of the shot would ruin four minutes of carefully executed filming.

And run we did, especially Dan. During every take, in his few seconds off camera, he ran an entire city block from the rehearsal space to the restaurant and another block back again. He had fifteen seconds to get from one end of the street to the other and make his entrances without huffing and puffing. It didn't help that the clothing stylist had dressed him in heavy black boots, or that a bicyclist had to roll through each shot and then swerve out of the way, right in front of Dan, who at that point would be running back to hit his next mark, clomping at full steam down pavement that was sprayed with water before each take.

Of course, there are no small parts.

Jake's part in the "Closing Time" video:

Enter frame at beginning of song, pick up cymbal, walk to drum set, put cymbal on stand, and secure it with a wing nut. Don't put wing nut on upside down, turn it in the wrong direction, or drop it.

Play first chorus on the drums with Dan and John without flaring nostrils or stretching lips.

Play second verse drums as Dan leaves the frame. Rock out during second chorus. Maintain eye contact with John. Ignore the pressure. Don't start laughing. Don't freak out and yell, "Cut!"

As camera pans away, quickly stow drumsticks; grab newspaper and glass of cranberry juice so as to look like John and I are on break when the camera pans back and Denise enters the frame. Don't spill red juice on white pants. Try to look halfway intelligent while making "I dunno where he went" gesture to Denise. As camera pans away, quickly stow juice and newspaper, grab sticks, and resume drumming. When camera pans away again, run from behind the drums to the doorway in time to be the first out of the room. Don't trip over cymbal stand. While running to door, lick outside of upper lip to remove cranberry juice mustache in time for big close-up.

Walk out to car, open driver-side door. As camera pans away, run to front of rock club and look relaxed as Dan enters club. Don't grab mouth to soothe pain of having bitten tongue while running and licking upper lip in previous sequence.

Lean against car with John while waiting for Dan. Look as if we're talking about nothing in particular, but have conversation planned in advance so as not to make John laugh, thereby ruining the entire four-minute shot. When Dan comes, make "What happened? . . . Oh well" gestures. Don't look dumb. Don't look too pop, too triple-A, too rock, or too alternative.

It took us three nights to get it right. (The second night was rained out, costing us well over a hundred thousand dollars.) The actress who carried the tray of drinks between Dan and Denise, a crucial element in the story, kept mistiming her steps across the frame. (To be fair, her one bit of action came at the very end of each take and the pressure on her was enormous.)

By the end of the filming, Dan had run dozens of city blocks in his big black boots. Marcis, the Steadicam operator, had walked for several miles carrying an eighty-pound Steadicam and keeping it in focus. Between takes, he lay on the ground, catching his breath while his assistants brought him water and food and massaged his cramping calves. Chris's voice had been reduced to a rasp, having spent three nights yelling, "Yes!" and "No!" and "Sassy!" and "Where's the fucking drink tray?" Everyone exhausted but thrilled to have pulled it off, and though it was fun to spend three days at or near the center of the film crew's attention, I was personally relieved that they would not have to hear "Closing Time" again until the next time they tuned in to K-ROCK. Days later, after the film was processed and the left and right sides of the frame were aligned, the video was finished. Amazingly, it worked. More amazingly, the MTV executives gave their approval and put it into rotation.

The end of our opening week of sales drew near. Jim speculated about what the official tally might be, and his weekend estimate, informed by MCA's reports from various megaretailers, proved to be accurate. Still, hearing him say "Twelve thousand" was a positive thrill. *Feeling Strangely Fine* attained the number-one ranking in *Billboard*'s New Artist category. It sold more copies in its first week than *Great Divide* had in its first four months.

The telephone rang incessantly as Jim called to fill in our calendars with appearances at radio festivals, on MTV, and on network television. Every opportunity brought with it scheduling upheaval. It was the blur of action I had once feared but now had been craving since *Great Divide* had been put to rest.

Our *Feeling Strangely Fine* tour began on the West Coast, where in our *Great Divide* days we played in small clubs for scant crowds. With our growing presence on the radio, we graduated to larger clubs. In Los Angeles, K-ROCK DJ Jed the Fish squeezed through the capacity crowd and walked up on stage to give our introduction. "Enjoy this show, everybody, because the next time these guys come to town, I don't think you'll be seeing them at the Troubadour." In Seattle, we moved up from the Crocodile to the Showbox, and in San Francisco, from the Paradise to Slims. And all of the shows were sold out.

Seeing all of those faces staring at us, many for the first time, I was in no mood to show mercy on the drums. *I'm gonna leave a big hole here and make these people hold their fucking breath!* As the night pressed on, the fans in the front row positioned themselves to swipe the setlists from the stage at the show's end. Some mouthed their pleas for drumsticks from the very first song. My embarrassed drummer's smile of two years earlier now relaxed into the blankness befitting a platinum-blond rock-and-roll enigma.

More packed houses awaited us in the Southeast, again where previous shows had been scantily attended: Charlotte, Orlando, Charleston, Columbia, Winston-Salem. Fans pressed up against the stage, called out song titles from our two albums, and shook their hips en masse. I had the fewest singing chores and thus the greatest freedom to turn from the microphone and scan the faces in the front rows. The veteran Semisonic fans watched me and frowned if I gave too much attention to their cultural nemeses, the flirts. I worked both sides of the room—a game of badminton with the coquettes to my left, professorial nods to the scholars who knew all the words on my right.

The CDs and T-shirts flew off the merchandise table. After each show, we walked out of the club and into a flock of autograph seekers hovering around our tour bus. The attention swarmed around Dan, leaving me in the awkward position of fishing along the timid edges of the crowd. "How's it going?" They smiled and stared. These shyer types, it seemed, wanted me to start things off. "May I sign that for you?" *Points off for doing the asking.*

"Um. Sure."

Soon four or five people would inch forward with their CDs. *Where's that woman with the green eyes?* Few autograph seekers ever came equipped with a Sharpie (the marker of choice), and this posed another dilemma: Should I walk out of the club with a Sharpie in my pocket? *That looks lame.* I finally asked Chris, our tour manager, to follow us out after every show with a pocket full of Sharpies.

Occasionally, an obsessive fan would pull me aside to answer a long list of questions: What model year is John's P-bass? Why does Dan have two Rat pedals? Why hasn't anyone responded to my demo tape? Fifteen feet away, Dan fended off admiration and lust. (Wearing the crown of accessibility is a common fate of drummers. Ringo, for instance, received much more fan mail than his bandmates, but I suspect many fans addressed their letters to Ringo figuring that he was the Beatle most likely to answer questions about the lives of John, Paul, and George.)

I said good-bye to the shy ones and received an awkward silence in return. As a gathering crowd pressed in on Dan, I worked my way through—"Excuse me"—feigning determination to get on the bus. Alas, they were all too willing to let me through. I climbed the bus steps, paused, closed the door, and walked to the back lounge, where I plopped down, always surprised that my shirt smelled of cigarettes and beer. Over the whirring of the bus generator I could hear chattering voices, Dan's laugh, and shouts of recognition when John emerged from the club. Sometimes, after ten minutes or so, John or Dan stepped onto the bus out of breath and said, "Jake, where'd you go? You got some people out there who want your autograph!" I hurried off the bus and signed for the two last fans on the empty sidewalk, the shyest ones of all.

More cities. More shows. More headlines from Jim: "We SoundScanned fifteen thousand last week."

And the MCA locals: "We just went top five alternative."

"SoundScan went up to nineteen thousand."

"Number three alternative."

In our morning and afternoon radio interviews, the DJs obsessed over the "Closing Time" lyrics. "I love that line 'The end of the beginning is an old end to a new . . .' No, wait. How does it go?"

Of all of Dan's lines, "Every new beginning comes from some other beginning's end" has the distinction of being the most memorable and the hardest to remember. The philosophical flavor of that line and other lyrics of Dan's became the focus of our interviews. As a result, we were positioned as "smart guys," a potential selling point and incalculable liability. Ironically, when we recorded the song, our producer Nick Launay had said, "That's one for the punters, then." Jim agreed, maintaining that the line most responsible for winning over the masses was "Finish your whiskey or beer."

"Closing Time" continued its ascent, reaching number two on the alternative-radio charts and teetering on the edge of number one. One local told me that the distance between "Closing Time" and the song ahead of it was a matter of just thirty spins from the nationwide total. Dan and John had only a passing interest in our sales and radio chart status, leaving me to conceal my fixation on SoundScan numbers and the quest for number one. However, when the New England local greeted us in Providence with the news that "Closing Time" had gone number one, I ran up and down the bus pumping my fists and whooping like an obnoxious sports fan. Dan and John were amused by this victory dance. That night I celebrated on the drums, launching a veritable fireworks display of flamboyant fills that drew oohs and aahs from the front row fans and approving laughter from my bandmates. Afterward, Dan quipped, "Someone should tell Jake that we just went number one before *every* show."

It was late spring, radio festival season. Thanks to "Closing Time," we had better offers than in past years. First up was HFS-tival, a huge show sponsored by WHFS, an influential alternative station based in Washington, DC. The concert took place at RFK Stadium. Two years earlier, we would have played on the secondary stages in the parking lot, but with a number-one song, we were given a slot on the big stage inside the stadium.

The festival staff led us from our bus to our dressing room, through the cement corridors under the stadium, where we could hear the sound of a very large rock concert already under way as we passed a series of dressing rooms marked for the bands on the bill: the B-52s, the Foo Fighters, Everclear, Green Day, and finally, Semisonic.

Modern Rock Tracks™

T. WK	L. WK	2 WKS ON	WKS ON	TRACK TITLE ALBUM TITLE (IF ANY)	ARTIST IMPRINT/PROMOTIONG LABEL
				★ ★ ★ No. 1 ★ ★ ★	
①	2	2	12	**CLOSING TIME** 1 week at No. 1 FEELING STRANGELY FINE	◆ SEMISONIC MCA
2	1	1	15	**THE WAY** ALL THE PAIN MONEY CAN BUY	◆ FASTBALL HOLLYWOOD
③	3	6	8	**IRIS** "CITY OF ANGELS" SOUNDTRACK	◆ GOO GOO DOLLS WARNER SUNSET/REPRISE
④	4	4	8	**DON'T DRINK THE WATER** BEFORE THESE CROWDED STREETS	◆ DAVE MATTHEWS BAND RCA
5	5	5	8	**PUSH IT** GARBAGE VERSION 2.0	◆ GARBAGE ALMO SOUNDS/INTERSCOPE
⑥	9	—	2	**AVA ADORE** ADORE	THE SMASHING PUMPKINS VIRGIN
⑦	8	8	12	**SHIMMER** SUNBURN	◆ FUEL 550 MUSIC
8	7	7	14	**WISHLIST** YIELD	PEARL JAM EPIC
9	6	3	17	**I WILL BUY YOU A NEW LIFE** SO MUCH FOR THE AFTERGLOW	◆ EVERCLEAR CAPITOL
⑩	10	10	4	**HEROES** GODZILLA THE ALBUM	◆ THE WALLFLOWERS EPIC
⑪	11	11	8	**FLAGPOLE SITTA** WHERE HAVE ALL THE MERRYMAKERS GONE?	HARVEY DANGER SLASH/LONDON/ISLAND
⑫	15	19	8	**JUMP RIGHT IN** MASTER OF STYLES	◆ THE URGE IMMORTAL/EPIC
13	12	9	31	**SEX AND CANDY** MARCY PLAYGROUND	◆ MARCY PLAYGROUND CAPITOL
14	13	15	9	**REAL WORLD** YOURSELF OR SOMEONE LIKE YOU	◆ MATCHBOX 20 LAVA/ATLANTIC
⑮	14	17	6	**SPARK** FROM THE CHOIRGIRL HOTEL	◆ TORI AMOS ATLANTIC
16	18	16	13	**ZOOT SUIT RIOT** ZOOT SUIT RIOT	◆ CHERRY POPPIN' DADDIES MOJO/UNIVERSAL
⑰	22	21	6	**REDUNDANT** NIMROD.	◆ GREEN DAY REPRISE
18	16	13	27	**MY OWN PRISON** MY OWN PRISON	◆ CREED WIND-UP
19	17	12	20	**MY HERO** THE COLOUR AND THE SHAPE	◆ FOO FIGHTERS ROSWELL CAPITOL
				★ ★ ★ AIRPOWER ★ ★ ★	
⑳	27	31	5	**INSIDE OUT** EVE 6	◆ EVE 6 RCA
21	19	14	11	**LOSING A WHOLE YEAR** THIRD EYE BLIND	◆ THIRD EYE BLIND ELEKTRA/EEG
22	20	20	12	**FROM YOUR MOUTH** LIFE IN THE SO-CALLED SPACE AGE	◆ GOD LIVES UNDERWATER 1500 A&M
㉓	25	26	6	**WHAT I DIDN'T KNOW** [RADIANCE]	ATHENAEUM ATLANTIC

Shortly after noon, our tour manager, Chris, led us from our dressing room back through the halls and up the stairs to the massive outdoor stage where our crew was in the final seconds of the fifteen-minute changeover from the previous band. We had an early set time, well ahead of the headline acts. Even so, when I peeked out through the scaffolding on the side of the stage, I saw tens of thousands of people standing on the football field in front of the stage, a few of them wearing Semisonic T-shirts. One held a sign that read "Sing it to me Semisonic!" Some near the stage waved at me as I took out my camera to snap pictures. I snuck out on stage and crouched to take more shots and then retreated to the wings as the crew finished checking the equipment.

We walked on stage to scattered whoops. Dan's "How's everybody doing?" got a healthy response, and we launched into our thirty-minute set. In contrast to previous festivals, I felt that the entire crowd had fixed its attention on us. The older songs brought shouts of recognition from Semisonic fans, and the new songs stirred up even more: "Play 'California.' PLEEEEEEEZE!" The cheers from the swelling crowd swirled about, and as we marched forward through the set, each song drew a bigger response. The cheering soon fluttered about the entire volume of space enclosed by the stadium seats. And then we came to the last song in the set.

During the *Great Divide* tour, Dan had struggled to find a satisfying way to end our shows. Our sets never felt truly done, even after we left the stage. Writing a set-closer was very much on his mind when he wrote "Closing Time." It filled that role perfectly, especially now that it was the Semisonic song everyone knew. Dan strummed the opening chords on his guitar, and screams rippled back through the crowd. John plunked out the piano part and Dan began to sing, joined by a chorus of thousands. The first verse, absent drums and bass, built up line by line as more and more people joined in until, by the verse's end, the massive crowd shouted in unison, "YOU DON'T HAVE TO GO HOME BUT YOU CAN'T—STAY—HERE!"

As the band landed on the downbeat of the first chorus, a titanic roar swept across the field and slammed into the stage with such force that it shook me. Only concentration kept me from screaming. My skin tightened, and I swung my sticks as a football field full of people jumped up and down to the beat, raising their arms and screaming out the words: "I KNOW WHO I WANT TO TAKE ME HOME!" Crowd surfers were tossed about on a sea of outstretched hands.

As we settled into the next verse, I looked over at John, who looked back at me and mouthed something like *Holy shit!* Another verse, another chorus, another tidal wave, another whoosh of shivers up my arms and down my legs. The stage shook as my head swam through joy and my limbs attended to the drums. The dizzying bridge came next, followed by the guitar solo, a soft verse, and the suspenseful "Clearmountain pause," which we lengthened into a twenty-second, teasing cliffhanger of band silence. The crowd yelled, pleaded, begged, demanded the final chorus, filling the air with an extended "AAAAAAAAAAAAAAAAAAAAAAAAAA-AAAAAAY" like a stadium full of football fans waiting for a kickoff.

Then we unleashed it. Pandemonium. The loudest chorus of our lives. A raging, jumping, screaming, stomp-box-crushing, guitar-scrubbing, bass-thumping, cymbal-smashing, drum-pounding, crowd-surfer-tossing, stage-shaking, football-field-quaking triple chorus—twenty-four bars of rock-festival bedlam.

Finally, blessedly, the song washed into its soft coda. As the last chord rang out, Dan waved and shouted into the mike—"Thank you"—detonating a final explosion of white noise from the crowd that thundered up through the upper decks of the stadium and showered down upon us as we walked off the stage.

Chapter XI

"SEMISONIC BOOM HEARD NATIONALLY"

week after our album had been released, I opened a small package from my mother, a gift-wrapped three-pack of Rolaids. Thanks to the hit status of "Closing Time," we were days away from making our national television debut on *Late Night with Conan O'Brien*, so this care package was much appreciated. The news buzzed through Minneapolis, and a friend stopped me on the sidewalk near my apartment.

"Dude. Are you excited?"

"I'm nervous as hell."

"Oh, come on. What's the worst thing that could happen? You could drop your sticks and throw up."

That was precisely the kind of imagery I was hoping to banish from my mind. Two years earlier, I had watched our road friends Aimee Mann and The Verve Pipe perform on Leno and Letterman and felt envious. Now that it was our turn, I was grateful that our first performance on national television would be on Conan's show as opposed to his higher-rated and higher-pressure counterparts'.

Days later, in New York City, we were escorted through the doors of NBC's studios in Rockefeller Center. Jim, Hans, and our MCA publicist, Christine, had left work in the midafternoon to keep us company in our dressing room. I looked over the several shirts I had brought, still confused about the instructions we had received regarding television apparel. T-shirts with words on them were not allowed, and there were color restrictions regarding blue backgrounds and the strong opinions of my hairdresser, Mimi, to consider. How to dress myself continued to be a vexing issue. I remained wary of following Dan and John's forays into flamboyance but knew that my clothes should say, "rock star." If only they could say, "Thoughtful rock star, skeptical of stardom and fashion, who nevertheless manages to dress with an unassuming panache." I slipped into the bone-white pants and black Calvin Klein shirt I had worn in the "Closing Time" video and added a new touch, a silver necklace that John's girlfriend Penny had made for my birthday. Meanwhile, Hans and Jim raided the chip bowl and speculated on the size of our viewing audience— "What do you think for a Tuesday night? Two million? Three million?"—a conversation I tuned out in the interest of nerve management.

Soon our NBC chaperone collected us for camera rehearsal, leading us down the hallway to the stage doors, which opened up into a studio that was much smaller than my television-viewer's preconceptions. The shallow stage, the narrow and steep audience seating, everything half the size of what I had anticipated—it all testified to the distorting power of the television camera. A short, bald man rehearsed the reading of jokes off cue cards as he slouched over the desk, sitting in for the tall, redheaded O'Brien so the cue-card wrangler could practice his timing. The director then brought the cameras and their operators over to the band area for music rehearsals. "Okay, guys, can you run through the song for us?"

The length of the song had been dutifully shortened in advance. Network airtime is a precious commodity, and Conan's staff had told us a week earlier that our time limit was four minutes. That forced us to trim thirty seconds from our normal version of "Closing Time," which we accomplished by skipping a few bars here and there. For the past week we had practiced the abbreviated version, drilling the new arrangement into our heads so that in the glare of the lights and cameras none of us would diverge from the others. At a recent wedding, the three of us had witnessed the kind of mishap we were hoping to avoid on national television. The members of the string quartet assembled for the occasion had failed to agree on which passages of the processional music would be repeated before moving to the next section. As they played, the musicians peeled away from each other, each waiting for the others to join him, and soon they were scattered across several pages of music. Mothers-in-law-to-be and music lovers alike dabbed their eyes as the bride made her veiled advance down the aisle and the tranquil strains of Bach's "Air in D Major" slowly awakened into screeching modernism.

We ran through "Closing Time" repeatedly as the camera crew explored various shot possibilities. As I drummed, I practiced looking into the camera with my rock face, pretending that millions of people were watching, trying to imagine what the pressure of the actual performance might feel like. I came down on the crash cymbal with a big swoop. The camera crew looked up. I lifted my sticks up high for a tom-tom fill, and they looked at me again. While Dan and John focused on the placement of their pedals and the new song form, the camera crew appeared to decide that my showy gestures made for more interesting television than the equipment fiddling that occupied the attention of my bandmates. Naturally, I felt no need to alert Dan and John to this fact.

Back in the dressing room, more MCA people dropped in. "Jake! Are you excited?" I nodded and pulled out a fresh pack of Rolaids.

"Jim?"

"Yeah."

"Since they're taping the show, if we fuck up the song, can they reshoot it?"

"What do you mean, 'fuck up'?"

"Well, like if I drop my sticks or something."

"If Dan breaks a string—maybe. You'll be fine. Don't drop your sticks."

The dressing-room conversation turned to Conan's other guests this night and their impact on the ratings, an angle I had not considered. We would appear in the final segment of the show—the standard slot for bands—and therefore would rely on the guests who preceded us to attract and retain viewers. From the band's perspective, an ideal lead guest would be a major film star on the order of Julia Roberts or Brad Pitt, preferably someone who had just broken up with another film star or celebrated a recent murder acquittal. God forbid the lead guest should be an author.

Leading off this night was Matt LeBlanc, followed by Christina Applegate. Their names were vaguely familiar to me, and I was told that they were stars of the television shows *Friends* and *Married with Children*. The consensus was that our fellow guests made for moderate appeal. No one bothered mentioning that Semisonic's unfamiliar name brought the average down.

From the closed-circuit monitor in our dressing room, we could see the final cue-card rehearsals and then the studio audience filing in. Occasional bumps of the camera jostled the picture on the monitor. Eventually, the live camera shot of the milling crowd was replaced with the show's logo, a cartoon of a crescent moon. The audio, however, continued to feed the bustling sounds of the studio—swelling audience chatter and warm-up music from the house band, the Max Weinberg Seven. Dressing-room pulse rates continued their steady climb. Through an adjacent wall, we could hear a few wails from an electric guitar, and we were told that it was Conan, whose preshow ritual includes a few solitary minutes in his office with his guitar and amp. I peeled off another Rolaid as we heard the audience being led through practice cheers by the applause coach. Finally, the crescent moon logo disappeared, the band struck up the theme song as the opening credits scrolled, and Conan walked out to a well-rehearsed ovation and opened with the jokes we had heard repeatedly during rehearsal.

I looked at the clock: fifty-five minutes to go before our slot. A blast from the house band signaled the first commercial, and a chaperone knocked on the door and grabbed Dan for makeup as the music blared and a surge of applause marked the segue back into the show. Conan introduced the first guest, Matt LeBlanc, who made a shy entrance. Jim and Hans frowned, commenting that he looked nervous. I walked a slow figure eight behind the chairs gathered around the monitor as Hans and Jim complained that LeBlanc was losing viewers. I looked closer, and sure enough, LeBlanc was a powerful sedative. Conan prompted his reticent guest to tell various anecdotes. LeBlanc took the cues—"Yeah, this is kinda funny"—but his punchlines fell flat: "And the funniest thing about the whole thing was the pilot's name. Are you ready for this? Jim Harder."

Hans shook his head. "Jesus! This guy is killing us."

Jim agreed. "Well, Jake, I wouldn't worry about the Rolaids. The way this show's going, no one's gonna be watching by the time you guys play."

"Really?"

"Just kidding. We'll have a lot of viewers. Settle down. You look nervous."

The chaperone brought back Dan and grabbed John. I looked at the clock. Forty minutes to go. I walked to the mirror in the back of the room and practiced my blank drumming face as I thought through the revised "Closing Time" arrangement. More loud going-to-commercial music from the house band. More applause. More adrenaline. I vowed that after the show I would meet Max Weinberg, the leader of the house band but best known as the drummer for Bruce Springsteen's E Street Band.

John returned, and it was my turn to be escorted through the empty halls to the makeup room. There, in the presence of another television monitor, I sat in a chair, determined to impress the makeup person with a face that allowed itself to be smeared, wiped, powdered, and drawn upon with professional calm. She smiled and asked, "What's that white chalky stuff on your lips?"

Five minutes later in the dressing room, Dan stood in the corner, strumming his guitar and singing softly. John leaned against the wall, glassy-eyed. Finally, the chaperone knocked and escorted us down the hallway and motioned for quiet before leading us through the large doors in back of the stage. We stood behind black curtains, feeling a cool draft and hearing a trace of Conan's voice, loud audience laughter, a gust of applause, and a blast from the Max Weinberg Seven, indicating a commercial break. Work lights came on, the chaperone pulled back the curtain, and we walked out onto the stage and into the stares of the audience, stepping over cables and taking our places as the house band blared at us from point-blank range. Technicians scampered here and there, and people with headsets guided cameras into place around the band. A surge of applause caught me off guard, but it was only a brief camera pan across the audience between commercials; we still had two minutes to go. We tested our equipment. I moistened my lips, wiped off my palms, and checked my drumstick holster where spare sticks waited in case of an unfortunate slip. A minor technical issue with the guitar was fixed with pit-stop intensity by Toby, our guitar tech. Chris, our recently hired road manager, made eye contact with each of us to confirm everything was set. The floor director clapped his hands and shouted, "Ready? Here we go." We nodded back as the applause swelled again and the house band soared through a flourishing finale. *It's gonna be good. God, please let it be good.*

The applause died down. I looked up and saw Conan, pale under the bright lights across the stage. "Our next guests . . ." The angled stage and the fun-house proportions of the studio made it hard to gauge how close he was. "Is it Sem-eye-sonic or Sem-ee-sonic?" At twenty after six in the evening, we were all pretending it was twenty past midnight. "Please welcome Sem-ee-sonic."

The crowd coach whipped up applause, hoots, and whistles as I counted in the song. Dan began strumming and singing, and I waited for my entrance, focusing all thought on the first item on my mental checklist: *Don't rush the first chorus.* John and I landed with confidence and settled back nicely into the verse. Thus assured, I felt a calm stare in my brows as I thumped the drums. The cameras moved in and out, asking for and receiving all of the showy gestures I had made in rehearsal—lifting my sticks over my head, crashing the cymbals, pounding the tom-toms, cracking the snare drum, and chewing the high hat. I shot a friendly snarl toward the camera to my left, a blank stare to the camera in front of Dan, a half-smile in John's direction, and then a neutral glance at the audience.

I lost track of seconds and minutes and found myself suspended in a reverie of music and light, from which I emerged with a final cymbal crash. Dan sang the last words on his own and I sat back, holding my sticks at my side, stealing a friendly nod from Max Weinberg. *Definitely got to talk to him later.* As the final guitar chord rang and the applause burst forth on cue, Conan stepped forward to shake our hands, joking with us as the applause segued into a commercial break, "I never know if I'll ruin the sustain of the last chord by making the guitarist shake my hand."

We chatted with him briefly before a technician stopped by to say, "Okay, the tape is good. You guys are done." I was relieved to hear that we were dismissed but alarmed to think that a technical glitch could have forced us to do it all again. The dressing-room crowd congratulated us. I sat down and felt a week's worth of tension dissolve. Twenty minutes later, walking to the elevator, we came upon Max Weinberg standing in the hallway and talking with one of the guards. I walked up and introduced myself. "I'm a huge fan of yours—and fellow drummer, of course." I blushed.

"Thanks." Max nodded, then turned away and resumed his discussion with the guard. The conversation I had hoped for crashed to the floor. I smiled and followed the rest of our party to the elevator, out to the street, and up the block to a nearby restaurant, where Hans bought us dinner. I felt relieved, and yet I was anxious that the performance, in a sense, was still approaching. Back in my hotel room, I endured a night of prime-time television. "Later, join Conan and his guests Matt LeBlanc, Christina Applegate, and musical guests Semisonic." That goosed my pulse. I watched all of Jay Leno. Finally came the crescent moon, the opening theme and credits—"and musical guests Semisonic"— applause, Conan O'Brien, the same old jokes, Matt LeBlanc, and Christina Applegate. The commercial breaks were exhausting.

And then: "Our next guests are from Minneapolis. Their new album . . ." I wanted to tap the drummer on the shoulder and tell him to enjoy himself. "Please welcome Semisonic." The camera zoomed in on Dan as he sang the opening verse. From behind his head I could see my elbow and neck. As we blasted into the chorus, a new angle showed the whole band. The giant sphere of time that I had occupied a few hours earlier with mythic cymbal crashes and thunderous pounding was now flattened out on the television screen, an image that was being beamed across the sky into living rooms everywhere. *That's a good shot of me. Ew. Not that.* I wondered if we looked special enough. Was I smiling too much? I tried to enter back into my performing self on the screen on the one hand and absorb the performance coming out of the TV on the other, but the song was over before I could do either. I watched Conan shake our hands, and then the show cut to commercial and returned to the speedy scrolling of the end credits and the network's onward rush to the next show. A silent and invisible audience of millions went to the kitchen, changed the channel, or doused their sets. Dan, John, and I had survived our first venture onto national television, and I fell asleep in my complimentary "Late Night with Conan O'Brien" T-shirt, owning a vague sense of triumph and a desire for more.

Back in Minneapolis, my mailbox was filling up with copies of early album reviews forwarded by MCA's publicity department. Most of them were positive.

"Pop in the present perfect tense" *(Press Enterprise)*

"Brilliance defined . . . an amazing achievement" *(A&A)*

". . . *Feeling Strangely Fine* is an absolutely exhilarating pop experience" (Greg Siegel, *Audio)*

Some straddled the fence.

"Of the gaggle of middling pop-rock bands likely to be shoved down your throat by modern-rock radio in the coming months, Semisonic may be one of the more palatable" (David Peisner, *Creative Loafing)*

"I regret having been snide about this excellent band previously" (Rob Kemp, *Time Out New York)*

And one or two raised a stink.

"Semisonic plow their way through 11 execrable tracks before finally giving up" (Nevin Martel, *Raygun)*

Headlines made reference to a "sonic boom," and the writers predicted massive success. After our experience at RFK Stadium, it didn't seem far-fetched. The outside walls of record stores were painted with giant replicas of our album cover. Our video climbed into MTV's top ten, and having made our first network appearance, I noticed the cumulative effect of this exposure. While in New York, Dan and I strolled through the Metropolitan Museum of Art. Three teenage girls walked up. "Are you the singer for Semisonic?" Dan smiled and signed autographs for the three of them, and they walked away giggling. Soon afterward, he made a guest appearance on *House of Style*, a half-hour show on MTV where a camera crew follows a rock star and a model as they shop for clothes. Hairdresser Mimi swooned over this as she applied another round of bleach to my hair. "And did you see that model? She was a hottie!" As our shows, e-mails, exploding Internet message board, street encounters in numerous cities, and an article in *Entertainment Weekly* attested, "Dan Wilson is getting the heartthrob treatment." Headlines proclaimed Semisonic "Modern-Day Romeos," and others dismissed us on the same score: "Semisonic thrills girls, plays nice pop rock."

John, whom some at MCA had tagged as the band's sex symbol, complicated his fate by growing a biker 'stache. E-mail from fans was sharply divided, for and against, as were the opinions of our Minneapolis friends, some of whom said that with his new facial hair John was "sexier than ever" and one who protested, "He looks like a car thief!"

The controversy throbbed its way through Jim's temples and from there to my telephone receiver. "Have you seen the message-board fight over John's mustache? He's scaring off the kids!" The louder the complaints, the more brazen John's delight. A soul patch on his chin soon followed.

Compared to my bandmates—Dan, the singer-songwriter/hottie, and John, the hottie/car thief—I received little public attention. *Rolling Stone* Online reported that I grinned "goonishly" on stage. Once in a while, a more complimentary reference slipped through at the end of an article:

"Drummer Jake Slichter impresses with his ability to play drums and keyboards simultaneously" *(Hollywood Reporter)*

"This Will Be My Year," my solo songwriting contribution to our album, was often reworded for a headline or closing observation: "This will be their year." A few reviewers listed it as a favorite track, making my day, though one singled it out as the album's only flaw. *Yuck.*

We did interviews every day, over the phone as individuals and in person as a group. During group interviews, I held back. Though sometimes given to long rambles on stage, Dan was reliably crisp in his responses to interviewers' questions. I answered the perfunctory questions that came at the beginning of an interview, questions concerning our origins and the pronunciation of Semisonic. "We pronounce it sem-ee-sonic." As the questions continued, however, I leaned back to let Dan do the talking. On any given day, his message might change ("I wanted to make a bedroom record" / "I'm not embarrassed by the spotlight"), and I did not want to interfere.

Over time, I began to take on questions requiring moderate levels of mental dexterity. For instance, "Does it help to have a big record company behind you?" I knew what not to say—that, on the one hand, MCA had fucked up our previous record, and on the other, they had spent $700,000 on radio promotion to push "Closing Time" to number one. No, the way to avoid praising or criticizing MCA was to say this: "A record company can only do so much for you. It really comes down to what the people think."

We did most of our interviews from the road, calling from our hotel rooms or a bank of pay phones at a roadside restaurant. While Dan was talking with *Rolling Stone,* the *Los Angeles Times,* and the *New York Post,* John and I spoke to less-experienced reporters.

"Hi, this is Jake from Semisonic, calling for our three o'clock interview."

"Oh, hi! I'm sorry. I'm finishing a term paper. Can you call back later?"

I was the rock equivalent of a client at a barber's college.

"Hi, it's Jake from Semisonic again."

"Thanks for calling back. Okay, let's see. First of all, how has the success of 'Semi Charmed Life' affected you?"

"I think you're confused. 'Semi Charmed Life' is a song by Third Eye Blind. I'm in a band called Semisonic."

"Oh, my GOD! That is so embarrassing! Okay, I'm totally sorry." These journalist trainees sometimes mislaid their prewritten questions and kept me on the phone as they groped about for something to ask. "Um. Oh, I know: How do you like doing interviews?" I felt like an adult who had stopped by school to participate in show-and-tell.

Weeks later, however, when the published interview made its way to my mailbox, courtesy of MCA, I was aghast to realize that these novice interviewers had been justly paired with a novice interviewee.

"Semisonic's Jake Schlicter dishes info on life of a rising band"

Q: Is what you're going through right now what you wanted when you longed for success?

A: It's not what I imagined when I was in the early stages of "I think I want to be a musician," and "wouldn't it be cool," because then you're sort of—you're listening to records and your [sic] imagining playing shows and your [sic] imagining writing, but you're not imagining waiting for the bus or waiting in the airport. You think about traveling but you don't think about the fact that even when you travel you have all kinds of other things that might keep you from just being a tourist.

What?! Where was the succinct voice that I hear in my head all day long? Jim suggested that for now I should keep my interviews short. "Don't give them more than five minutes." For my part, I was mad at myself for failing to prepare smart answers to the obvious questions. I realized that I had a long way to go before I was worthy of a stroll along the Hudson, musing about life, politics, art, and religion with Jon Pareles of the *New York Times*. For now, I rambled across the pages of the *Lincoln Journal Star*, the *Topeka Capital-Journal*, and the *Pointer*, the student publication of the University of Wisconsin at Stevens Point, and reading those interviews, I had a newfound appreciation for Matt LeBlanc.

Aside from the issue of my meandering answers to questions, I had failed to give adequate consideration to how I would present me, the person, assuming that it would be a matter of just being myself. That turned out to be terribly naive, as I found out on *Loveline,* a late-night syndicated radio talk show offering frank advice on sex, drugs, and relationships to callers from a nationwide audience of teenagers and young adults. The hosts, comic Adam Carolla and a physician known as Dr. Drew, regularly invite rock bands on the show to perform new songs and chip in with their advice to callers. Five minutes into the show, the first caller, a teenage girl, complained that "My boyfriend won't go down on me."

Adam asked her, "Do you go down on him?"

"Yeah."

"Dan, John, Jake . . . any advice for Amanda?"

Dan and John felt at ease, and Dan said, "Don't do anything for him he wouldn't do for you." I kept silent, secretly pining for the 1950s. The next question came from a twenty-year-old guy.

"Yeah, my girlfriend's vagina is so big, I really don't feel much when we're having sex. Do you think I should break up with her? Are there exercises she can do to make herself smaller?" Of course, his girlfriend may have had her own complaint about the size issue, but I kept that observation to myself. Minutes later, when the conversation turned to music, I spoke up, using as much sarcasm as possible to mask my discomfort with my newfound role as national sex adviser. More calls came in.

"Yeah, I'm pregnant, but I think my boyfriend and I are splitting up. He's kind of a jerk. Anyway, I don't know whether to keep the baby or get an abortion." Adam pressed her for details, and sure enough, she didn't want the baby and hated her boyfriend. Adam recommended abortion and then polled the band. Dan and John felt the answer was obvious.

"And Jake? What do you think she ought to do?"

"Um . . ." I closed my eyes and swallowed a quart of air. "I'm pro-choice, which means it's her decision, not mine." *Now, can we please get the fuck out of here?*

Adam cracked a suspicious smile and pushed me further into the open. "Are any of you guys religious? John?"

"No."

"Dan?"

"No."

"Jake?"

Please God. If I say "yes," I'll alienate the nation's blow-job-seeking teens and get a flood of e-mail from Christian rock fans. What am I supposed to say?

"Yes."

As the summer warmed up and "Closing Time" enjoyed its thirteen-week roost atop the alternative charts, a bit of rock-star confidence worked itself into my posture.

In Orlando, as I strode with scuffing heels toward the stage of a downtown block party, I was summoned by a forty-year-old beer drinker who spotted me in my dressy show clothes and dyed hair. "Hey, you. Come here. Are you in a band or something?"

"Yeah."

"What's the name?"

"Semisonic."

"Never heard of you. I guess I better get your autograph in case you turn out to be famous or something."

Our growing popularity and well-dressed image made us into inviting targets for mockery. In Miami, we played an alternative-rock festival in a muddy field made muddier by tens of thousands of shirtless, jumping, stomping, crowd-surfing, and mud-throwing tattooed teenagers. We watched from the side of the stage as the band before us, Black Lab, was showered with a barrage of mud so relentless, it appeared as if the crowd had commandeered a piece of farm equipment. Black Lab were good sports about it, taunting the crowd to throw even more, and by the time they left the stage, their shoes, pants, guitars, shirts, faces, and hair were caked in swampy Miami clay. The mud kept flying during the equipment changeover, and we wondered what we would do when the first splotch of mud hit one of us. Would we leave the stage and cast ourselves as sissies, or submit to a public humiliation? Just then, the singer for Stabbing Westward, the day's biggest attraction, walked out to the mike at center stage. "Hey! If one more fucking piece of mud comes up on stage, Stabbing Westward will not play. Got that? No more mud." After our mud-free set (two handfuls went wide right), we found our way to the Stabbing Westward tour bus to kneel in gratitude.

Degradations of female fans by some of the bands we encountered put literal mud-throwing to shame. Their tour buses were rolling frat-houses where stoned and drunken women were asked to pose nude for the stoned and drunken tour bus cameramen. Then these women would disappear into the back lounge with one or more of the band members. The next day, in the next city, the previous night's pictures were added to rows of similar photographs, mug shots of breasts (no faces) mounted on a bulletin board on the bus or on a crew member's workstation on the side of the stage.

I patted myself on the back for being above such crudity, but I practiced my own more insidious form of the rock-and-roll cult of male vanity and power. Occasionally, in the backstage hallways, I might have a conversation with a young woman whose eyes and body language expressed sexual interest, and I encouraged this with my tone and posture. I deflected the rare overture—"So, mister drummer, how do I get to see the inside of a tour bus?"— but not without savoring the fact of being propositioned, shaking my head with a teasing smile. As we traveled the country for various television appearances and to make videos, I was all too happy to be set up on dates by friends eager to help me exploit the long-awaited moment of my success. "She wants to have dinner with you. I told her you're a rock star. She's psyched!" *Yeah, but when we meet at the restaurant, I'll pretend to think she doesn't know who Semisonic is and avoid the subject. Let her bring it up and act surprised that she knows. She'll think I'm the down-to-earth kind of rock star.*

By early July, we had been invited to play *The Tonight Show*, yet another milestone marking our ever-widening appeal. The experience of playing on *Late Night with Conan O'Brien* proved invaluable. As soon as we walked into the dressing room, Dan turned off the closed-circuit monitor, remarking that watching the live taping of Conan had frazzled our nerves. During rehearsal, we ran through an even shorter version of "Closing Time"—*The Tonight Show*'s standards were fifteen seconds stricter than Conan's. I wasted no time in unfurling my best moves for the camera crew. Dan and John had yet to learn that face-time was won and lost in rehearsal. Back in the dressing room, Jim, having watched the camera rehearsal from the control room, said, "Wow, Jake, you're getting a lot of shots. I feel bad for John." John emerged from a side room, and I lowered my head behind my book. Dan walked in and sat down, and for the next half hour I watched my bandmates read. Then Jay Leno knocked on the door. I couldn't tell which was more disorienting, the fact that he was dressed in blue jeans and a windbreaker, or that in real life his eyes seemed darker and his jaw even larger.

The lead guest this night was Danny Glover, who went missing at the last minute, sending the *Tonight Show* staff into a panicked search. He was found reclining on the couch in the wrong dressing room.

This second network appearance felt much easier. The rumble of the house band and the cheering crowd through the dressing-room floor was just part of the routine. So were the soft voices and affectionate manner of the makeup artists, whose art lies not only in beautifying but also in calming each guest, like a parent preparing a child for bed with a bath, a fluffy towel, pajamas, and a story.

Danny Glover's interview was followed by a visit from a zookeeper who brought an assortment of baby animals for Jay to cuddle and be nipped by—classic *Tonight Show* fare. Our chaperone brought us down from our dressing room during this segment, and as we approached the studio doors, some of those wolf pups and baby jungle cats were huddled along the sides of the hall, innocent reminders of the millions of viewers who would be watching us.

During the break, we walked through the studio doors and into the surreal surroundings of the television studio, with its sharp angles and shrunken dimensions, as the house band played and the crowd cheered. I grabbed my drum key and gave an extra twist to the nut holding my bass drum beater in place, then made sure the clamp holding my top high-hat cymbal was also secure. I surveyed the room and shared a nervous chuckle with John. Another surge of applause marked the end of the commercial break, and the house band slammed to a stop. The ovation evaporated into the faint echo of Jay's voice as he spoke from across the stage as his face was lit by a blasting light, a startling effect that is unnoticed by the television viewer. I listened closely for my cue— "Please welcome Semisonic"—and clicked my sticks to count in the song.

The mental list of arrangement changes and camera opportunities kept me comfortably task-oriented. *Sticks above the head for the crash into the chorus. Give Dan a nod to remind him about the half-bridge. Here comes the guy with the handheld camera.* This denied me the existential thrill of thinking, "I'm rocking out on *The Tonight Show* in front of six million fucking people!"—but such thoughts were exactly what I wanted to avoid.

As the crowd applauded and Jay shook our hands, my mind turned immediately to thoughts of joining Jay and the other guests for a brief on-camera chat. *Just one good line. That's all I need. Two good lines and maybe Jim can get me on* Politically Incorrect. Unfortunately, the show had run long, and there was no such opportunity.

We grabbed our "Tonight Show" hats from the dressing room and left behind the welcome basket with its nine square yards of cellophane wrapping and the standard trimmings—tropical fruits, macadamia nuts, bonbons, pralines, and so forth—too much to consume backstage, too fragile to pack in our bags. We drove off the NBC lot hours before sunset, and after dinner I returned to my hotel room, where once again I watched myself from the edge of my bed, all alone in an audience of millions. This time, I made no attempt to reexperience the taping or savor the broadcast. Instead, I made notes. Maybe my hunching and scrunching looked OK to everyone else. Did I look like every other drummer? Did we look like every other band? If we got on *Saturday Night Live,* would they put me in a skit?

Our television appearances continued with MTV's *Beach House,* hosted by Carson Daly. This celebration of surf, sand, and singles culture featured an audience of fun-loving and improbably slim young women and men, handpicked by the producers. In our first bit, we were handed a microphone and asked to feed pickup lines to one of the young men from the audience as he strolled along a public beach, repeating the lines he heard in his earpiece to passing females. I didn't know any pickup lines. Fortunately, Jim had warned us about this bit ahead of time.

"Okay, Jake. Give Ted a pickup line."

"Which way to the Captain Endurance contest?"

After a brief interview, the stunts continued when we were asked to throw wet sponges at targets painted on the bellies of bikini-clad women, audience volunteers, as they drifted around the beach-house swimming pool on inner tubes. Dan, aware of how ridiculous it would look, excused himself from this activity, leaving John and me to make underhand tosses from the balcony overlooking the pool. My first toss missed its target, making what I assumed to be a painful impact inches below one woman's navel; she kept a straight face. John's first toss went wide. My turn again. Staring down at these female targets with a soaking wet sponge in my hand—was there ever a more opportune moment to turn to the camera and lambaste MTV's horrid gender politics? Was there ever a more reluctant critic of MTV? A successful bull's-eye hit earned me a question from a member of the audience, a college-aged woman.

"Okay, Tanya, what's your question for Jake?"

"Yeah, what do you listen to when you want to get your groove on?"

The camera swung back to me. I tried to decide what she meant by the phrase "get your groove on." Then I ran down a list of possible answers, casting aside "Fake Plastic Trees" because maybe I was supposed to think of something with a pronounced beat, and deciding against *Portishead* because I didn't know anything about the record and might get killed with a follow-up question. Finally, I said, " 'Creepin' by Stevie Wonder," an answer that elicited blank nods from the audience and a disappointed shrug from the woman who had asked the question.

Back in Los Angeles, we appeared on the televised version of *Loveline*, roughly the same as the radio version except for the addition of cameras and a studio audience. There were no hiding places for those who might blush over a question about ribbed condoms, but Dan and John had plenty of advice, allowing me to maintain silence and depart with a complimentary "Loveline" bathrobe.

Meanwhile, "Closing Time" permeated American pop culture. As I watched *SportsCenter* from my hotel bed one night, I heard anchorman Stuart Scott comment on a highlight of a strikeout with the words "You don't have to go home, but you better get the heck up out of here!" *That's a "Closing Time" reference. Right?* Bars began to use "Closing Time" as exit music. Relief pitchers loved it as entrance music. Stadiums across the country blasted the song over the loudspeakers as the home-team relief pitcher jogged from the bullpen to the mound to close out the game. One of them, Todd Jones of the Detroit Tigers, adopted it as his theme song and hooked us up with tickets on a number of occasions. We even heard it while watching the World Series. New York Senate candidate Chuck Schumer and Minnesota gubernatorial candidate Jesse Ventura listed it as their favorite song. (And both won.) As tens of thousands bought our album each week, our shows were packed with fans both younger and older than the twenty-somethings who had already latched on to us. Now those post-college rock fans stood among soccer moms, Little League dads, and cheerleaders.

E-mails poured in from everywhere. Surgeons sutured patients while "Closing Time" played on the operating-room boom box. Graduating seniors made it their class song and prom theme. An obstetrician reported that as she delivered a baby, "Closing Time" was playing over the delivery-room stereo. She handed the baby to its mother just in time for the song's final words: "Every new beginning comes from some other beginning's end." The mother said to her newborn, "It's not ending time, it's beginning time."

A man ran up to Dan in a hotel lobby. "Hey! You're the 'Closing Time' guy, right? I just got back from my company's real-estate sales conference. At the end of the whole thing, guess what song they played? 'Closing Time.' Get it? *Closing* time."

As the song sustained its dominance of the airwaves, the critics began to hedge, and some even railed:

"An insinuating, repetitive song about the insinuating, repetitive nature of consumerism." (Ann Powers, the *New York Times*)

Two months later, the same writer felt positively besieged:

"A weary, repetitive song about the weariness and repetition of urban life, and of modern rock, too." (Ann Powers, the *New York Times*)

Friends of ours expressed concern: "The radio's playing your song too much. Tell them to stop before people start hating you." The idea that we could or would ask radio programmers to back off the song seemed laughable to me, but that was exactly what MCA was doing. The radio add-date of our next single, "Singing in My Sleep," was approaching, and MCA wanted radio stations to hold back "Closing Time" and clear the way for its follow-up. The radio stations' research, however, found that "Closing Time" continued to be an overwhelming favorite with listeners; no way were the programmers going to let go of it.

The radio dial was wall-to-wall "Closing Time." A friend reported that Mel Gibson, appearing on a talk show, complained of hearing it nonstop. I wondered if his grousing about "Closing Time," "Closing Time," "Closing Time" had been followed by a plug for his latest film, *Lethal Weapon IV*.

In early autumn, we were invited to play on *Late Show with David Letterman*. My anticipation of this chance to complete the late-night television circuit had by now grown into arrogant impatience, even though rumors of Letterman's edgy persona suggested a minefield of bad possibilities: "If you see Dave in the hallway, don't look at him, don't try to talk to him, don't even say 'Hi, Dave.' " The studio was said to be freezing, and the three-and-a-half-minute time limit for music, according to another Letterman legend, was strictly enforced by an angry man with a stopwatch.

The reality proved much less daunting. After walking through the Fifty-third Street side entrance to the Ed Sullivan Theater, I exchanged a friendly "Hello" with Paul Shaffer. The studio itself was frigid as promised, but our interactions with the crew during camera rehearsal were pleasant, the man with the stopwatch smiled, and the nasty picture painted by the rumors slowly disintegrated.

We observed Dan's "no monitoring of the show taping" rule and kept the dressing-room television tuned to a soccer game announced in Spanish. Dan took over one of the two small dressing rooms to warm up his voice, Jim and Hans bantered in the hallway, and John read a magazine as the soccer game blared on. I walked up and down the six flights of stairs to our dressing room several times, hoping to run into Mark McGwire—who days earlier had broken the single-season record for home runs—only to learn that we had read the schedule incorrectly; the lead guest was Kelly Preston. In the makeup room, I bumped into Peter Boyle, who was the second guest on the show. He had no idea who Semisonic was, but he graciously returned my compliments of his performance in *Taxi Driver* with curiosity about the band.

By the time our chaperone led us down to the ground floor for our performance, a large crowd had gathered on the street outside the side entrance. We walked through the stage doors to the freezing studio, crossing paths with Boyle, who surveyed us with a genial smile. We walked onto the set as Paul Shaffer and the house band romped through the break. There was Dave, sitting at his desk, under bright lights on a tiny set. All around us were the familiar faces of the technical crew, people regularly featured in

Letterman's comic bits. Biff Henderson, the stage manager and most familiar of those faces, smiled at me amid the chaos. *He's actually managing the stage!* It was a brainteaser on the order of watching French children speak French.

The crowd applauded and settled down, and Dave began to talk. On the periphery of my awareness was the strange sensation I had also noticed on Conan and Leno—the experience of realizing that I was no longer a Letterman viewer but someone he was about to introduce with a backward stretch of his arm. He cracked a joke, and I laughed along with the audience. I could feel one of the cameras catching my grin, and I wondered if I hadn't looked goofy by laughing along. "Please welcome . . . Semisonic."

It was all business. We were now unveiling "Singing in My Sleep," our follow-up single. On this particular song, I played drums and keyboards simultaneously (keyboard with my right hand, clutching the stick between my thumb and palm, the other three limbs attending to the drums), and managing two instruments at once left no mental space free for existential freakouts. Time passed quickly whenever we performed on television, because I did not allow my mind to process more than five seconds at once. The big picture was off-limits. The crowd applauded, and Dave walked out to shake our hands. *Don't stare at him.*

We didn't get to see the broadcast of our performance, because we flew back to Minneapolis immediately after the taping, leaving me to trust that we had made a reasonable impression on the households blinking 30,000 feet below us. I saw a video of our performance a few days later, but I missed the electric sensation of watching with millions of others.

In spite of the dominance of "Closing Time," Jim felt that MCA had failed to raise public awareness of the band and Dan in particular. He was smart, handsome, a great songwriter, a highly quotable interviewee, and yet he received a fraction of the coverage given to other artists of his stature. MCA's publicity department defended itself, saying that Semisonic came off as too serious. Jim thought this dodged the real issue—MCA's reputation of bungling the careers of its rock bands made journalists and editors wary of devoting time and column inches to Semisonic—but he agreed to meet with the publicity staff to address this issue. One of the MCA publicists, Kymm Britton, suggested we try to shake up our earnest image and display our humorous side by appearing on the Howard Stern Show. Stern was the Anti-Earnest, and his radio ratings would assure us of massive exposure. Jim liked the idea and called each of the band members to get our reaction.

"Howard Stern? He'll tear us to shreds!"

Jim, however, told us that Stern was said to like the band, and there were other upsides. For months we had heard that we were not as "marketplace" as other pop-rock bands who sold more records—Matchbox 20 and Third Eye Blind, for example. "Closing Time," these voices said, was a "marketplace song," but Semisonic was not a "marketplace band." We gagged on this language. Nevertheless, feeling that we were close to breaking through to wider acclaim, we agreed to risk our egos with an appearance on the Stern show. Jim passed the word to Kymm, and she sought and received an official invite. "Howard is psyched!" *Now we're fucked.*

I wanted to prepare for Stern's questions, but how? Stern was known as a ruthless cross-examiner. He might like us. He might hate us. He might like us, and then if one of us—the drummer perhaps—seemed a little too quiet, too circumspect, he might press that person for an embarrassing revelation, pull on that loose thread and watch it unravel. Then, having denuded his unfortunate guest, Stern could proceed to dissect and devour him while millions listened and laughed.

Jim reassured me. "This is your big chance, Jake. Everyone will get to hear how funny you are. In fact, if Howard goes after Dan, you should step up and say, 'No, you don't want to mess with *him*. Talk to *me*.' You and Howard—it'll be hilarious. I'll send the tape to the people at *Politically Incorrect*."

Certainly, I had become a more confident and experienced interviewee, occasionally capable of spicing up the perfunctory responses to standard questions. (When an interviewer on VH1 asked us where we got our name, I answered that I had won it in a high-stakes poker game.) As the Stern interview approached, I rehearsed answers for a variety of embarrassing questions.

Howard: So, Jake, you must get laid a lot.
Jake: Sure.
Howard: When was the last time you got laid?
Jake: Um . . .
Howard: You don't remember?
Jake: I, um . . .
Howard: You LIED to me?

Shit, that won't work. What about . . .

Howard: So, Jake, you must get laid a lot.
Jake: Ha! That's a good one. Me? Get laid? I haven't been laid since . . . When did the Mets beat the Sox in the World Series?
Howard: Oh, I see. You're trying to be funny. Do you think you're funny?

Fuck!

The morning of the interview, Kymm met us in the hotel lobby for the ride over to the midtown Manhattan broadcast studio. She had appeared on the Stern show with other artists—the Ramones, Sammy Hagar, and Live—and had volunteered to accompany us in order to draw fire away from the band if things turned bad. With that in mind, she dressed in tight black leather pants, a tight black leather coat, and gave her hair an artful tussling. Perhaps the publicist in her knew that following us into the studio in this getup would lend the earnest lads of Semisonic the hyper-hetero legitimacy that the world of Howard Stern demanded.

As our town car pulled up in front of the tall midtown building that is home to the *Howard Stern Show,* a man with a video camera walked up, training his lens on us. Kymm explained that he worked for the show and would film the entirety of our visit, from the time we entered the building to the time we left. Footage from this camera might be used on the televised version of the original radio broadcast. I gathered that this meant if one of us scratched his ass or picked his nose, the producers would splice it into the televised rebroadcast of the show. We got on the elevator, and the cameraman followed, filming us as we looked down at our feet.

The camera watched us sit in the reception area and then followed us through the halls to the room where we would wait for the next forty-five minutes. Its constant presence kept our conversation restricted to weather and sports—nothing about our approaching encounter with the fearsome king of shock radio. Eventually, the room fell silent except for the camera's whir and the creeping feet of its operator. My nose itched. My lips felt dry. My underwear needed adjustment. My fingers could feel the pack of Rolaids in my pocket, and yet how would I sneak one into my mouth? "Excuse me. Where's the rest room?"

A minute before our interview, we were led to a room adjacent to the studio. One of the show's producers interviewed us, also on camera, wondering if we were nervous. "I ask because, as you know, Howard can get kind of rough with some of his guests." *Fuck me.*

Through the speakers in the hall, we could hear Howard on a vicious tirade against one of his talk-radio rivals, Don Imus, railing about what a worthless, whimpering dog Imus was. The producer nodded at us. "Ready?" Just then I noticed a blotch of toothpaste residue on the crotch of my pants.

Howard settled down from his rant and continued. "All right, let's meet the guys from Semisonic." We walked through the door. "Look at these guys. Very serious musicians." We sat down. I rested my folded hands over the toothpaste stain.

Howard looked us over. "That's what I like, three guys in a group. If you get ten guys, like Chicago or something like that, you gotta split it all up. By the time you're done, you got no money left."

I giggled.

Howard asked about how we divided the money. Dan told him we split it equally, but Howard suggested Dan reconsider his decision to split the songwriting royalties. I laughed again, and as the conversation proceeded, I continued to giggle and chuckle in Dan's shadow.

Then Howard leaned back and smiled at Dan. "What are you wearing? A wedding ring?"

"Yeah."

"What about you other guys—you married, too?"

"No." I giggled.

Howard beamed and shook his head at Dan. " 'Dear journal, today we played a show in Schenectady. Fifty hot chicks came on to me and they came up to the room. John and Jacob banged them.' "

From giggles to wincing cackles. Howard pressed for details on Dan's wife. "She must be hot? A white girl?" Retreating to a nervous chuckle.

Dan remained unruffled: "No."

"Really? You're married to a black chick?"

"No."

"Asian?"

"Yeah."

Howard nodded his head. "No kidding. I go for that. Never had that." He applauded softly. "Very subservient—true or false?"

I held my breath. Dan said, "I'm the subservient one."

Howard continued. "I love Asian people. Good service is so important. I've always dreamt that I would be in Japan in a kimono in my hotel room—"

Dan interrupted. "Servicing Asian people?" Touché.

Howard smiled. "Yes. Never seems to happen—none of them want me."

I exhaled, and the conversation moved on to other topics, salted by my endless supply of giggles. They came reflexively, punctuating everything Howard said. Once or twice, a softball came our way, and I stepped forward to answer, then resumed my servile laughter. How long would the interview continue? Never before had the prospect of playing the drums for millions seemed like an escape. Howard and Robin, his sidekick, focused some of their attention on Kymm, the welcome diversion for which all of us had hoped. For the most part, however, Howard directed friendly questions toward the band. He was delighted to know that we were Prince fans. Did we know any Prince songs? Yes. That won us more points.

During a commercial break, we took our places behind our instruments, and the show resumed with a performance of "Closing Time," for which we received a small but approving ovation from Howard, Robin, Kymm, and ourselves. Then, at Howard's request, we played the Prince song "Erotic City." The lyrics included many occurrences of the word "fuck," which we replaced with "funk." Howard walked around the studio, nodding his head and smiling as we played. He remarked on the fact that both John and I played keyboards while playing the bass and drums. "Imagine, keyboards and drums at the same time. Anybody got a flute in their ass?"

"Ha HAH!"

Our time was up. Howard thanked us, shook our hands, and posed for a few pictures during the commercial break. We collected our things and walked quickly to the elevator, leaving behind the cameraman for the bright blue autumn Manhattan morning. It was nine o'clock.

Jim caught up with us later to offer his congratulations. Then he pulled me aside. "Jesus, Jake, you really choked." True, but neither had I been ripped apart. In fact, by now I had played my drums for millions of people on radio and television without once dropping my sticks or throwing up.

Chapter XII

CARPE PER DIEM

With our burgeoning popularity, we were offered and accepted the chance to go on tour with Matchbox 20, a band whose multiplatinum success was well under way. They needed an opening band for their late-summer tour of outdoor amphitheaters—a "shed tour," as it is known in the music business. (The term was probably coined in reference to earlier generations of these venues, which were cheaply built structures with metal roofs.) We were offered the first slot on a three-band bill: Semisonic, followed by Soul Asylum and Matchbox 20.

We hesitated before accepting the offer. Playing the first slot was less appetizing, since many of the fans would not yet have arrived. Also, we felt unsure about how appearing on the same bill with Matchbox 20 might affect the broader perception of Semisonic. We saw ourselves as cosmopolitan, in the ilk of U2, R.E.M., and Björk. Might a tour with Matchbox 20 peg us as suburban? Jim regarded this concern as vain self-delusion. Basically, Jim suggested, we were not as cool as we thought we were, we came off a lot more like Matchbox 20 than we realized, and maybe that wasn't such a bad thing. So we accepted the offer. In late August, we arrived at the Merriweather Post Pavilion in Columbia, Maryland, for the first of eighteen shows stretching over twenty-five days.

Most of our time on the road is spent on a tour bus. Tour buses come in a wide variety, and those who travel in them argue over which makes—Prevost, Eagle, Van Hool, and so on—provide the best ride. But the real differences lie in the modifications made by the bus-rental companies to the individual buses. Except for the driver's seat, the forty-five-foot interiors of the buses they purchase from the manufacturers are empty shells. The rental companies take these empty vehicles and install luxurious lounges, entertainment systems, bunks, kitchenettes, toilets, and sinks. A finished bus might cost a million dollars, though the state-of-the-art models—equipped with technology that allows them to expand in size when parked—cost two to three times as much. A standard tour bus costs a band $3,000–$5,000 per week (including rental, fuel, and the driver's pay and hotel rooms), but for those willing to endure a noisier and bumpier ride, older buses are available at a discount.

A typical tour-bus interior includes a front lounge (couches, a TV, stereo, kitchenette, and a bathroom off to the side), a bunk compartment, and a back lounge. Some, like the bus we had on the Matchbox 20 tour, include small televisions with built-in videotape players mounted within each bunk compartment. A pair of headphones allows surreptitious daytime viewing behind the drawn curtain of the bunk. Impressive, yes, but the veteran bus rider steps aboard and checks to see if the satellite dish works. Can it be accessed from the TV in the back lounge? How about a DVD player? How's the collection of bus movies? Are there enough outlets in the back lounge to charge eight cell phones and five walkie-talkies? Is the bathroom clean? Are the carpets? A dirty bus is a telltale sign of a neglectful driver, the most central bus feature of all.

Because so many people are packed together in such a small space, bus etiquette must be fastidiously observed. Keep the front door locked and the curtain drawn. Store your large items in the bays underneath to free up space in the living quarters. Keep your books, laptop computer, and dirty socks off the seats. No renegade thermostat tampering. And woe to the person who violates the most important rule of all, sometimes posted in the bathroom: "Pee only. No poo!"

Our bus was not as nice as Matchbox 20's, especially considering that they had three buses—one for the band and two for the crew. Ours, however, was nice enough to be our home for a twenty-five-day trip across the country. Here is my memory of one of those days:

7:30 A.M.—Wake up in bunk to beeping sound bus makes as it backs into its parking space.

7:33—Three-minute segments of sleep, punctuated by revving of bus engine and slamming of bus door as driver gets on and off, repositioning the bus several times. Finally, the driver kills the engine, depriving me of the sound I associate with sleep. He then starts the generator, and its whirring will be the soundtrack of our waking hours.

8:53—An important decision: keep resting or risk missing out on the first crack at the backstage amphitheater shower and a dry bath mat?

9:21—Gather fresh clothes and shaving kit, step off bus. The bus drivers are hanging out together, waiting to be driven to their hotel rooms, where they will spend the daylight hours sleeping, in preparation for the next night's drive. I say hello to our new bus driver, John. He's a welcome change from two others who were fired in quick succession. One of them almost tipped the bus over on a sidewalk full of fans in Dallas when he backed over the curb. The second of those two, Earl, could not read a map. We'd go to sleep as Earl began a two-hundred-mile trip, wake up eight hours later, and find that we were still sixty miles from our destination. Sometimes I'd wake up in my bunk in the middle of the night feeling the bus lurch forward and back, and my inner compass would tell me that Earl was making a U-turn on a country road somewhere. If, as the search for our destination dragged on, anyone bothered to ask Earl why it took five hours to cover 120 miles, he had plenty of excuses. "I got two words for you: road construction!" The crew coined the phrase "As the Earl flies" to describe his circuitous routing.

Life with Earl got worse when he combined bleach and ammonia in the toilet, creating a toxic vapor that stung our eyes and induced splitting headaches. In Montreal, he parked the bus in front of a café, and when a patron complained of the diesel fumes from the idling engine, he leapt off the bus and punched out the patron, screaming, "I've killed better people than you in 'Nam!" Five minutes later, our tour manager, Chris, was on the phone finding another driver. That was a month ago. Now it's nice to have John, a solid driver with a mellow vibe.

9:22—Take a look around at the backstage parking lot of the Coca-Cola Star Lake Amphitheater in Burgettstown, Pennsylvania, half an hour from Pittsburgh. Look around for showers. Hear from someone in charge that towels aren't ready yet. Asking the Matchbox 20 production manager about towels will only piss him off first thing in the morning, when he's got semi trucks full of gear being unloaded and a stage in the process of being assembled. Return to bus, get back in bunk, and lie there for forty seconds, listening to snores, tossing and turning, and the muffled sound of the bus generator, before deciding to get back up and eat breakfast.

9:30—Go through catering line. The pancakes look good. Recall the days before our record deal, when we would lose weight on the road.

9:34—Finish eating. Pick up my copy of Bertrand Russell's *History of Western Philosophy*.

9:35—Put down *History of Western Philosophy*. Pick up cell phone. No messages. Explore the built-in game options. There's a game called Snake where you use the number pad to steer a snake, one dot in length, around the small screen toward another dot, which the snake then eats, lengthening itself in the process. After a while, when the snake has grown to twenty dots in length, it becomes challenging to steer toward the next randomly placed dot without running the snake into itself or off the edge of the screen, ending the game. As I play, I wonder how long it would take to create a snake so long that it fills the entire screen, thus attaining the maximum possible score.

9:37—Check messages on my home phone. None.

9:40—Locate someone who knows about the towels. The towels are ready. Return to bus for shaving kit and clean clothes. Shower and shave.

9:52—Stare at mirror, recalling Mimi's instructions to "make it look kind of messy."

9:56—Walk around the parking lot. It would be nice to walk around a city, but we're not in Boston, we're at the Great Woods Performing Arts Center in Mansfield, Massachusetts, half an hour away. Pick up *History of Western Philosophy* and return to catering area.

10:00—*Do I really believe I'm going to finish reading this book?*

10:08—Dan, John, and soundman Brad file into the catering area.

10:30—After three more failed attempts to make progress in book, get back on the bus and hear the sound of a television coming from the TV in guitar tech Toby's bunk. Toby loves television. Once, on a day off in Toronto, he stayed in his hotel bed and watched a twelve-hour *Little House on the Prairie* marathon, leaving his bed only to answer the door and pay the pizza deliveryman. Now, as I sit in the front lounge, the theme song to *The Price Is Right* serves as a brief reminder of why I brought *A History of Western Philosophy* along.

10:42—"No, you fucking idiot!" Toby can't believe that one

contestant, ignorant of basic *Price Is Right* strategy, has blown an opportunity to make a one-dollar bid and win the grandfather clock. He turns off the TV, gets out of his bunk, pulls on some socks and shoes, and steps off the bus, muttering groggy complaints about the decayed state of the American mind.

10:53—Brad gets back on the bus. "This is some shit coffee."

11:02—John and then Dan return to the bus.

"Hey."

"Hey."

"Hey."

11:06—Tour manager Chris steps aboard to hand out the per diems, $210 for each member of the band and crew. "Carpe the per diem!" jokes Toby as he steps on the bus halfway through this weekly rite. Chris then tells the band about the rest of the day. A radio visit in the midafternoon. Dan has a phone interview at 1:30. Also, last night's set ran three minutes long. Finish on time tonight or we'll be in trouble with the Matchbox 20 tour manager. I pick up my cell phone and check my home messages. None.

11:08—Step off of bus to explore concert venue grounds. The PNC Bank Arts Center in Holmdel, New Jersey, evokes memories of the Merriweather Post Pavilion in Columbia, Maryland. Also, John is irritated. Why is the only car in the parking lot parked underneath the basketball hoop? Watch as John makes a polite inquiry into getting the car moved, only to receive overdramatized sighs expressing inconvenience. He steps back on the bus and picks up one of his Chinese books.

11:15—Over to catering to ask what time lunch is served. Back to bus.

11:16—*What the fuck am I going to do for the next hour and fourteen minutes?*

11:17—Peer out of the corner of my eye at *A History of Western Philosophy*.

11:18—Nyeaahh.

11:19—Dan is in the front lounge, writing songs on his guitar. I head to the back lounge, haul my acoustic guitar out of the closet, and strum aimlessly for ten minutes. Open my lyric notebook and flip past the various ideas that seemed promising when I wrote them down. I close the lyric notebook, a nice one bought months ago. Only the first five pages have any writing on them. Ratchet my expectations as a songwriter down one more notch and stow guitar. Grab *Law and Order* videotape number two of six (recorded for us by Toby's girlfriend, Kathy), crawl into my bunk. With the curtain drawn and the headphones plugged into the television, I can watch without being detected by anyone who may wander on and off the bus, and then, a year later, hear me complain about how little time there is for songwriting.

12:29 P.M.—One minute until lunch. Walk to catering in the spiritual limbo that lies between a television viewer's shame and satiation.

12:30—Cheeseburgers, chips, diet Coke.

12:33—Look at watch. Ask catering staff person what time dinner is. Look at watch again.

12:39—Wander along the row of dressing rooms at the Blossom Music Center in Cuyahoga Falls, half an hour from Cleveland. The Matchbox 20 tour manager has posted signs on the doors to those rooms. Two rooms are reserved for Matchbox 20's production offices. Then comes the "Matchbox 20 dressing room," followed by "Matchbox 20 hospitality room" and "Matchbox 20 therapy room" (where the tour masseuse keeps the band limbered up) and the "Matchbox 20 warm-up room." Only after the "Matchbox 20 tuning room," "Matchbox 20 guitar room," "Matchbox 20 wardrobe room," and several others, do I pass the door to the second-smallest room, "Soul Asylum," and turn the corner to find the littlest room of all—"Semisonic." I peek in. Catering has not yet delivered our snacks. Chris has set up his computer, and I don't want to encroach on his space or sit under fluorescent lights. I step out into the hallway and bump into Adam, one of the Matchbox 20 guitar players. He has the same-model cell phone as me, and informs me that last night, after several hours of concentrated effort, he conquered the game Snake, creating a snake that filled the entire screen. "And when the snake ate the last dot, it just said 'Game Over.' "

"How long did it take?"

"Like, a couple of hours."

"Wow."

"I know."

"All right."

"See ya."

Return to bus. Lie in the back lounge trying to think of a self-improvement regimen that will make use of all the downtime on the road. Get out cell phone and play Snake. Quit. Dial home phone. "You have no messages." Open curtain. Look outside. Close curtain. A voice squawks over one of the walkie-talkies left on the bus: "Has anyone seen Jake?" I turn it off.

1:09—Take out practice pad, sticks, metronome, and *Stick Control* by George Lawrence Stone. Follow instructions to play each exercise "twenty times without stopping." The repetitive nature of the exercises and the tapping of my sticks clear my mind, leaving a white page with black notes. On that mental backdrop I project images of Danny Seraphine and James Gadson, my two favorite drummers as a teenager.

1:33—Put away *Stick Control* and pull out *Accents and Rebounds*, by the same author. More repetitiveness. Now images of other drummers give way to visions of me playing with masterful dexterity. How many more years of this regimen will it take? *How good am I, really?*

1:58—MCA local knocks on the bus door. He's here to take us on a few radio visits. Luckily, the Deer Creek Music Center, on the outskirts of Indianapolis, is not far from the station. We ride as the local makes a wrong turn, and then another, and soon he's on his cell phone getting directions from the station receptionist. I inform him that this will cost him in the "Semisonic Promo 500," a joke contest I invented: The first MCA local to drive us 500 miles in the right direction will win an unspecified prize. Miles traveled in the wrong direction are deducted from a driver's total. Teasing the local about this earns me a friendly "Fuck you."

The DJ starts our interview by saying, "So, being on the road, I'll bet you guys have some great stories." We don't. Pictures with the program director follow the interview. As we ride back to the venue, I stuff another complimentary station T-shirt under the seat of the local's SUV.

5:07—Back at the Kiel Center in Saint Louis for soundcheck. The crew has been at work for several hours, and now here come the musos (mew-zohs), the crew word for *musicians.* A muso doesn't know the difference between duct tape and gaff tape. (Duct tape leaves a sticky grunge behind; gaff tape is cleaner and available only from theatrical supply houses.) A muso might refer to the soundman as "a roadie." Don't. A muso might meddle where he shouldn't—for instance, in the guitar tech's toolbox. As far as the crew is concerned, everything would go a lot easier if the musos would just stick to playing their instruments and leave the equipment the hell alone.

The stage is a dangerous place. On this day, a friend of ours and longtime crew member for The Verve Pipe, Boo Bruey, is in the middle of a six-month hospitalization and rehab following his forty-foot fall from a catwalk, which broke his back and shattered his heel and both wrists. At the last second, one of his crewmates stuck out his hands to cradle Boo's head before it hit the ground, saving his life. Three months from now, on a small stage in Germany, our guitar tech, Toby, will be electrocuted by a faulty power transformer. Our tour manager, Chris, will save Toby's life by kicking a cable out of his hand and stopping the 220 volts surging through his chest. Amazingly, Toby will spend only one night in the hospital. Every crew person has witnessed similar terrifying episodes. Some of the people on the crew, when they aren't working for us, tour with other bands. Other crew folks we know have gone on to work for rock stars who can fill stadiums. Some of those stars are prone to violent stage tantrums, throwing microphones at the nearest crew member if something goes wrong.

Because we are the opening band, we rarely get a soundcheck, during which we play through several songs and adjust the balance of voices and instruments that each of us will hear. Today we get a quick line check—a quick test of each microphone and guitar, and a few plunks of the piano keys, enough to say, "It's working." We have enough time left over to run through half of one loud song and half of a soft one. Sometimes we don't even get a line check. Then the first few minutes of the show are chaos.

5:28—Back on the bus, Matt, our monitor engineer, plays a video game on the television in the back lounge. In this game, which I still don't understand, a rabbit runs through a forest, hopping over tree stumps and elves, kicking yellow boxes that explode, and jumping improbably high on and off of bridges and walls on his way to doing something. I grab *A History of Western Philosophy* and head for the catering room.

5:31—Spaghetti with meat sauce and salad with Newman's Italian dressing. Read next eight sentences out of book. Reread sentences seven and eight. Replace bookmark. Sit in a state of confusion and leftover scholastic guilt. Then, overcome by laziness, head back to bus.

5:36—Front lounge of the bus. Channel-surf on the satellite television. Dan climbs aboard.

"Has anyone seen my glasses?" The search brings noise and upheaval to the front lounge, where Toby and I are trying to watch Columbo close in on a murderous wine connoisseur. We join the search halfheartedly and quickly direct Dan to the bunk compartment and the rear lounge.

John steps on the bus. "Why hasn't Fucko moved his car from underneath the basketball rim?!"

6:40—Get dressed. No reason to use the dressing room since our clothes are on the bus, and anyway, the bus is nicer. I have three light-blue shirts and two pairs of black slacks. Each night, I entertain other options. What about the nice black shirt and the bone-colored slacks from the video? I put them on and stand in front of the closet mirror, looking confused.

John sees me. "What's up?"

"I'm just wondering how this looks."

Dan joins in. "What about your light-blue shirt and black pants?"

John agrees. "Yeah, that always looks good."

6:52—Dan goes to the back lounge to warm up his voice. John sits down with his Chinese book. I grab my CD player and headphones and listen to my favorite snippets of drumming. The first CD is a compilation of my favorite drum fills. I made it myself. Each selection is a few seconds long, with just enough song on either end of the drum fill to place it in context. It starts with examples of simplicity—Andy Newmark's suspenseful silence, broken with loud tom-tom booms in Carly Simon's "Anticipation"—and gradually progresses to mayhem—John Bonham's hilarious chorus fills in "Misty Mountain Hop." I pull out *In the Jungle Groove* by James Brown, absorbing the funky stylings of Clyde Stubblefield and Jabo Starks. Then I flip through my CD cases to my Spinners collection and listen to Earl Young pave a simple but silken groove under "I'll Be Around," which ranks among the most instructive drum performances ever.

7:13—Dan opens the door to the back lounge and hails John and me for a group vocal warm-up. This consists of first deciding which songs we need to run through, then getting distracted and running through other songs instead. Just as we come upon a section that needs work, Chris comes to tell us it's time for the show. We put in our in-ear monitor system, custom-molded earplugs with tiny speakers mounted inside them, feeding us a mix by way of a wireless transmitter pack. Thus, with our "ears" in and our packs switched on, we can hear the sounds of the crowd milling around the amphitheater even while we're still on the bus. I check my blood sugar one last time, and drink cranberry juice to ensure against insulin shock. One by one, each band member remembers something he forgot. Chris is straight-faced, though surely he is dreading a lecture on tardiness from the Matchbox 20 tour manager and wondering why, after years of shows, Semisonic still can't make it to the stage without three last-minute trips to the bathroom.

7:21—Walk from the bus up the loading-dock stairs to the back of the stage. We stand next to the monitor board in the wings. Toby looks over our clothes. Fortunately, he makes no jokes about our appearance, as he sometimes feels is necessary. Two-thirds of the seats at the Sandstone Amphitheater in Bonner Springs, Kansas, are empty, a familiar sight for an opening band. A few Semisonic fans in the front rows spot us and send up a small whoop. We wait as Toby walks the stage, making a last check of the connections on Dan's guitar rig, pressing his lips up to Dan's mike while holding the plugged-in guitar to make sure Dan won't get shocked. He gives Chris the ready sign. Chris nods to the Matchbox 20 production manager, who sends word out over the walkie-talkies. The house music playing over the speakers stops, and we take the stage to modest applause. It's still daylight. The colored stage lights shining down from above us are barely noticeable. Behind our equipment is a clutter of drums and amplifiers that will be used by the other two bands. I step up to the drum riser and sit down at the drums. I check for my spare sticks and setlist. The September sun is shining in our eyes.

7:25—Dan says, "Hello." The few Semisonic fans scream some more as Dan scrubs the opening riff of "f.n.t." The drums and bass follow. Within seconds, I locate the faces in the crowd that will shine reliably for the next thirty minutes: three high school kids in front wearing Semisonic shirts, two twenty-something women dancing halfway up the middle section, and a father with his ten-year-old son in the third row.

As soon as Dan begins to sing, I look toward the monitor board and catch Matt's eye. Then I look toward Dan and motion "up" with my face, and seconds later, Dan's vocal level increases in my ears. On days when we don't get a soundcheck, Matt is swamped with pleas from the various band members. As the singer, Dan is Matt's highest priority; I may have to wait a song or two before getting rid of the guitar screaming in my left ear. John's mix is the hardest to perfect, because the heft of the bass guitar cannot be satisfactorily conveyed by way of the in-ear monitors. It drives John, and thus Matt, insane. As for me, I need to hear vocals, guitar for tuning, bass for groove, and drums. If I ask for too much drums, then I'll have to ask for more of everything else, and soon I have a deafening mix. But if I don't hear enough drums, I'll compensate by hitting them too hard, doing injury to the groove.

Communicating my requests is hard while playing the drums. Plus, I try to keep technical troubles from the audience's view. Thankfully, tonight the mix is right. With the drums dialed in nicely, I play with a sweet touch. And I'm enjoying a nice boost from the crowd mikes, which are pointed at the crowd and fill our plugged ears with the most glorious of all sounds—applause. Sometimes, as I play, I notice myself moaning and groaning. Most of the time I'm unaware of it until the show is over and my throat is sore from all of my rasping.

The set is tightly timed. We can just squeeze seven songs into thirty-five minutes, with room for a detour or two during one or two songs. I know which songs Dan will speak between. Thanks to the preshow warning from Chris, "Rambling Dan" takes a night off. More and more seats fill. The twenty-something women are still dancing, irking the Matchbox 20 fans seated behind them. If I'm off my game, my mind starts to wander, thinking a few songs ahead, or wishing that the crowd were as loud as the crowd at the Rosemont Horizon in Chicago a few nights ago. We had a lot of Semisonic fans there. It was a good show for my family to have seen.

Over the course of the set, I build the groove into a wave where I can surf. I like to lie back where the top of the wave curls over me—the pocket. On my best nights, I am lord of the pocket, the wave, and the ocean. With a large spacious fill, the wave becomes fifty feet high, and I glide along the top, enjoying the ride as I send it crashing down, a rush for the audience. At other moments, I still the water and skim over its glassy smoothness. Drumming is a game: Make the audience shimmy and shake, then knock them over. Give Dan and John a surprise kick in the ass. They love it. The ten-year-old boy and his father love it, too.

The seats have filled up, and now I can see why the Red Rocks Amphitheater, seated in the mountains overlooking Denver, is prized by so many musicians and crew members. Dan gets the audience shouting during an extended breakdown in "Delicious," notated *Delish* on our setlist. If I'm on my game, the beat flows hypnotically from the drums, seducing the crowd into unison hip-shaking. It won't matter if my high hat has come loose and Toby can't understand me as I gesture for him to fix it. If I'm off my game, however, the loose high hat is one more calamity in a night spent worrying about having forgotten the name of the VH1 personality who interviewed us on camera before the show. On an off night, the drums give nothing back; I hit harder, yanking out an effortful groove. But tonight I'm on. The father enjoys watching his ten-year-old son wave at me, and I smile in return.

When Dan starts "Closing Time," the entire crowd stands up.

A beach ball bounds down from the rearmost seats, punched up in the air by a crowd high on this summer night. Some of them think of this concert as "Matchbox 20 plus 'Closing Time,'" and they will savor the next four minutes, as will we. The sun has set, and the stage lighting now adds color to the stage, and though we have no light show (the Matchbox lighting crew throws in a few basic moves for us), the additional wattage heightens the drama for the crowd and the band. The crowd loves the Clearmountain pause. We rock through the last chorus and a loud rock-show ending, which we tacked on to the song's quiet coda so we can leave the stage on a bang. As Dan and John bear down on the final held note, strumming and thumping furiously, my arms fly around the drums, thrashing the cymbals. Over these fireworks, Dan points the neck of his guitar at the different sections of the crowd, ten thousand people by now, and then turns back toward John and me and slashes downward once—WHAM—and then four times—WHAM WHAM WHAM WHAM. The end.

The crowd erupts. We exit the stage, getting a nod from Chris as he hands us towels and bottles of water. I hand my sticks to Toby and point to the ten-year-old kid. "For him. Thanks." We were under our time limit. Through our in-ear monitors we can hear the applause sustain and then fade abruptly as the between-set house music kicks in, a reminder of our status as openers. Chris walks us out to the bus and unlocks the door. On the perimeter of the backstage area, fans press their faces against the Cyclone fencing, shouting at us from afar. On the first night of the tour, I made the mistake of walking over to someone yelling, "Hey, drummer from Semisonic! Oh, my God! Come here. Please!"

"Hi."

"Hi. Can you give this note to Rob from Matchbox 20?"

I didn't make that mistake again. Tonight, we step aboard the bus and sit down, observing a few minutes of restful silence. Then we change out of our show clothes.

8:20—Over the bus generator's whir, I can hear Soul Asylum

begin their set. I flip through the channels of the satellite television as Dan resumes his nightly search for his glasses. He pulls apart his bunk and the closets with all of their contents, rummaging through suitcases and handbags. I've told him many times, "I pick a place where each important thing goes, and I never put it anywhere else." Then, every night, I see him laying out his belongings on his bunk, thinking up a new system, which he is certain to forget by the time he wakes up.

I step off the bus and roam around backstage as Soul Asylum finishes. Dave Pirner sees me and flashes his evil grin as he walks to his dressing room. In our dressing room, Chris is packing up his computer. He's spent the day advancing shows for our next tour, which will begin in October and take us to rock clubs around the East and Midwest. The load-in times, soundcheck times, door times, equipment and stage specifications, our dressing-room buffet, hotel reservations for the bus driver—all of that and more has to be arranged for every show. It doesn't help that many club managers don't answer the phone or return messages. Chris's life is further complicated by special appearances that may be inserted into the schedule. In spite of his longing for simplicity and order, his mind is covered in mental Post-it notes, many of them placed there by Jim. "Book a hotel near the airport in case we have to fly out the next day." Chris has to remember which of Jim's multiple backup plans are still in play, which hotel reservations need to be canceled, which airport limousines need to be booked. He once was a guitar tech and traveled the world with the Eagles and Elton John. His days were shorter then.

In the catering area, which by now has been cleared of food by the catering staff, Dan is on his cell phone with Diane. They talk every night for half an hour. Later, Dan will report to us that Coco is doing well, but last night a thunderstorm knocked out the power to the house and she had to be taken to the hospital, where the medical apparatuses that she still relies on would have electrical power.

A huge roar from the crowd signals the beginning of the Matchbox 20 set. By the beginning of the second song, I watch from the side of the stage. The crowd loves it. I don't, but I understand the appeal. The singer, Rob Thomas, roams the stage, gripping a wireless mike, and the band's performance is driven by the conviction in his voice and onstage persona. He lifts the mike up, points out into the audience, and sings, and at certain moments, his words and gritty tone elicit screams. He pounds his heart with the fist of his free hand, producing still more screams. This is the culmination of Matchbox's tour, which began two years ago, in 1996. As one single then another broke through, they worked their way up through clubs and theaters. Now they're headlining sheds. As they play, I think about our next single, "Singing in My Sleep." That should be a hit, I tell myself, followed by "Secret Smile," or perhaps "Never You Mind." We've got plenty more songs where "Closing Time" came from, and there's little question in my mind that next summer, with a string of successful singles, we'll be headlining a shed tour of our own.

11:00 (sharp!)—Bus driver John returns from his daylong sleep at a nearby hotel. We have a long drive to Salt Lake City. Chris makes sure everyone is onboard and says to John, our driver, "We're a bus," which means, everyone's on, let's go. John may stop in the middle of the night to get fuel, and if you want to walk into the truck stop, perhaps to buy some milk to go with the Oreos you took from the dressing room, you must leave your laminated "Matchbox 20—All Access" artist's pass on John's seat, so that when he gets back on the bus, John will know he has to wait. Failing to leave a sign of your temporary absence puts you at risk of being "oil-spotted." That happened to our friends the Tropicals when they traveled on our bus and moseyed into a restaurant and ordered breakfast, not realizing that our driver had stopped only to make a phone call. An hour later, someone realized, "The Tropicals are missing!" Two taxis and a train ride later, they caught up to us.

In the back lounge, a few of us gather to watch a *Law and Order* episode. We're near the end of tape number five, in danger of exhausting our supply before the tour ends next week. We generally wait until the bus is on the interstate before popping in the tape. Afterward, the crew wants to watch a movie, something from the video library that came with the bus. There are eighty-five movies to choose from. I've seen the five good ones. The bulk of the selection consists of B-minus action flicks starring the likes of Steven Seagal. Occasionally, someone unearths a shoot-'em-up classic like *The Magnificent Seven*, or even a recent gem like *Unforgiven*. In that case, I stay up with the crew to watch. But if it's *Under Siege 2: Dark Territory*, I head for my bunk and draw the curtain.

3 A.M.—I get up to use the bathroom. As I step into the front lounge and close the bunk compartment door behind me, I can hear talk radio punctuated by CB chatter blasting in the driver's ear. Sometimes I've made the mistake of pulling back the curtain and sitting next to the driver, talking to him. That's a risk. Some drivers listen to a lot of crazy talk-radio shows and want to chat about what they've heard. "Jake, did you know that the IRS isn't even part of our government? They're a private organization!" Some drivers hate visits from the band, but most are all too eager for a conversation, and it might take me half an hour to work up the nerve to say, "Well, I better get back to bed."

Tonight, I sit on the couch, hidden from the driver's view by the curtain drawn behind him. Only trucks and buses roam the interstate at this hour. Out west, the roads are long and smooth—much better than the twisty and bumpy Northeast—and you can drift off to sleep on the couch. The Northeast—how long ago was that? We've been out three weeks. It feels like either three days or three months. As I walk back to my bunk, I can see light underneath the door to the back lounge. I open it. It's Matt, all by himself, playing the jumping rabbit video game.

Chapter XIII

UNPLUGGED

We walked off the stage at the end of our Matchbox 20 tour, waving to thousands of cheering fans at the Universal Amphitheater in Los Angeles. Jim met us in our dressing room and led us on a long walk through the backstage corridors. He held open a door and we walked into a room full of MCA employees, who greeted us with a burst of applause. Then three of them stepped forward with gold records, one for each member of the band.

My very own gold record—that was a thrill. The band photo and album-cover artwork were set into a frame behind a twelve-inch gold record and a small inscribed plaque:

> *Presented to Jacob Slichter*
> *To Commemorate RIAA Certified*
> *Sale of more than*
> *500,000 copies of the*
> *MCA Records*
> *Compact Disc and Cassette*
> *"Feeling Strangely Fine"*

The MCA folks, veterans of these celebrations, smiled upon us like parents watching their child unwrap a first bicycle. And as I posed for photographs with them, I felt a child's embarrassment, especially as I kept examining my new prized possession.

I quietly asked Jim about the sales figure. Had we really sold over half a million records? "No. That's how many we've shipped." That bothered me. Why not wait until we've actually sold the required amount, just to be sure? Jim waved that off. I asked one of the MCA old-timers about the gold record itself. Was it a golden vinyl copy of our album? No, he said. It was probably an old Frank Sinatra overstock spray-painted gold. I congratulated Hans, who as the album's A&R person would later receive a gold record of his own, and whispered my appreciation to Nancy Levin, whose intervention had rescued the record from the hesitation of her bosses. One of those bosses, a vaguely ominous man I referred to privately as Dr. Evil, stood nearby with his teenage son, and I toasted them, too. "Here's to multiplatinum." They smiled.

It was September, and the second single, "Singing in My Sleep," was now in the hands of radio programmers. Jim and Hans both believed it to be as strong a song as "Closing Time." If "Closing Time" had made us into stars, a second single could make us into megastars. I knew the progression. We had already moved up from clubs to small theaters. Soon we could be playing 20,000-seat arenas.

There was no guarantee. It was the fourth quarter, when the competition for playlist slots is fiercest. With a flood of new singles from major acts, the programmers would be unwilling to let anything but the most obvious hits into their rotations. As it had been with "Closing Time," early listener research on "Singing in My Sleep" reflected indifference.

Soon, we were told that Dr. Evil had begun to bad-mouth Semisonic as being "too old." That perspective, our sources told us, was largely drawn from his discussions with his teenage son, whose opinion always weighed heavily in Dr. Evil's decisions.

Little did we know that behind a teenager's bashful smile and cracking voice lurked a judgment that might bring our careers squealing to a halt. Perhaps this adolescent was unaware of how far his opinions reached into the world. "That kid might as well come to our marketing meetings," one person at MCA told me. Another person reported that Dr. Evil had brought his son in to hear a video pitch: "This is my son. If he likes the pitch, you've got the deal." Dr. Evil walked through the halls of MCA trashing Semisonic and advocating a different act, the New Radicals, whose song "You Get What You Give" was becoming a hit on alternative stations. According to Dr. Evil, the New Radicals—a band his son reportedly loved—represented the future for MCA.

Meanwhile, the response from influential program directors at alternative radio was that "Singing in My Sleep" and perhaps Semisonic's music in general was too soft for their format. Perhaps this, rather than Dr. Evil, was our ultimate obstacle. Pushing through this resistance, or perhaps pushing the song at other radio formats, would cost hundreds of thousands of dollars, and the executives atop MCA were ever mindful of trimming costs from the balance sheet. A few weeks into the single, MCA killed it.

MCA promised us a third single, though that would have to wait until after Christmas. For now, we would coast on the diminishing momentum of "Closing Time." That momentum earned us an invitation from Fox television to perform on the Billboard Awards, a nationally televised ceremony broadcast live from the MGM Grand in Las Vegas. Unlike the Grammys, the Billboard Awards are based not on votes but purely on sales and airplay. On that basis, we already knew that Semisonic would not win an award, but the producers asked us if we would fly out and end the show with "Closing Time," and we agreed.

So, on a Saturday morning, we boarded a plane for Vegas along with a hundred jolly Minnesotans with luck in their eyes. Those near me traded stories of friends who had won hundreds of dollars on previous trips. "Blackjack and craps," said one man. "You've got much better odds with those." His neighbor countered with stories of friends who had hit big on the slots. I hid my disdain behind the pages of J. M. Roberts's *History of Europe.*

Upon stepping off the plane, I heard the familiar sound of Las Vegas, the binging, bonging, ching-chang of slot machines—*Bing bong, ching chang, youloozayoulooza bong, riiiiiiiiing*—and, excited by those sounds, some of the arriving tourists made their first donations to the Las Vegas economy. *Bing bong loozaloozalooza.*

We checked into the Hard Rock Café and Hotel and walked around the first-floor casino to the elevators. A roomful of gamblers hiked up their pants, sipped rum and Cokes, tossed betting chips and smiles at the straight-faced blackjack dealers, and shoved silver dollars and prayers into the slot machines. The elevator doors closed on my smirk, and I rode up several floors to my room, conveniently forgetting the fact that the past sixteen years of my life represented an enormous and foolish gamble. I lay on my bed and read my book, killing time until our afternoon rehearsal. For each page read, I rewarded myself with twenty minutes of channel surfing.

The Monday-night show would be a vast production, so we had flown to town in time for the rehearsals, which began on Saturday. We arrived at the MGM Garden, the arena attached to the mammoth hotel complex, promptly at four o'clock. By then, rehearsal was running well behind schedule. We were the final act and the least known, so waiting was no surprise. As the crew fiddled with the TelePrompTer and various electrical connections, however, I knew that arriving on time, though unnecessary, lent us an aura of professionalism. So did our smiling forbearance in the face of continuing delays. *These guys have been dealing with a bunch of whiny rock-star prima donnas all day long.* After more than an hour of waiting, the crew invited us to the stage.

"Sorry about the wait, guys."

"No problem." *We're the nice band.*

From a technical standpoint, our bit was easy—easier than we would have preferred. To avoid the additional production requirements of another live performance, the producers had invited us to lip-sync to the prerecorded track. At Dan's request, Jim negotiated a live vocal mike so Dan could sing over the instrumental mix, aptly referred to as a "television" or "karaoke" mix. As for me, I had only to look the part, playing on deadened drums and stick-synching as I do in videos. After a half hour of Semisonic's cheery cooperation, the crew dismissed us. "Thanks, guys. You've been great. See you on Monday afternoon for the final run-through."

Saturday night in Vegas. It was too cold to walk the strip. Not liking to gamble or drink, I locked my door for three hours of reading and surfing the barren television landscape. Finally, Toby and Chris called me down to the casino. I followed them around, getting laughed at by the slot machines. *Bingabonga chinga changa looza looza.* Forty dollars later, I returned to my room.

I kept to my room for most of Sunday as well, imprisoned by a renewed hatred of gambling and a light dusting of snow. At five o'clock, as the December afternoon faded into darkness, we gathered in the lobby, dressed for our appearance as presenters on the pre–awards show televised on VH1. This was a precursor to the big Monday-night show, an opportunity to give winners of lower-profile awards some camera time. Kymm Britton and Leona Megerdichian, another MCA publicist, had flown in to escort us, along with Dennis Boerner, who handled MCA's video promotion.

We rolled up to the MGM in a stretch limo, and a series of attendants opened the limousine doors, the doors to the hotel, and still more doors. Finally, we entered a giant room jammed with reporters, photographers, and video crews. A whistling mob of spectators looked down from balconies at the stars making their way along a red carpet, lined with velvet ropes and security guards, which parted this sea of chaos. I realized I had underestimated the magnitude of the Billboard Awards and perhaps of Semisonic's profile.

We walked down the carpet as reporters leaned over and yelled questions at us like merchants at a loud bazaar. Kymm and Leona led us past most of these shouters and steered us toward a select few. Flashbulbs went off all around us in rapid fire, and if I managed to keep my jaw closed for most of the photographs, it was quite an accomplishment.

A television reporter lobbed an infotainment softball: "How does it feel to be here?"

And we swung our infotainment bats: "Great."

"What do you think of Las Vegas?"

"Incredible energy."

"Are you planning anything special for the show?"

"We're gonna blow the roof off."

"And finally—"

That was Kymm's cue to move us along. Depriving the interviewer of at least one answer reinforced the perception that Semisonic had heat. I trailed behind my bandmates, bedazzled by the noise and the lights, staring at the shouting mouths of reporters begging me for a response. Leona waved me forward. It took us five minutes to cover twenty yards of reporters and flashbulbs. It felt like half an hour.

We disappeared through some doors into a backstage area and exhaled. Were we really that famous? Did the event make us look more famous than we really were? Were the reporters inflating the importance of the entertainers in order to make the whole affair appear worthy of coverage?

In the hallway backstage, Everclear front man Art Alexakis was standing about with his bandmates. Two years earlier, he had told the crowd at the BCN River Rave, "I just saw this band called Semisonic on the side stage and they blew me away." We introduced ourselves. He gave his head a slight shake, as if he had never heard of Semisonic. Was he feigning ignorance to establish his superior rank, or merely spacey and forgetful? In the world of rock, either explanation seemed plausible.

Kymm introduced us to our Billboard Awards guide, a woman who knew when and where we would be needed and would help us navigate the sprawling layout of the back hallways of the MGM to get to those destinations. As it turned out, she had no knowledge of the MGM hotel layout and an acute fear of getting lost. As she led us, she stopped several times to look left and right down intersecting halls, blushed, and then took us backtracking as she hyperventilated. By the time she delivered us to our destination, we had no time to spare. An assistant for VH1 handed us a script to review and walked us through a small door, snatching the script from our hands as we stepped onto a small stage in front of lights and cameras. Having conquered the world of late-night television, standing confidently at the podium and reading from the scrolling TelePrompTer was well within our grasp.

"Hi, we're Semisonic and we're here to present the award for . . . And the 1998 Billboard Award winner for Adult Top Forty is . . . Natalie Em-BREW-lee-ah."

Thankfully, *Imbruglia* had been spelled out phonetically. The small crowd applauded. Natalie Imbruglia walked out, the picture of poise, and delivered her thank-you speech, an amazing display of memorization or perhaps extemporaneous speaking from this Australian soap-opera star turned pop star. Her fluid eye contact with every person in the room, I thought, set a standard Semisonic should try to equal. Members of the Australian Parliament, had they been watching, might have glimpsed in her a formidable rival of the future.

We disappeared backstage and someone pointed out the Sugarhill Gang, who twenty years earlier had launched the hip-hop explosion with "Rapper's Delight." I walked up to one of them. "Wow, I'll never forget the first time I heard 'Rapper's Delight.' I was at a party, and—"

"Where's the food?"

"Upstairs."

"Thanks."

On Monday afternoon, we rode to the MGM Grand for dress rehearsal, wearing new suits that our ever-reliable stylist, Shari, had picked out for this occasion. Mine was a gray sharkskin, for which Shari had chosen a black shirt. The rehearsal was already in progress. On stage, Bette Midler and Carole King rehearsed their award presentation to Celine Dion, who would accept via satellite from Canada. A technician flagged us down and said the rehearsal was behind schedule, and we camped out in a small area behind a curtain and waited. After a while, I heard Shania Twain singing the opening bars of "From This Moment On." I peeked out from behind the curtain—no Shania in sight, only a tape. We waited some more. A stand-in for Mariah Carey improvised a thank-you speech. More bits of taped music and yawning stretches of nothing. The technician found us and again apologized for the delay, and we reassured him that we were fine.

Over the course of the next two hours, he returned several times to report further delays, but we were unfazed. Finally, he came to tell us there was no time for us to rehearse. "I'm really sorry. You guys have been so patient, but I promise you, everything's going to go great tonight."

Here was a grand opportunity to complain, but instead we invested in goodwill, knowing that somewhere a jackpot of brownie points awaited us. "Hey, we understand." The technician smiled. With even-keeled professionalism, Semisonic, the little band at the end of the show, had won not only the respect but also the hearts of the production staff.

We followed Kymm and Leona out a side door to a gleaming

black limousine. The driver opened the door. We got in and stretched out, absorbing every last luxurious inch of legroom. The driver got in, started the engine, drove fifty feet forward, stopped, got out, and opened the passenger door to let us out. The seven-second ride had taken us from a side exit of the auditorium to the hotel's front entrance and another red carpet, the purpose of our short limo ride being to make an impressive entrance for the army of television crews, reporters, and photographers crowded about. A phalanx of security guards stood behind the press corps, holding off hundreds off screaming fans. Teen pop stars Hanson were midway down the carpet ahead of us, smiling, answering questions, and whenever someone screamed one of their names—"Taylor!"—waving to the crowd.

Kymm cued us and we began our slow stroll. We heard a few screams of "Dan!" and "Semisonic!" *Try not to look like some happy-faced goon.* Kymm guided us toward a television reporter.

"You've burst on the scene so quickly—are you nervous about performing on such a star-studded show?"

"We plan to get up there and rock."

A firing squad of photographers—the first row kneeling, the second row crouching, and the back row standing—waited at the end of the carpet.

"Hey, guys, look left."

"On your right!"

"Left, guys. Left!"

Dan, sensing the need for order, asked me to point at one set of cameras and then another so that we could all look at the same lenses at the same time. This produced twenty seconds of me pointing and Dan and John doubled over laughing. Then we noticed future Australian prime minister Imbruglia demonstrating the proper handling of this situation. Standing in front of the next group of photographers, she faced right and slowly turned her picture-perfect smile to the left across a fusillade of flashing bulbs. We tried mimicking this technique, but since we rotated our heads at different speeds, the photographers caught us staring in three different directions.

Reaching the end of the gauntlet, we walked through the doors and were delivered once again to our guide, who nervously led us to the makeup room. Courtney Love and Hole were on their way out as we walked in. The three Hanson brothers were taking turns ahead of us. Middle brother Taylor spotted Dan and introduced himself, saying that he owned both *Great Divide* and *Feeling Strangely Fine*. That was an exciting revelation, even though I knew none of Hanson's music. Zac, the youngest brother, bounced around in camouflage-pattern sneakers. "Nice shoes," I said.

"Yeah, they're great for paintball," he said, striking a gun-firing pose and blasting an imaginary opponent while vocalizing theater-quality gun sounds. I think he was thirteen.

We walked out of the makeup room just as Garth Brooks walked in. Our guide got lost again, and we made several passes down long hallways, walking repeatedly past various stars, some of whom I recognized—Jay-Z, K-Cee, and Jo Jo—and many others I didn't. It was amazing to think that of all the high-profile artists present, we were the ones closing the show.

Inside the auditorium, the ceremony was already under way. Garth Brooks was on stage performing. In the time it had taken our guide to find her way to the auditorium, he had sat for his makeup, walked to the back of the auditorium, climbed up to the catwalks, and, we were told, made his trademark flying entrance to the stage suspended by an invisible wire. We sat down three chairs over from Magic Johnson. Throughout the show, various performers stopped by to pay him tribute.

This was by far the most elite list of performers and personalities with whom we had ever shared a stage. Stevie Wonder, Mariah Carey, Lauryn Hill, James Taylor, Carole King, Bette

Midler, Shania Twain—the legends and new faces who paraded the stage were not only our fellow performers, they would compose the most impressive audience we had ever entertained. The idea that Stevie Wonder, whose records I had long memorized from start to finish, would hear us, and perhaps congratulate us after the show, was an exciting prospect. As Lauryn Hill and her band turned out a crushing live rendition of "Doo Wop That Thing," I wished Semisonic had been allowed to perform live instead of mimicking to a prerecorded track.

I had been vaguely aware of who the Backstreet Boys were, but when they took the stage and received the explosion of shrieks one normally associates with Michael Jackson, I realized I was out of it. Later, 'N Sync walked up to the podium to present an award, and again I was shocked by the hormonal torture expressed by the teenage girls in the audience.

Thirty minutes before our performance, we were summoned backstage. As we walked through the halls, we heard some female voices stirring together in a rich vibrato, accompanied by finger snaps. We turned the corner and came within two feet of Whitney Houston and her background singers, huddled in the hallway, warming up their voices and sweating up a storm. After our quick touch-up in the makeup room, our tour manager, Chris, relieved our flustered guide and walked us to the green room, a small tent behind the back of the stage. One person stood inside—Cher. Her facial-expression control unit was switched to the "off" position. Don't even think of saying hello to Cher when her face is turned off. A television monitor showed the action on stage: Courtney Love and Hole. We sat down, careful not to block Cher's view of the screen. I peeked to see if she had switched her face on. No, not until Drew Barrymore rushed in and gave her a big hug. I looked at my watch. The show was already past the ten-o'clock network cutoff time.

The nervous technical crew hustled us to the stage. The time overrun was a big problem. With seconds to go, the system was up and we were introduced. The cameras closed in as the music started, but the fact that I would only be mimicking my part allowed my mind to wander more freely than it had during previous television appearances.

Dan started to sing: "Closing time, open all the doors and let you out into the world . . ."

How's my hair? Hair—shit, I've got a brand-new bottle of Aveda shampoo in the hotel shower. Don't forget it.

"Closing time, one more call for alcohol so finish your whiskey or beer."

I'll pack up tonight. We've got an early-morning flight. I wonder if I got upgraded. Remember to call Northwest.

"You don't have to go home but you can't—stay—here."

Just make it look real.

I crashed on the downbeat of the chorus. On we rocked, or pretended to rock—Dan swinging his hips, John shaking his full head of hair, and me estimating the number of frequent-flier miles on a round-trip from Minneapolis to Vegas. We came to the end of the second chorus in full swing and launched into the dreamy bridge section. Suddenly, the bottom fell out. Dan stopped. So did John. The music had stopped. The sound had been cut halfway through our song! "What the fuck?"

The houselights came on. A voice thanked the crowd for coming and wished them a good night. Fifteen thousand people— Stevie Wonder, Whitney Houston, Lauryn Hill, James Taylor, Mariah Carey, the Backstreet Boys, Magic Johnson, Jay-Z, Carole King, Garth Brooks, Bette Midler, Cher, and 14,984 others— headed for the exits while we stood on stage with our guitars and drums, looking around, confused and severely humiliated.

I felt like throwing something. "Who cut the power?" I shouted. No one answered. "What the hell happened?" Silence. Jim showed up, and soon he learned that the technical crew had turned off the music as soon as the television broadcast had ended. At least television viewers had not seen us standing on stage like three confused idiots, but had the technical crew bothered to remember that we were still on stage in the middle of our song in front of 15,000 people? Of course not. Who cares about the quiet, cooperative band? We had been so accommodating all weekend, so naively easygoing about the whole thing, of course they forgot about us. "Welcome to Vegas, you fucking saps." *Binga bonga looza looza looza!*

After an hour of backstage sulking, we went to a large after-party held for the performers in the hotel bar. I didn't want to show my face, but Jay Boberg had flown out for the event and had invited us to dinner afterward; it would have been rude to decline. The music blared as I scanned the room for various stars. I spotted Jay-Z standing in a corner and puffing on a cigar. I walked over. "Hi, I'm in Semisonic. . . . I just wanted to say I really loved 'Hard Knock Life.' " He opened his mouth. Out came a cloud of smoke and a few inaudible words. I nodded. "Cool. Nice meeting you." At the end of the night, I walked through the casino at the Hard Rock Café and Hotel and stepped into the elevator as the loud-speakers blasted the New Radicals' "You Get What You Give," Dr. Evil's pet song. I patted my thigh in time with the music, the sound of MCA's slot machine denying us our follow-up single, "Singing in My Sleep."

In early 1999, MCA sent our third single, "Secret Smile," to radio. It was softer than the first two singles and therefore an unlikely choice for alternative radio. Jay Boberg had long identified "Secret Smile" as a potential single, and his strategy was to release it to all formats simultaneously. That would mean spending a fortune in promotion costs at alternative, top 40, and every format in between. It was an aggressive plan for a multifront war.

We shot a video in which Dan and the actress playing his girlfriend are at home, making a home video of each other, when a snooping camera crew barges into their living room and follows them as they flee out the door. Other camera crews (a local news team and crews working on various feature films) join the chase, which eventually drags in John and Jake. It was a $350,000 production, an elaborate affair using a number of cameras, a helicopter, a few dozen extras, and cameos by Paul Rudd, who had starred in *Clueless,* and Laura Prepon, star of *That '70s Show.* Filled with such promising elements, nevertheless the video was a disappointment. Dr. Evil was said to have proclaimed it a huge waste of money: "Stick a fork in this record. It's done."

Furthermore, though we agreed with the choice of "Secret Smile" as the third single, the fact that Jay had so visibly advocated it raised doubts about the song within MCA, owing to the poor reputation of Jay's ears. "It was Jay's choice for a single," one person was quoted as telling other members of the staff. Translation: "Don't bother. This song's going nowhere."

Negativity and doubt within MCA combined with the familiar difficulties at radio—"It's too soft for alternative, and pop won't add it until it hits on another format"—and soon after the single's launch, MCA shut it down. That was it. No more singles. The album would slowly lay itself to rest on the laurels of "Closing Time."

But what laurels! The song lingered in the public consciousness. As President Clinton's impeachment trial dragged on, the *New York Times* published an editorial urging its quick and graceful end. Perhaps you can guess the headline. At the end of February, we received the exciting news that "Closing Time" had earned a Grammy nomination for Best Rock Song. My dad's reaction—"Even *I* know what a Grammy is!"—summed up the mood among family and friends. Mimi summoned the three of us in for a pre-Grammy trim.

Though John and I were not up for the award (which goes to

the writer of the winning song), MCA bought plane tickets for all three of us so we could take advantage of the flurry of press and photo opportunities surrounding the ceremony. I stretched out among strangers in first class with a conversational ace up my sleeve: "So, what brings you to L.A.?"

The day before the awards, a limousine picked us up at the Sofitel and drove us to the Shrine Auditorium, which had become an encampment of broadcast trucks topped with satellite dishes and antennas. Our MCA publicists escorted us into the nearby press tent, jammed with journalists from around the world, and led us through the maze of tables, microphones, lights, cameras, and computers. They waved off interview requests from reporters for small papers and delivered us instead to prearranged interviews with magazines, television shows, and an online chat, where the three of us crowded around a computer screen flashing dozens of messages at once.

Sabbath RULES!

yer cute.

is creed gonna do a chat?

i love closing time!:)

shut up about creed!

There were few actual questions.

r u single?

George Clinton walked by with his rainbow of dreadlocks. We shook hands with B. B. King. Two young reporters from China's national radio, who had been roaming the tent like stowaways, sidled up to me with their tape recorder, held out a mike, and quietly asked, "What band you are in?" I recognized a rare opportunity, and before our publicists realized what was going on, I waved John over. As I had hoped, he shocked the two reporters by conversing with them in Mandarin. Finally, Christine and Kymm called an end to it, leaving the two journalists in stunned delight. Somewhere in China the next day, there must have been an hour-long feature on Semisonic.

We were not the only MCA artists Kymm and Christine had to look after. Back at the Sofitel, drunken members of another MCA act had smashed a marble coffee table in their room to tiny bits. The hotel announced it would add a several-thousand-dollar charge to the room bill for the table, at which point the gentlemen who had smashed it asked for the table's remains. "Now that we've paid for it, we want the pieces." This sent the hotel manager over the edge, and he ordered all MCA acts out of the hotel. Only intensive diplomatic intervention by the publicity department saved Semisonic's rooms.

As for our chances of winning a Grammy—Dan's chances—the competition was stiff. The other songs nominated in the same category formed an impressive list: "Bittersweet Symphony," "Celebrity Skin," "Have a Little Faith in Me," and "Uninvited." "Bittersweet Symphony" from the Verve's album *Urban Hymns* was originally credited to the band's singer/songwriter, Richard Ashcroft. Soon after the album's release, however, a lawsuit swirled up owing to the fact that the recording contained an unlicensed audio sample, lifted from a recording of an orchestral rendition of "The Last Time" by the Rolling Stones. As part of the settlement, the names of Mick Jagger and Keith Richards were added to the songwriting credits for "Bittersweet Symphony." Lawsuit aside, I loved the song, and who would bet against the Grammy going to Mick and Keith? Hole's song "Celebrity Skin," written by Billy Corgan, Eric Erlandson, and Courtney Love, was not the best song Corgan or Love ever wrote, but the accumulation of great songs that they had written deserved recognition. "Have a Little Faith in Me" by John Hiatt

had been released years earlier, and I assumed it had been nominated because it had resurfaced in some other form. It was my favorite John Hiatt song, and who wouldn't be happy to see an
underrecognized hero like Hiatt raise up a Grammy statue? As
for "Uninvited" by Alanis Morissette, I had never heard it—a
good sign. I mulled this list over as we toasted twenty of our
music-business friends at an impromptu "Thank-You Dinner"
the night before the awards. I rolled the dice in my mind, and
they kept coming up "Closing Time."

I rolled those dice during the limousine ride to the ceremonies
the following afternoon. *"Closing Time." Yes!* In my mind, I envisioned little stickers on our shrink-wrapped CDs: "Includes the
Grammy-winning hit 'Closing Time.' " All traffic within several
blocks of the Shrine Auditorium was virtually stopped. Onlookers
lined the sidewalks. A fifty-year-old unshaven man with an eight-
foot wooden cross and a sandwich board sign threatening God's
wrath wagged his finger with exaggerated disapproval at the long
train of limousines crawling by. We pulled around the corner,
stepped out in our glitzy Grammy threads (I wore the same gray
sharkskin suit and black shirt), and walked down the red carpet
with veteran self-assurance.

"Look left, guys."

"I need you to look right."

No problem. *You yell, we pose.* The cameras flashed. Ten steps
later, a network morning show reporter pleaded with us to sing a
few bars of "Closing Time." We wisely declined. John Lydon, the
former Johnny Rotten of the Sex Pistols, interviewed us for VH1.

"Who are ya?"

"Semisonic."

"Never heard of you. What are you nominated for?"

"Best Music." *Asshole.*

Inside, the afternoon ceremonies were under way, the untele-
vised segment of the show when lower-profile awards were
handed out. The pace of proceedings was much faster and more

businesslike than the dramatic prime-time segment would be. A rotating supply of nominees streamed into the room and took the seats vacated by those who had already won or lost, and the casual atmosphere suggested a PTA meeting. Those accepting the awards for Best Polka Album, Best Spoken Word Album for Children, and Best Recording Package—Boxed were mercifully concise. A tag team of emcees kept things moving along. We found some seats, and the Barenaked Ladies, for whom we had opened in Cleveland, said hello as they made their way to some newly vacated seats three rows behind us.

Former *Entertainment Tonight* host John Tesh stepped up to the podium, relieving the previous emcee. "Okay, where are we? Best Pop Collaboration with Vocals. The nominees are 'How Come, How Long,' Babyface with Stevie Wonder; 'Kisses Sweeter Than Wine,' Jackson Browne and Bonnie Raitt; 'I Still Have That Other Girl,' Elvis Costello and Burt Bacharach; and 'I'm Your Angel,' R. Kelly and Celine Dion. And the Grammy goes to . . ."

I rolled the dice. *Elvis Costello and Burt Bacharach.*

" 'I Still Have That Other Girl,' Elvis Costello and Burt Bacharach."

A quick thank-you from the winners and Tesh moved on to Best Male Pop Vocal Performance. "And the nominees are . . ." The names were read, and I rolled my dice again. *Eric Clapton.*

"And the winner is . . . Eric Clapton."

Before long, I had a streak of seven correct predictions. I turned to Dan. "Do you have a thank-you speech written?"

"No. Shit. Do you have a pen?"

Christ! "Pssst. Jim. Dan needs a pen."

"The nominees for Best Pop Performance by a Duo or Group with Vocal are 'I Don't Want to Miss a Thing,' Aerosmith; 'One Week,' Barenaked Ladies; 'Iris,' Goo Goo Dolls; 'Crush,' Dave Matthews Band; and 'Jump Jive an' Wail,' Brian Setzer Orchestra. And the Grammy goes to . . ."

Brian Setzer.

"Brian Setzer."

"FOR CRYING OUT LOUD!!!" The Barenaked Ladies shocked everyone by raising their voices in mock protest. "Brian Setzer isn't even here!" one of them shouted as Tesh scanned the crowd for the absent winner. Several members of the audience turned around and scowled at what they assumed to be an ungracious breach of decorum, much to the back-row snickering satisfaction of the Barenaked Ladies.

Jim leaned over. "If 'Closing Time' wins, all of you guys should go up together."

Dan tugged my sleeve. "Who do we thank if we win?"

"Well, Jim and Hans, the guys in the crew, Diane and Coco—"

"The nominees for Best Rock Song are 'Bitter Sweet Symphony,' Richard Ashcroft, Mick Jagger, and Keith Richards.' "

Nope.

" 'Celebrity Skin,' Billy Corgan, Eric Erlandson, and Courtney Love."

Nope.

" 'Have a Little Faith in Me,' John Hiatt."

Mmmm. No.

" 'Closing Time,' Dan Wilson."

OK, can I get a "yes" on "Closing Time"? Yes?

"And 'Uninvited,' Alanis Morissette."

Oh shit!

"And the Grammy goes to . . ."

Please, don't let it be—

"Alanis Morissette."

The audience applauded Alanis as she walked to the stage. I was too stunned to hear what she was saying. *Alanis Morissette.* I scrunched my cheeks into a smile and patted Dan on the shoulder. He was disappointed but also relieved to be crumpling up his hastily written thank-you speech, which certainly would have omitted some crucial name. We watched two more presentations, and then Jim suggested we head for the bar in the lobby. As we got up, the Barenaked Ladies called out, "Sorry, Dan. You shouldn't have sat up here in the LOSER section."

Waiting in line for drinks, we said hello to Bob Clearmountain and his wife, Betty. John stared as Beach Boy Brian Wilson ate a hot dog. I continued to replay the moment of losing. *Alanis fucking Morissette. I've never even heard that song.*

An hour later, the television cameras were in position as we took our seats twenty rows back from the seats reserved for the nominees in the major categories. One by one, those big-name artists made their entrances, none with more flair than Lauryn Hill, who strode in wearing a dazzling white dress. The lights went down. I stretched my legs out into the aisle, nearly tripping Jerry Seinfeld as a production assistant hurried him along.

I had not watched the Grammys since the eighth grade, when I had been outraged that "Love Will Keep Us Together" by the Captain and Tennille won Best Song. Sitting in the auditorium, watching a slew of great performances from a lineup of musical and cultural giants—Madonna, Aerosmith, Lauryn Hill, Sheryl Crow, Alanis Morissette, Ricky Martin, John Williams conducting the theme from *Star Wars*, a tribute to Duke Ellington featuring Wynton Marsalis, Clark Terry, and Natalie Cole, a duet between Eric Clapton and B. B. King—was a priceless musical education. Every idea was clear, every gesture simple and bold. No wonder Vince Gill was such a big deal. Celine Dion, whose massive success had always puzzled me, performed a duet with Andrea Bocelli, and the purity of their tone forced me to close my eyes and reluctantly concede my respect. By the end of the ceremony, my existing standards of greatness had been thoroughly eclipsed. If we wanted to be stars, we had to measure up to the grandeur we had just witnessed. I longed to come back to the Grammys the next year, throw down a showstopping performance of our own, sneak a laugh line into our acceptance speech, and walk out with a trophy.

Not tonight. We filed out of the auditorium with the crowd and into the parking lot, where thousands of people searched for their limousines. Soon, the freeways were packed with chauffeured rock stars, producers, record company presidents, and the winner of Best Engineered Album—Classical, all on their way to various Grammy parties. The biggest of these were those thrown by the five major music empires.

A year earlier, there had been six big parties, but Seagram, the parent company of the Universal Music Group, had just acquired Polygram and merged these two majors into one giant supermajor. Thus, A&M Records, Mercury Records, Motown, and Island Records were folded into the corporate structure that already included MCA, Geffen, and Interscope. In the ensuing consolidation, entire labels were shut down, thousands of record company employees were fired, and hundreds of bands were dropped from their contracts or shuffled around the newly merged conglomerate in a state of contractual limbo, the very fate we had avoided after the regime change at Elektra. Girls Against Boys, who three years earlier had been so hotly pursued by several labels, could not get their phone calls returned. Had it not been for "Closing Time," Semisonic would have been dropped.

In light of the thousands of layoffs, the Universal Music Group chiefs decided that a smaller Grammy party would be in better taste. Invitations to Universal's party were therefore restricted to corporate chiefs, artists, and their managers. Those lower-ranking employees who still had their jobs were left off the list, deprived of champagne and cake so that their corporate bosses might look less rapacious. Thus, when we walked into the party, we walked into the exclusive company of a hundred record-company moguls and rock stars. Jay Boberg walked up, and soon we were posing for a photograph with him and ten strangers. I shook hands with those I assumed were bishops and rooks on the music-industry chessboard. The body language told me that as a president of one of the several labels in the Universal Music Group, Jay was a mere pawn. I liked him for that. A photographer lined us up and snapped some shots. Afterward, Jim grabbed my shoulder. "So are you psyched that you just had your picture taken with Smokey Robinson?"

"Smokey Robinson! Where?"

"He was standing at the other end of the shot."

"Where did he go?"

"Right over there somewhere."

I made a slow lap around the room before bumping into Dan, who was sipping Champagne with a smile. "Did you see Bono?"

"Where?"

"I just spoke with him over there. He was talking with Jimmy Iovine."

John walked up. "Jake, did you check out Sting?" I made another slow lap around the room in a vain search for these stars. I met up with Dan, who now was savoring the three-minute chat he had just had with Elvis Costello and Beck, both of whom had also vanished. Jim brought us over to a table where Sheryl Crow and her band were sitting. *Shake hands and don't stare.* We were about to embark on a month-long tour with them. After quick introductions and congratulations on her Grammy, we dispersed. This time I managed to have a twenty-minute conversation with Lionel Richie, who graciously endured my recollections of how my high school funk band had performed "Fancy Dancer" and other songs by his former group, the Commodores.

Finally, Jim gathered us. "Everyone's left. Let's go to the Warner party and meet Madonna." By the time we arrived, however, the Warner party was also near an end. Someone pointed out the Goo Goo Dolls, one of whom swayed about drunkenly, wearing a shirt that announced that he had been nominated for several Grammys: "... And all I got was this lousy t-shirt!" Madonna was nowhere to be seen. I assumed she and all the other stars I had missed had driven off to ultra-exclusive private gatherings around swimming pools in the hills. We flew back the following day, and at my next haircut, Mimi was dying to know what it was like to meet Bono, Sting, Elvis Costello, Beck, and all the others.

Over the next month, we saw a lot of one of those stars, Sheryl Crow. We were her opening act for a month-long cross-country tour of theaters and arenas. I maintained a low-key front in her presence—"Hey" in the hallways backstage, and "How's it going?" in the catering line. After a couple of weeks, she invited us to join her on stage during her encores for renditions of "Drift Away" by Dobie Gray and "What Is Life" by George Harrison. It wasn't long before I was eating a slice of apple pie three chairs over from her in the catering room, scratching the ears of her dog, Scout, and receiving "Hey, Jake"s in the hallway. I got to the backstage Ping-Pong table too late to play against rising movie star Owen Wilson, whom Sheryl was dating at the time. And, of course, I retreated somewhat when the Artist Formerly Known As Prince showed up for a couple of shows on the East Coast, watching from the wings, then disappearing into the backstage halls. We wondered if he might take the stage during one of Sheryl's encores. (He didn't.) Perhaps the exciting thought of his presence played a part in my decision to throw my sticks into the audience as we walked from the stage at the Beacon Theater in New York. The sticks soared ten rows and hit an unsuspecting woman in the face, hastening my exit.

Backstage, I spotted the artist soon to be known again as Prince, walked up, and held out my hand. "We're huge fans of yours. In fact, we play a couple of your songs." He nodded and said something inaudible. "Well . . . cool, then. . . . Thanks." One doesn't ask Prince to speak up.

Jim and Hans invited us to a bar next door, where we were joined by a couple of MCA employees for the quiet presentation of our platinum records. Our sales had steadily declined since our gold-record party, which had celebrated a bright future. Six months later, our platinum records felt like grave markers of hopes long buried. The photographer snapped away. I stared at the lens and leaned over to Jim: "So I suppose this is another situation where we shipped a million but haven't sold a million."

"Yeah."

"That bugs me."

"Don't worry about it."

The camera flashed, and we smiled with the strained humanity of a runner-up to Miss America. Then John stepped over to the bar to have a beer with a friend, and Dan huddled with an English journalist for an interview. I set down my plaque, unable to silence the complaints that had been planted in my mind over the past six months.

"You guys got fucked on 'Singing in My Sleep.'"

"A song like 'Closing Time' should have sold two million albums, easy."

"Why didn't MCA release 'Never You Mind'?"

The shine of my platinum record was dulled by months of multiplatinum expectations. I thought back to the Grammy Awards, where the triumph of our red-carpet entrance was thoroughly eclipsed by the giants—Aerosmith, Madonna, and Sheryl Crow—who rocked the Grammy stage and walked off with statues in their hands, while I stared from my seat and asked myself, "When will we be that big?"

I looked over at Hans. He shrugged his shoulders. Jim patted me on the back. "Congratulations." I flipped through the channels on my emotional dial, but none of them felt right.

Chapter XIV

MISTER PHELPS

An hour after landing in Manchester, England, on an October morning, I stumbled through the city streets, doing my best to stay awake until local bedtime. In my groggy state, I was even more susceptible to the spell cast by foreign coins, menus, newsstands, traffic, and voices. Naturally, we had long believed that we would be an excellent match with foreign audiences, especially those in cities with fine dining and great museums. Now we were getting our chance. Universal had fired the executive who, two years earlier in Dublin, told us he would prevent his subordinates from releasing *Great Divide* in foreign territories. With the American success of *Feeling Strangely Fine*, MCA's president, Jay Boberg, insisted that the new international executives give proper attention to Semisonic, and in the fall of 1998 they agreed to explore our overseas potential by funding a quick tour through select cities in the United Kingdom and Europe.

Dana Collins, the MCA liaison to Universal International, accompanied us on this trip. He was a fan of the band and, with his boss, Eamon Sherlock, had long advocated on our behalf in the world of MCA and Universal. The day after our arrival in Manchester, he gave us an overview of what to expect of our tour through seven countries. The UK, he said, was the biggest prize but also the toughest to win. British taste was notoriously finicky, and in recent years had been disapproving of many successful American bands. (The converse was also true: the English band Oasis, who filled stadiums in their homeland, had a theater-sized profile and a modest radio presence in the US. Other British bands, such as Blur and Teenage Fanclub, were popular at home but largely unknown to the average American radio listener.)

Behind my polite smile, I confidently dismissed Dana's warnings about the UK. But that night, as we walked off the stage after our first performance in England to a mere trickle of applause from the seventeen people who came to see us, I accepted the reality he had warned about. We were starting off at the bottom. By the time we zoomed through the foggy off-kilter streets of London two days later, the UK felt thoroughly beyond our reach. When we walked into the BBC for a radio interview, one of the people in charge sneered at me and commented on my apparel. "If you want to be a rock star, don't wear a Viper Room T-shirt." (I'd received a free shirt after playing the Viper Room in L.A. two years earlier.)

Actually, I've always wanted to be a condescending asshole who works at radio. May I have your shirt? "Thanks," I murmured, still unsure about my dressing habits.

Here was the skepticism of which we had been warned. The BBC studio was thick with it. Our interviewer hid behind formality and withheld anything resembling warmth. "Closing Time," which had just surfaced on UK radio, seemed to impress no one present. As we walked out afterward, I wondered if our success in the States might have fostered more resistance than we otherwise would have faced. We hopped into the van, and I asked if we could swing by the hotel. Dan and John asked why, and when I told them I wanted to change shirts, they railed, "Don't let that asshole make you change shirts!" Would I spend the rest of the day as a wannabe in a Viper Room shirt or a clothes-changing coward? As we walked out of our next interview, Ruth Flower, who worked for Universal International and oversaw our visits to all foreign lands, handed me one of my other shirts, which she had mercifully arranged to have sent over from the hotel. We then drove off to MTV's London studios, where we endured an interview with another Semisonic skeptic.

That night, we played for a packed house at the Hundred Club, a small club on Oxford Street that, we were told, was a popular venue in the days of English punk. Though many in the crowd were Americans (slightly disappointing for a band that wanted to win new fans), a good portion were Brits, and we played well. Marilyn Manson, another of Universal International's artists, stopped by to hear a few songs. Afterward, Dan found himself dining with Manson as Ruth's guest at a local restaurant (yet another star encounter that I managed to miss). Music played over the loudspeakers, and as midnight approached, Manson leaned over to Dan and dryly observed, "If we stay here long enough, maybe they'll play your song." We spent the following day in our hotel, where we conducted interviews with journalists from Switzerland, Portugal, and other countries we would not be visiting. Then we left for the airport, but not before Ruth handed me a fresh bottle of Aveda Blue Malva shampoo, which she had kindly arranged to have delivered to the hotel after overhearing me complain that I had left mine behind in Minneapolis.

Over the next ten days, we traveled to Gothenburg, Munich, Cologne, Amsterdam, Paris, Madrid, and Milan. We returned a month later and hit most of those cities, as well as Barcelona, Hamburg, Stuttgart, and Stockholm. In each city, a different set of Universal representatives served as our hosts.

"Try the Torsk. Very good. Very Swedish."

"I got you lads some tickets to the Tate Modern. I'll send a car around at half ten."

"No. In Cologne, one never asks for Alt. Here we drink Kolsch."

"The models? They're here for Milan fashion week."

This was not the do-it-yourself indie-rock tour of Europe with sleeping bags, trail mix, and a VW minibus. It was a business-class excursion bankrolled by a multinational media giant (and then charged to Semisonic's ever-more-hopeless recoupable debt). In between our morning pastries and our nighttime rock shows, we conducted interviews, performed on the radio, and took in the local sights, when possible. "No, you do not have time for the Rijksmuseum. I myself do not have such time!" Our Amsterdam rep was not a big art fan. Dana straightened him out.

The charms of each city and the attentiveness of the Universal staff induced in us the rock-band version of traveler's myopia: The country we most wanted to become stars in was whatever country we happened to be in. I inquired into the price of apartment rentals in several cities, fantasizing about foreign living and a future as a polyglot.

In Germany, our hosts packed the days with interviews, photo shoots, video appearances, and on-air radio performances. Every five-minute segment of the day was accounted for, even the drive times between appointments, which were based on insane German highway speeds. I sat in the front seat of a minivan as the lane markers flew under us in a 110-mile-per-hour blur. Station wagons would weave over from the "slow" lane and our driver would sigh as he slammed on the brakes, sparing the lives of small children, then accelerated back up to speed, swerving to pass a freight truck on the right. As we leaned into wide sweeping turns, blood flow succumbed to the laws of Newtonian physics, the world distorted into a fish-eye lens, and nausea appeared in the rearview mirror gaining fast. When we pulled into the parking lot for our next interview, I remained in the van for a minute of reverent silence as I regained my equilibrium, took in the trees, grass, and flowers, and reflected upon the miracle of life and all I had ever taken for granted. At least our many speedy trips down the autobahn from interview to interview pointed to the German media's interest in the band.

In France, by contrast, a more liberal attitude toward time management prevailed. Our host from the label greeted us at the airport, checked us into our hotel, seated us at the hotel restaurant, ordered our lunch, offered us cigarettes, poured us wine, told us stories, ordered more food, poured more wine, laughed at our jokes, ordered dessert, smoked more cigarettes, ordered coffee, refilled our wineglasses, and then looked at her watch.

"Well . . . now we are very late. We should probably order a final espresso and then get going."

Then she lit another cigarette and leaned back. We did three interviews that afternoon and had the rest of the afternoon and the entire next day to explore the city.

As we waited in line for tickets at the Louvre the following morning, a day reserved entirely for sightseeing, an American kid ran up to me and blurted out, "Are you the drummer for Everclear?"

"No, I'm the drummer for Semisonic."

"Shit, I meant Semisonic. Anyway, can I have your autograph?" I signed the back of his Louvre brochure. He held up a camera— "And could we get a picture with you?"—and I smiled as he and his friends took turns posing next to me, attracting curious looks from others in line. I savored the idea of being spotted in the Louvre, paying no mind to the fact that this ego-nourishing fan encounter and our entire day of tourism were made possible by the French media's indifference toward Semisonic.

Spain had thrown off the tyranny of the clock entirely. We showed up for a television appearance—"She's kind of the Spanish David Letterman"—and waited on stage for the audience to show up. They dribbled in, and then we waited for the makeup artist, who eventually showed up and smeared our faces in front of the watching crowd. The taping did not begin until the host arrived twenty minutes later.

As for the interviews, the journalists hit us with questions we had never heard in the States. "I find the scansion of your lyrics to be beautiful," declared one English journalist. The most intense questions, however, came from the German interviewers.

"Can hope overcome despair in the real world, as it does on your records?"

"In what ways can music change the world?"

"Why are you so afraid to write a political song?"

Beneath these questions lay a philosophical heft that was both inspiring and intimidating. For the most part, John and I yielded these new topics of conversation to Dan, who enjoyed the chance to romp across unfamiliar terrain.

A few of the European journalists spoke flawless English. Others spoke no English, requiring our label hosts to function as interpreters. The majority spoke functional English—one or two verb tenses and confused syntax. "But I think you are writing some pop songs always. But for your next album, too?"

We answered, "But this is exactly what is not on our minds. We are not thinking to make our next record yet." Immersion is a powerful teacher.

We narrowly averted calamity on the Christian Luuk show. ("He's the Swedish David Letterman.") Luuk interviewed us on camera before we played. "So tell us about Minnesota. Many Swedes live there, I think."

Dan nodded. "Yes, many Swedes live there, and during the winter, Minnesota is much like Sweden—a vast, ice-covered, god-forsaken land."

Luuk tilted his head. "Well, I don't think Sweden is godforsaken." The audience stared at us in Swedish silence. Fortunately, a video error forced a retake, and this time Dan steered well clear of God, Sweden, and the weather. The misunderstanding was all the more startling because our Minnesotan manner seemed to have sweetened our various Swedish encounters. Every time I smiled and said, "Hey," the Swedes would smile back. "Hej."

Country after country, the hosts spoke of their excitement about the band, and their affection felt genuine. The variety of music we heard on the radio suggested that Europe was a less regimented musical world where Semisonic would not be penalized for being "too soft for alternative and too loud for pop," as was the case in the US. With the exceptions of France and the ever-skeptical UK, these new countries felt like fertile ground. The people who came to our shows hung around afterward, eager to know more about us, sometimes surprising us with their knowledge of the band's history. The plan was for us to come back in early 1999 to build on the growing momentum.

"Closing Time," however, made only small inroads in these new countries. It had modest success in Germany. In the UK it fell flat. Though this had been expected, it was also a problem. The UK is considered a "leader" territory. The press and radio in other countries look to the UK (and, to a lesser extent, Germany) to gauge the potential success of new releases in their own land. The label offices in "follower" countries will push harder to promote those acts that have proven to be winners in the UK and will avoid the losers. In our case, the top-level Universal executives did not share the enthusiasm of Ruth and her colleagues around Europe. Plans for a return trip were scrapped, and our album languished as a low priority.

We made several trips to Canada, where our record had gone gold. (The recording industry in each country sets a different sales standard for gold and platinum to account for differences in population. In Canada, a gold record certifies sales of 50,000, one-tenth the US standard.) In addition to club shows in Toronto, Vancouver, and Montreal, we added two horrendous outdoor experiences. The first was a poorly organized outdoor festival in Kenora, Ontario. Before arriving, we heard that advance ticket sales had been slow and pouring rains had cut ticket sales further. Then we learned that some of the artists had not been paid and that other artists who had heard this news had canceled their appearances. We arrived at the rain-soaked festival grounds and saw electrical cables strung through huge puddles of water—not a good sign. Fans yelled at the festival staff, demanding that the music start. We waited in the catering tent, and the catering staff quietly suggested we leave the grounds before a riot erupted. Minutes later, the security staff walked off the job—having not been paid themselves—and upon hearing that, we, too, departed, despite the pleas of the promoter, who promised everything would be all right if just one band, perhaps Semisonic, would play.

Our second outdoor show in Canada was a snowboarding festival in the Canadian Rockies for Much Music, a Canadian music video channel. We played on a stage set into the side of a snow-covered mountain at an elevation of 6,000 feet. The temperature on stage was twelve degrees Fahrenheit. Dan and John tried playing with gloves with the fingertips cut off, but these were too cumbersome. The TV crew then brought in powerful heaters and mounted them at the lip of the stage, providing Dan and John with a two-foot-deep zone in which their fingers would neither singe nor freeze to the metal strings of their guitars. The thick mittens with which I held my frozen drumsticks and the constricting snowboarding suit that covered the rest of my body dictated a vastly simplified approach to drumming. So did oxygen deprivation and hypoglycemia.

The Universal offices in Australia and New Zealand called us down for a weeklong tour. In Sydney, we rocked on stage with Rob Hurst, the drummer for Midnight Oil, who sat in for one of our encores while I played keyboards. In Auckland we played with Neil Finn, of Split Enz and Crowded House fame. I returned to the States with the familiar sensation of having impressed the local staffs and new national audiences. Then, as always, I learned that the response of the broader public was muted. As Jim put it, "Semisonic is not a reactive band." Indeed, for us the countries of the globe seemed to compose a box of wet matches.

After the Universal/Polygram merger in early 1999, yet another regime came to power in the London office. Jay Boberg continued to press the case for Semisonic with the international company. Executives in the newly merged London office—Marc Marot among others—believed that our album had been inadequately promoted in the UK and were determined to give it another chance. At the same time, the program director of Capital Radio, a dominant chain of stations in the UK, became interested in the band. His name was Richard Park. The word was that his wife had turned him on to Semisonic and that he was a fan of the band, and especially of "Secret Smile," which MCA had recently pulled from radio in the US. The new leadership at Universal encouraged his interest by flying him to see our opening set for Sheryl Crow at the Beacon Theater in New York. He loved the show and returned to England, determined to make "Secret Smile" and Semisonic a hit in the UK.

Jim, Hans, and Dana passed this promising news along, though I was now accustomed to dismissing good news from abroad. Nevertheless, we soon heard that "Secret Smile" was indeed a radio hit in the UK, and that Universal wanted to fly us back for more promotion.

As our July trip approached, Jim called to say that our popularity was such that the label suggested we come up with aliases for our hotel rooms. I called Hans. "So Hans, like, how big are we in the UK right now?"

"If you guys were any bigger, you'd be the Beatles."

"Are we as big as the Spice Girls?"

"No."

"Oasis?"

"No."

"Blur?"

"No."

"So, honestly, how big are we?"

Members of the newly merged Universal staff greeted us at Gatwick as we walked out of the customs area. One of them was a well-dressed man named Graham, whose air of distinguished cool set him apart from any record executive we had ever met. He generously invited us to ride back to the hotel with him in his $200,000 Mercedes. To receive such treatment from an executive of obvious high rank boded well for us. He turned on the radio, and soon—as Graham had predicted—"Secret Smile" came thumping over the speakers, and we sank confidently into the leather seats. After dropping us at the hotel, he said he'd return to take us to rehearsal. I asked one of the other Universal people what Graham's position was and learned that, alas, Graham was not a senior executive with a special love for Semisonic. He owned a luxury-car service.

Our rooms at the Royal Garden Hotel were booked under the aliases we had supplied to the label. I had considered using the name of some English rock star—Liam Gallagher, Sting—just for laughs, but I realized that if some rabid Oasis fan actually called for Liam and came to believe he was staying at the hotel, responsibility for the ensuing pandemonium would fall squarely on me. So I chose a different name, Jim Phelps, the name of the main character on *Mission Impossible*. All messages and deliveries, and even the tag on my suitcase, bore his name. Every day began with a wake-up call—"Good morning, Mister Phelps"—and I smiled, enjoying my spacious room, the view overlooking Hyde Park, and the fact that I was using an alias, even as I wondered if it was really necessary.

In the mornings, we walked out of the hotel to find Graham standing next to his Mercedes, each day in a different smashing suit. This was a man with a lot of closet space. From our hotel, we set out on our various appointments, all of which were designed to promote the upcoming release of "Secret Smile" as a commercial single.

In the States, MCA had not released a CD single of "Closing Time" for record buyers. That would have undercut album sales. (The absence of a commercial US single was quickly exploited by a guy in New Jersey who recorded a copycat version of "Closing Time" under the name Sokaotic—a word conveniently similar to our band name—and managed to sell tens of thousands of copies before MCA could track him down.) In the UK, however, all radio singles are made available for purchase. The UK singles chart is watched by everyone from radio programmers and record executives to fans who want their band to do well. The chart is so decisive in the fate of a song, album, and career that in addition to the weekly chart, which is published on Sunday, there is actually a midweek chart published on Wednesday, over which record companies and managers obsess. As always, the opening week would be crucial, and "Secret Smile" was a few days away from its debut.

So we rode in the climate-controlled stereophonic leather luxury of Graham's Mercedes to MTV's studios in Camden Town (where the interviewers were friendlier than in the fall), then Oxford Circus for *The Pepsi Chart* show, then interviews with print journalists, and then more videotaped interviews, all arranged by Ruth. Along the way, Graham played tapes of soon-to-be-released albums by our favorite British bands; it was unclear how he had come to possess them. In fact, there was something generally clandestine about Graham's methods— something that made us feel all the more important. If one of us mentioned a hankering for Thai food, we soon found ourselves entering the side door of a gourmet Thai restaurant. "Graham's friends? Your table is over here." While riding to our various appointments, we asked Graham questions and received his answers concerning the history behind various London landmarks— Trafalgar Square, the Royal Albert Hall. He pointed at some statues of lions: "We nicked those from the Egyptians."

He drove us past the autograph seekers at the gates of BBC Television to tape a performance of "Secret Smile" for *Top of the Pops*, a legendary British show in the vein of *American Bandstand*. Whether or not our taped performance would actually air would depend on how well "Secret Smile" placed on the singles charts. Inside the eerily empty BBC complex—long, dark hallways of locked doors—we walked through the studio doors and waited our turn to lip-synch our song, the standard routine for *Top of the Pops*. (Television producers love lip-synching because playing a tape is vastly simpler than recording a live performance.) The fact that we sat in the studio and watched Blur and Jennifer Lopez do their own lip-synching made this prospect easier to stomach. A roomful of teenagers stood in front of the stage and jumped, clapped, yelled, and did whatever the man in the headsets shouted at them to do. Between acts, they were quieted and then suddenly revved back into a teenage frenzy for the next performance, sometimes being hushed briefly for last-second technical adjustments before being unleashed again for the cameras. From what I saw, they were having a blast, and that eased my guilt as we delivered our own faked performance. At the end of the song, their applause overtook the fading track and we stood still for the camera. After the taping, we were escorted out to the fans at the front gate to sign autographs. "Jake, can we please get a picture with you?"

They even know my name. Click.

We made more radio visits, punctuated by Graham's stealthily arranged detours to fine clothiers, where the mere mention of Graham's name prompted the tailors to bring out their very best suits for us to try on. More press interviews, more fine dining and tourist activities arranged and paid for by Ruth and Dana, more television shows—CD:UK, TFI—and more lessons in English culture.

"Graham, what does T-F-I stand for?"

"The first three words in 'Thank Fuck It's Friday.' "

Outside the TFI studio, a hundred people lined the street waiting for tickets, and a few shouts followed us as security guards escorted us into the building. Inside, we walked past dressing rooms for the Manic Street Preachers, Alice Cooper, and Lenny Kravitz. After camera rehearsal, we followed the various performers and the technical crew outside, lining up with everyone else to have our picture taken with the biggest star on the show, Kermit the Frog.

Throughout the week, we waited to see how "Secret Smile" would fare in the singles charts. We were hoping to place in the top ten and came in at thirteen. (The consensus was that our true chart position was actually higher. A reporting glitch had omitted the counts of several stores where "Secret Smile" had sold especially well.) Jim, Dana, and Ruth insisted this was good news, though I couldn't help privately wondering if in fact thirteen was a disappointment. From the bed in my hotel room, I watched the television broadcast of England's biggest rock festival, Glastonbury, and saw the end of R.E.M.'s performance, longing to be on that stage myself.

As we departed, the prevailing mood remained optimistic. Graham dropped us at the airport, and when we told him we hoped to see him again, he nodded confidently and replied, "Oh, I have a feeling you'll be seeing quite a bit of me." A few weeks later, our album was rereleased in the UK, a year after being released the first time. (As "Secret Smile" became a hit, Universal had the album pulled off the record store shelves in order to build pent-up demand.) It debuted at number nineteen among all albums and moved up to seventeen during the second week, far beyond even our best weeks in the US album charts.

In August 1999, we stepped off the plane in Mexico City and a man came up to Dan and asked, "Are you the man who . . . who . . . 'Nobody knows it'?" It was a quote from the opening line of Mexico's number-one song:

"TFI Friday"
London
25/6/99

Nobody knows it but you've got a secret smile
And you use it only for me

We stopped for a brief lunch, and then the Universal staff whisked us off to our first press conference ever. We sat at a table in the front of the room, each of us with his own microphone. Behind us hung a large Coca-Cola banner, advertising the corporate sponsor of the concert, and the table was flanked by two women, who stood in swimsuits and high heels, looking straight ahead like statues. Strange that we should be framed so extravagantly when only ten of the fifty chairs set out for reporters were occupied.

The sleepy reporters crossed their legs, and the questions came forth slowly, timidly. During the long, awkward gaps between each answer and the next question, I auditioned various postures and facial expressions, hoping somehow to span the distance between the fantastical staging and the tepid reality of the silent few journalists sitting among the empty chairs. The gaps between questions grew longer, and the reporters began to look at each other. Perhaps they had been duped into coming and thought we were to blame. Or maybe this was all completely normal.

Our show that night at the Palacio de los Deportes was a welcome contrast. The arena was filled to capacity—10,000 people— the largest crowd ever to see a Semisonic-headlined event. A third of the available tickets had been bought, and Coca-Cola had given away the remaining 7,000 seats. Ticket giveaways generally guarantee a poor attendance, since people who have nothing invested in the tickets are more likely to make other plans. However, from the stage we couldn't see an empty seat.

From the very first note, the crowd showed their familiarity with our songs. Row by row, section by section, an arena of spectators swayed their hips back and forth. During our fourth song, a softer mid-tempo number titled "DND" (for "Do Not Disturb"), hundreds of people hauled out lighters and flicked them on and off with the backbeats, as if my left drumstick were literally lighting up the room with each smack of the snare drum. I laughed in amazement, nearly falling off the drum throne. The opening bars of "Secret Smile" produced a tingling shower of screams, and the entire arena sang along. At the end of the show, I let Dan and John exit before making my way to the front of the stage for an exaggerated "thank you" wave. We boarded the plane the next morning cradling gift bottles of Don Julio Tequila from the Universal staff, looking forward to our return to Mexico. It never came.

Dana called from his MCA office to report more international successes. "You guys are all over the radio in South Africa." Rumors of a South American tour floated, briefly. And we received e-mail from fans around the globe—Thailand, Japan, Costa Rica, Singapore, Germany, Brazil.

It had been a year since "Closing Time" had slipped from the number-one spot on the US alternative-radio charts. Since then, we had tried to rekindle our American success with singles released in a variety of formats. "Delicious," a single on the second *Friends* soundtrack album, went nowhere. Other Semisonic songs made their way into films—*Ten Things I Hate About You, American Pie, For Love of the Game,* and *Never Been Kissed*—but as I soon learned, the songs were buried in the body of the films, audible for a few seconds at a time. Other soundtrack offers came in, some of them lucrative, but MCA forbade us from accepting these because the soundtrack albums would be released by other labels, thus depriving MCA of potential Semisonic recording proceeds.

Each time Jim called with the good news that another song of ours was going into a film, I felt like a sap for entertaining hope. In all likelihood the movie would suck, our song would be buried, the soundtrack album would tank, and various industry folks would associate us with failure. Then I'd fake my way through phone calls from friends who were excited to have seen Semisonic listed with other bands in a television ad for the film.

Back in the UK, however, Universal was about to release "Closing Time." It had been released a year earlier in the UK but had made a poor showing. Now, in the wake of "Secret Smile," it returned to radio as a follow-up single. We flew back to London to do more promotion. Unlike our frustrating reception at home, our UK success felt sturdy. There, we were something like stars. Whenever we had time to walk through the city, we were stopped on the streets and asked for autographs. A small crowd would form and rival autograph seekers would warn us about others present. "You know, those guys with the blank cards are just going to sell your autographs on eBay." Somehow, having my autograph sold on the Internet was a form of exploitation I could live with. And there were always the kids who held up their cameras: "Do you mind?"

"Not at all." *I fucking love this place.*

Click.

What a difference from the US. In New York, we played at the 600-capacity Bowery Ballroom; in London, we sold out the 2,000-plus-capacity Shepherd's Bush Empire. "Get ya kit off!" one of the women in the audience yelled at Dan. Translation: Take off your clothes.

"Closing Time" came in at twenty-four on the singles chart, a shocking disappointment. Our album, however, remained in the UK top thirty. After our return to Minneapolis, we received our platinum records from the UK. Having been told how difficult it would be to break through there, I treasured my new plaque all the more. In February 2000, we were nominated for the Brit Awards, the UK version of the Grammys, in the category of Best International Newcomer. We were too busy making our next album to attend the ceremony, and we did not win, but the names of the others nominated in our category—Britney Spears,

Eminem, Jennifer Lopez, and the winner, Macy Gray—suggested how much bigger our profile was in the UK than in the US. Indeed, when we returned to England in June, and the three of us stood in front of separate immigration officers at the airport, one of them asked, "Aren't you chaps Semisonic?"

The adjacent official winked and said, "Semisonic? They've got a secret smile, haven't they?"

We drove south from London to Glastonbury to play for 100,000 people at the music festival there. The previous year, I had watched it on television from my London hotel room and dreamed that we might become popular enough to make an appearance, and now it was so. Half an hour after passing Stonehenge, we crested a hill and saw a sea of tents spread out across the horizon. Some of the fans had camped out all week in anticipation of the weekend festival, and many had come from foreign countries.

We played decently, not brilliantly, that afternoon. After months in the studio recording new songs, our live show was rusty, and perhaps we were a bit overexcited about playing such a marquee event. I had hoped our performance would be legendary, like the Travis set the year before when their song "Why Does It Always Rain On Me?" opened the skies over Glastonbury and produced a downpour of rain on an ecstatic crowd. I wanted a moment like that, but we would have to wait.

After our set, I took a walk through the crowd. Ocean Colour Scene, a band Graham had introduced me to, was playing, and as I wandered farther from the stage to the very edge of the crowd, I was moved by the reverent silence of the listeners. It was a welcome contrast to the moshing and mud throwing we had seen at US festivals. *Maybe we're more cut out for the UK than the US*, I thought as I stood on the grass beyond the fringes of the onlookers, enjoying Ocean Colour Scene and all who watched them. Next year, we might come back and play again; 2001 might be the year of our complete conquest of the UK and beyond. Until then,

I resolved to enjoy what we had right now, a life where we walked along the misty edges of stardom.

We flew home the next day. As I walked through the Minneapolis airport upon our return, two teenagers spotted me. The first one smiled and whispered to the second, and he smiled, too. The first one got out his camera. *Here we go.* They approached bashfully. *Be friendly. Fame is a privilege.* "Would you mind?" the first one asked, holding up his camera.

"Not at all," I said, fixing my collar. Then he handed me the camera and put his arm around his friend. "It's the red button on top."

Click.

Chapter XV

THE RUSH FORWARD

Our success in the UK pleased the executives at MCA, but in their minds it was inconveniently timed. "Closing Time" was hitting the radio in the UK eighteen months after its debut in the States, and MCA feared that our British touring was pushing back the recording and release of our next album, a delay that could cost us momentum with American listeners. If we didn't hurry, Hans and his bosses warned, listeners would forget Semisonic.

Dan had spent months locked in hotel rooms and the back lounges of tour buses with his guitar and notebook, but the ever-changing scenery and lack of privacy made it nearly impossible to write on the road. Jim, meanwhile, wanted to continue to build our fan base at home and booked us a month of shows with the Barenaked Ladies. That, in turn, outraged Jay Boberg, who wanted a new record as fast as possible. He had already announced to MCA employees that our record would be released in the spring of 2000. That release date was laughable, given that the announcement was made in the summer of 1999 and we would not be able to begin recording until the fall.

Adding to MCA's anxieties was Dan's insistence that we be allowed to produce the record ourselves. "We've earned it. We've made records with producers, and now I want to do one on our own." Once again Hans called me, hoping to employ me as an emissary.

"If I were Dan, I'd want to work with the best producer I could get. Here's his big chance."

And, having delivered Hans's messages to Dan, I'd hear the response: "They say that, and then whenever I name a producer that I'd work with, they tell me, 'Well, you can't work with him.' "

An example of such a producer was Nick Launay. We had loved making the last record with him and had established a good rapport. MCA, however, balked at this idea. Over and over I heard the confounding words "We can't have another *Feeling Strangely Fine* on our hands." That thinking continued to amaze me. *Feeling Strangely Fine* contained songs that had reached number one in several different countries. It had gone platinum in the US and UK as well as gold in Canada. *Rolling Stone* and others had picked it as one of the best albums of 1998, and one of the songs was nominated for a Grammy. By any measure, these distinctions ought to constitute a great achievement. Not, however, by the standards of the music business. Our interest in working again with Nick brought nothing but scowls.

Dan agreed to work with some engineer/producers, who were flown to Minneapolis. The results were mediocre, in one case because the songs we recorded were unfinished, and in another because the engineer attempted to rework the songs and the arrangements, much to the band's frustration. Finally, MCA relented and stopped insisting we hire a producer. We cut some tracks with a producer friend from Minneapolis and then proceeded largely on our own. Brad, our trusted live-sound engineer, recorded most of the record with Dan, John, and sometimes me, sitting next to him in the producer's chair, speaking into the control-room microphone to whoever was performing. "Okay, let's try another."

"How was that?" asked the performer.

"Good, so let's do another," came the reply.

"I've already done five takes. What was wrong with the last one?"

"I guess it just wasn't as special as the one before."

"You guess? Then why don't we use the one before?"

"Because . . . Just do another."

All of the producer's chores now fell on our shoulders, including the maintenance of the $35,000 computerized recording system that we purchased, which required endless hours of data backup and disk-space management. At times, the advantages of computerized recording—intricate editing possibilities and portability—seemed to be offset by the incumbent hassles—the brilliant performances lost to computer crashes, the recording sessions halted by mysterious malfunctions, and the endless nights spent backing up the data. Furthermore, now that the music showed up on a computer screen, it was hard to resist the temptation to judge the music not by how it sounded but by how it looked—rows of green, red, blue, gray, and yellow waveforms extending horizontally across the screen. By magnifying the view, one could see that the bass drum was hit three milliseconds late on the downbeat of bar 64. "Slide it over." One mouse click at a time, the various eccentricities of an expressive performance could be "corrected," and if we were not careful, a slew of incremental fixes would transform a spirited performance into something soulless and flat.

The portability of our computerized recording equipment allowed us to record much of the record outside the expensive confines of a proper recording studio, thus sparing us thousands of dollars in studio costs. The bulk of our recording time was spent at our rehearsal space, a room in a converted auto-parts warehouse that now rented spaces to hundreds of bands. We did a lot of work individually, Dan recording in his basement on a digital workstation and John and I pulling shifts that barely overlapped at the rehearsal space. Sometimes Dan would call with an idea—"See if we can develop the second verse and then do something about the clutter on the bridge"—and I'd spend hours in front of the computer screen and speakers, surrounded by the windowless cinder-block walls of our rehearsal space, searching my mind for inspiration. I'd record new keyboard ideas, cut and paste existing tracks in new places, and eliminate ideas that were now obsolete. At midnight, I'd make a rough mix, dub a CD for Dan, drive it over to his house, and drop it through the mail slot. The next day we'd confer, and I proceeded accordingly. It was ironic that, working long hours separately, we were recording an album that came to be titled *All About Chemistry*.

Dan felt we should avoid revisiting the sound and mood of our previous album. If *Feeling Strangely Fine* was grainy in sound, melancholy in mood, and intended to be heard by lone listeners lying in a dark bedroom, he wanted our new record to sound shinier, to feel sassier, and to be the kind of record you might play at a party. The demo tracks he recorded in his basement pointed the way, sometimes shocking John and me by how sharply the songwriting and arrangement ideas contrasted with our previous albums. We wondered if the new songs sounded like Semisonic, to which Dan would respond, "But this is what I'm writing." Over time, John and I caught on. Dan, meanwhile, decided that some of his new songs sounded like they belonged on a more introspective solo album, and he kept those in a separate pile for a future solo project.

The recording continued for months, and MCA grew ever more impatient. We heard that Doug Morris, chairman and CEO of the Universal Music Group, had recently asked Jay Boberg about the upcoming MCA records. Jay played Morris an early demo of one of the songs, "Chemistry," and Morris was reportedly ecstatic. Such an emphatic reaction from his boss may have further convinced

Jay of the song's hit-worthiness. We, however, were not so sure. For one thing, "Chemistry," with a prominent piano part and trombones and flutes in the bridge, was too bright for the dark and ever-more-aggressive textures of alternative-rock radio, where we had enjoyed our biggest success. Then we heard that a top MCA executive had taken the unusual step of playing this early demo of "Chemistry" for a gathering of influential alternative-rock radio programmers. They shook their heads. "We like Semisonic, but we'd never play that." Thus, they were prejudiced against "Chemistry" before we had even recorded the final version of the song.

Another high-ranking MCA executive heard "Chemistry" and declared, "I can get that played on K-ROCK this afternoon." That sounded to us like a reckless boast. K-ROCK's playlist was now centered around the violent sounds of Limp Bizkit and Linkin Park. We missed the trusted ears of Nancy Levin, the former head of promotion who had helped launch "Closing Time." She, alas, had quit.

The official MCA view was now this: Semisonic had a winning single and therefore should wrap up the album quickly and get it released. Jim, however, was not sold on "Chemistry" and wanted us to take time to write and record more songs. He looked skeptically upon the label's rush to release the record. "They've got Semisonic factored into their financial projections. Let me deal with their pressure. You guys keep working."

As the recording stretched into the spring of 2000, past Jay's initial release date, Gary Ashley, the head of A&R, flew out to Minneapolis to meet with the band and "discuss the progress of the recording." I spoke up several times, saying that we didn't feel we would finish anytime soon and that we wanted to make the best record we could. Gary smiled and assured us that no one would take the record out of our hands until we felt it was done. "But let's not rule out the possibility that it might be done in time for the fall." The next day, Jim spoke with Ashley over the phone, and Ashley claimed that the band had agreed to finish the record quickly to allow a fall release.

Jim corrected him. "No. The band tells me that you agreed to let them finish the record, even if that takes us past a fall release."

"Your band are a bunch of liars."

The greater the pressure from MCA, the more I agreed with Jim's view that the label bosses were more concerned with hitting their fourth-quarter financial projections than with the quality and long-term sales potential of our album. The jobs at the top of the company were always rumored to be in jeopardy. Since Jay took over as president four years earlier, I had heard dozens of rumors about his imminent firing and of executives conniving to take his place. Though Jay had made his share of missteps with Semisonic, I felt uneasy about the prospect of a new label president. If Dr. Evil, the MCA executive who was rumored to have trashed Semisonic in the hallways and meeting rooms, took over the label, as some rumored he was trying to do, we'd be in big trouble. Clearly, Jay liked us, he had played an important role in getting our last record released overseas, and he was optimistic about the band's future. His desire that we declare the record finished, I thought, was shortsighted but also proof that he was focused on the band and believed we would deliver a hit.

Dan refused to be pressured into finishing early, and MCA backed off and agreed to postpone the release until early 2001, almost three years after the release of *Feeling Strangely Fine*. The extra months of recording allowed Dan to finish some of the best songs on the album. For years, he had asked our representatives at Warner Chappell Publishing to find additional writing opportunities, but with no success. As the entity that owned some of the publishing (and therefore royalty) rights to our songs, it was in their interest to find opportunities for Dan to write with other artists, but they had not delivered those chances. Finally, the ever-persistent Jim called one of the publishing reps and complained: "When are you going to set up Dan with some outside writing?"

"Well, Jim, the thing is—wait a minute, can you hold?" A minute later, the rep came back on the line. "Jim? Does Dan want to do a cowrite with Carole King?"

"Fuck you. I'm being serious."

"I *am* serious. Carole's on the other line, and she likes Semisonic."

"Really?"

"Yeah. Can you get him to L.A. on Friday?"

A few days later, Dan flew to Los Angeles and a limousine drove him, not to the mansion he had imagined but to a bungalow that was a project studio of an engineer with whom Carole works. She greeted him at the door, and soon he found himself in a drab little room with his guitar, a couple of chairs, an electronic keyboard, and a songwriting legend whose hit songs defined decades of pop music: "Will You Love Me Tomorrow," "Up on the Roof," "The Locomotion" "(You Make Me Feel) Like a Natural Woman," "You've Got a Friend," "I Feel the Earth Move," "It's Too Late," and many more.

Carole began by praising Dan's songs, which made him blush all the more. In advance of his arrival, Dan had reviewed the breadth of Carole's discography and responded to her generous words by reeling off the names of some of his favorite Carole King songs, mentioning as a special favorite one of her collaborations with Gerry Goffin, the Byrds' "Wasn't Born to Follow." Then, as he had hoped would happen, she took this cue and sat down at the keyboard, reacquainted herself with the chords, and sang it from beginning to end.

Thoroughly enchanted by this point, Dan took out his guitar and proceeded to show her some of his recent song ideas, enjoying both a rush of excitement when she grabbed hold of certain ideas—"Great! Wait a minute, yeah, keep going"—and a cold thrill when she dismissed others with abrupt firmness—"No! Get away from that." Over the course of their morning together, they wrote a song called "One True Love." After returning to Minneapolis, Dan completed the lyrics.

The extended recording deadline allowed us to record the song and send a rough mix to Carole, and she overdubbed a backing vocal and electric piano part. She sent the tape back to us, and we recorded her additions onto the computerized master. Of the many hours spent in front of the computer, my most glorious moment was typing "Carole—vox" into the computer track list and pressing Record.

We continued to work long days in the poorly ventilated confines of our rehearsal space. In the winter, it had been too cold. Now, in the summer, we gagged on the heat. Fifteen-hour days inside our rehearsal-space prison of cinder-block walls and fluorescent lights numbed my consciousness. I had hoped to write more than one song for the record, or failing that, to write a song worthy of being considered a single. Now the end was approaching and I had finished only two songs. I hoped that the better of those, "El Matador," a lyrical song that moved forward in a slow oceanic trance, would make the cut. Its tempo and elegiac tone would disqualify it as a single, but perhaps it would make a good last song on the record, a place of honor. As the summer dragged on, I longed to sit on the couch in Bob Clearmountain's studio and hear "El Matador" wash out of the speakers in its finished form.

In the last weeks of recording, I wrote some string arrangements for five of the songs, hoping to enlarge them by using a palette of violins, violas, and cellos to paint an aural horizon that might suggest the plainspoken grandeur and heroism of Aaron Copland's orchestral works. Jim booked my flight to Los Angeles to record the parts with a Hollywood string section in the famed A Room at Capitol Studios, a magnificent acoustic space where Frank Sinatra had recorded "Fly Me to the Moon" and other classics.

Unlike my previous experiences as a string arranger, when Dan and John were present to offer their opinion, I had to rely on my own judgments. Standing on the podium and staring at fourteen Hollywood string players, I did my best impersonation of a man who knew what he was doing, a performance that was dealt a setback after the first five bars of music when the baton I had specially purchased for the occasion flew out of my hand, bounced off the podium, and rolled around the floor under the feet of the musicians as they bowed away. I didn't touch it after that. However, with the help of a musically inclined engineer, Neal Avron, and a confident and supportive concertmaster, Joel Derovin, things came together nicely.

The arrangements sounded so good that at times I could not resist standing up and swaying my arms about, exhorting the players to higher heights as they pulled and pushed their bows, but for the most part I gave my nonexistent conducting skills a rest. Hearing them stir through the arrangement for my beloved "El Matador" was, of course, the biggest thrill of the day. Shaking hands with Neal at the end of the five-hour session, I felt enormous relief at having successfully completed my assignment, my biggest moment ever in the studio. I had planned to hook up with some of my L.A. friends to celebrate the completion of my daunting day, but as soon as I got back to my hotel room in the late afternoon, I collapsed on the bed and stared blankly at the ceiling for hours as tears of exhaustion rolled out of my eyes.

Two weeks later, I returned to Los Angeles, this time with Dan and John. Dan had already spent a week in Miami, mixing some of the songs with Tom Lord Alge, another of the A-list mixers we had used in the past. Now we would mix the remaining tracks with Bob Clearmountain. (Alge's trademark sound, with its crunchier guitars and vocals, is more compact and aggressive than Clearmountain's, which in turn offers more aural spaciousness than Alge's.) The mixing routine at Clearmountain's was by now familiar: resting poolside, eating food prepared by Bob's chef, and reveling in the sounds. Hans pulled me aside for his now standard speech. "Congratulations, Jake, your drumming has finally arrived." I nodded. He seemed unaware of having made this observation after each of our previous albums.

The studio door buzzed one afternoon and I rushed to answer it, wanting to be the one who greeted Carole King. I opened the door and lurched forward to give her a big hug. As we walked to the studio, I was slightly embarrassed for springing such a familiar welcome on someone I'd never met, though she seemed quite comfortable with it. As she was well aware, millions of people feel as if they know Carole King, and given the chance, most of them would go for the hug. She walked into the studio and everyone stood up, pop royalty that she is.

This would be the first time she listened to the finished version of "One True Love," the song she had written with Dan, and I was anxious to hear her verdict. After an agonizing ten minutes of exchanging niceties, we all sat down, and Bob rolled the tape. Carole sat at the mix console, and as the music played she moved about in her chair and rocked her head with a huge smile. At fifty-eight, she had an adolescent glee I had never seen in a studio, but that glee could disappear instantly as her face narrowed to focus on something unexpected and then widened back into a smile.

After listening twice, she pressed her hands onto her legs and beamed. "I love it." Somewhere in her first paragraph of observations she said, "Great drumming. Who's the drummer?" I raised my hand. "You have a really nice feel. I love the way it bounces."

"Thanks." I remember little else of what she said that afternoon. At the end of her visit, we took turns posing for pictures with her, and after I walked her out, I returned to the studio, where everyone had wilted into giddiness. A few days later, we mixed "El Matador" and I took the final mix out in the rental car, playing it over and over as I drove up and down the Malibu coast.

Eight years earlier, I had been terrified of the music-business machinery. Not only had I survived, I had outlasted many of the

people I had been scared of. Dr. Evil had cleared out his office at
MCA. The Minneapolis program director who had shut us out
and taken delight in engulfing the rival station that had played
our music—he had been fired, too. The word was, he had created
a phony "food shelf for the homeless" fund, for which he solicited
donations from record companies in return for airplay. One day,
the station receptionist got a call from a local mini-mart. "Someone keeps coming in here with one-hundred-dollar certificates
from your station, buying a can of peas, and pocketing the rest of
the money."

"What certificates?"

"The ones for your food shelf for the homeless."

"What food shelf for the homeless?" Later that day, the PD
was fired.

The songwriting royalties from "Closing Time" and "Secret
Smile" had been coming in for a year. (Recall that songwriting
royalties are not subject to the band's recoupable debts to the
record label.) We did not have millions, but we were now making
as much money as our friends in various professions. I had junked
my '82 Toyota Tercel and stepped up to a '92 Corolla. I had given
away my futon bed and futon couch and purchased a bed, sofa,
and matching chairs. In ten years, my Minneapolis existence had
been transformed from that of an office temp to that of a
semi–rock star with gold and platinum records. But I longed to go
further than that. I flew to New York, found an apartment in the
Park Slope area of Brooklyn, and signed a one-year lease. I now
had two apartments, two beds, two couches, two televisions, two
DVD players, and two closets between which I divided my rock-
star wardrobe. After finishing the mixes in L.A., I flew to my new
home.

Once in a while, someone, usually a fellow transplant from the
Midwest, would stop me on the street and say, "Are you Jake from
Semisonic?" I'd stop for a quick chat and then resume my heel-
scuffing strolls through the city, going nowhere in particular,

parading along in my ankle-length Dries Van Noten overcoat. As the colder weather moved in, I added a luxurious long red wool scarf, made by my friend Delight, a clothes designer. I first met her backstage at one of our shows with the Barenaked Ladies (she was there to see her friend Kevin Hearn, the keyboard player). We had become close friends, and once in a while she'd send me a package of clothes made especially for me, one of the ridiculous perks of being a rock musician.

I knew only a handful of people in New York, but that anonymity allowed me to emerge from my cocoon of midwestern humility and walk with 20 percent more swagger. I priced brownstones and mused about the elegant furnishings that would fill mine when the day came. I pictured a large living room with a giant Turkish carpet, on top of which I would park a sumptuous grand piano. "El Matador" had made the cut, and some of our musician friends singled it out as being a favorite. My days as a songwriter of note would soon be here. On that piano that I would soon buy for the brownstone I would soon own, I would write songs, small worlds of euphoria to which people would return again and again and think of Jacob Slichter whenever they did.

The fantasy I had spent my life chasing after was now within my grasp. Over the past two years, the autograph signings, the television appearances, the sound of myself on the radio, the sight of myself on television, the sensation of stepping out of a limousine into a blizzard of flashing cameras and cheering crowds—all of those experiences gathered into a strong wind blowing at my back. I knew how I wanted to look, how I wanted to carry myself, what I wanted to say. A photograph of me in *Rhythm*, an English drum magazine, captured me in a black turtleneck and freshly dyed platinum hair looking coolly into the lens. Underneath that picture, the magazine editors wrote a caption that predicted, "A rewarding alternative career as a Bond movie villain awaits Jake."

The routines of my life—the eruption of cheers that I had heard every night when the houselights went out and we took the stage; the heart-pounding anticipation of counting in the first song right before we flooded the room with sound, light, and joy; the shouts of "Jake" after a song I wrote or a special drum fill; the faces smiling at me from the front rows; the waves goodnight and the knowledge that we would be called back for one, two, and sometimes three encores; the triumphant mood of the dressing room, where I reveled in the adulation of our backstage guests: "best fucking show ever" / "completely blown away" / "oh, my fucking God"—those routines had transformed my exterior into an armor. I enjoyed wearing that armor and found it hard to remove. At times, every word out of my mouth seemed to be an interview-quality sound bite or story. During our brief layovers in Minneapolis I had begun to avoid contact with friends, because it took me several days to rein in the personality that had expanded to fill the stages and airwaves. It was hard to shrink back down to size, and now as I walked around a city of strangers, I didn't have to. As Dan had predicted when I first started touring and was terrified of the lonesome coldness of the road, I now savored that coldness.

My head was full of our new songs. The word was, our album was going to be big. As the holidays arrived, the executives at Universal International announced that in 2001, U2 would be the number-one priority. And of the hundreds of remaining acts on the many Universal labels, number two would be Semisonic. It was going to be a very good year.

Chapter XVI

ALL ABOUT CHEMISTRY

n a busy London intersection, workmen installed a nine-foot sculpture of two laboratory beakers shaped as male and female, joined at their heads and midsections. In other words, the giant beakers were having sex in front of thousands of London commuters who might also have noticed the sign next to the sculptures that announced "Semisonic: *All About Chemistry*, the fantastic new album, out March 5."

Thousands of miles away, on Hennepin Avenue in Minneapolis, a gigantic photograph of Dan, John, and me looked down from a billboard also advertising our album. Colorfully dressed in designer clothes, with artfully coiffed heads of copper, dark brown, and platinum hair, and seated three abreast in the white void of a photo studio—we had graduated from the arch smiles of do-it-yourself indie-rockers to the relaxed stares befitting pop icons. Magazine pages and the television cameras awaited, and I was determined to enjoy myself. During the photo shoot for the album artwork, I sashayed around in front of the camera, doing my impression of a fashion model's runway catwalk, pouting for the lens, and cracking up my bandmates, the stylist, and the photographer, who laughed as she clicked away.

And if our appearance had taken a step toward the glossy, our sound had more polish as well. "What a strange but wonderful thing it is when a band's Great Leap Forward so obviously happens." Thus began a review in the UK's biggest music journal, *Q* magazine, which gave *All About Chemistry* a five-star rating, a distinction that in recent years had been bestowed on only two other bands, Oasis and Radiohead. The rave review ended with the following flourish:

> Slichter's El Matador, a lonesome elegy to a lost summer, closes the whole album. Such is the quality of Wilson's work that El Matador is Slichter's only opportunity to shine—and that, correctly, is how it works at this level—but you'd still revel in hearing another heap of his songs. Not big, not clever, not hip, not trendy. Just fantastic.

I reread these closing sentences a dozen times. Something big was happening. This five-star review was a bottle of vintage champagne christening our album, a luxurious ocean liner.

We were more aggressive this time. Jim hired an outside publicity firm, Sacks and Company of New York, to help us sharpen our media presence, an arena where Jim thought MCA had come up short. On the musical front, we hired a side musician, Chris Joyner, to play piano for our live shows. Jim had always complained that we needed an extra musician to sound bigger, an opinion I disputed. But the material on the new album was heavily keyboard driven, and adding a keyboardist to our live shows not only freed Dan to remain front and center with his guitar, but made us sound bigger than ever. All we needed now was to get our single on the radio.

MCA flew us around the country for the standard blitz of key stations in advance of the single's add-date. The platinum records hanging on the lobby walls no longer awed me; I had two of my own. As we walked down the hallways to the broadcast studios, the DJs were eager to greet us. "Jake, I took your advice. Guess what? It worked!"

"Glad to hear it." I had no memory of that DJ or my advice to him. On the air, we were presented as stars on the verge of megastardom. We performed acoustic versions of old and new songs and let the DJs spin our new single, "Chemistry," which they predicted would become another hit.

But what did the program directors think? More important, what did *influential* program directors think? As we traveled across the country, I called Jim for updates. Had K-ROCK added the single? No. Neither had WBCN, WHFS, or other influential alternative stations. "It's too soft for alternative." Once again, our inability to squeeze nicely into a preexisting radio format became an issue. MCA turned its attention from alternative and to "triple A, modern adult, and hot AC." ("Hot AC" stands for hot adult contemporary.) The reverie of five-star reviews and billboards was now lifting. We were back in the jargon-cluttered landscape of a record launch, where soon we'd hear reports of "phones," "research," and "SoundScan."

In New York, we played a short set at MTV headquarters for a gathering of employees. A few months earlier, MTV had included Semisonic in a special on one-hit wonders. Now as I absorbed the employees' response, I couldn't decide if their applause signaled newfound excitement about the band or gratitude for a thirty-minute work break. That night we had dinner with a number of executives from MTV, VH1, and some of the senior MCA executives, including Jay Boberg and the new head of promotion, Craig Lambert. At dinner, Lambert had cornered Dan and said, "What's past is past, but this time around, you guys are gonna *work.*" Dan chuckled incredulously at this suggestion that we had somehow done too little touring and promotion. After dinner, Lambert corralled me for a nightcap at a hotel bar with a member of his promotion staff, and as with Dan, his tone toward me was vaguely threatening. For instance, he told of a band at his former label whose singer had come down with a sore throat and thus had to withdraw from a major radio festival. The station's program director called Lambert to say that, although the reason for the band's cancellation was understandable, he felt he had to drop the band from his rotation to dissuade other bands from canceling in the future. "And I thought about it, and I said, 'Yup, you're right. You got no choice.' " He took a few swigs, and before I could escape, he started musing out loud to his staff assistant about an MCA local he wanted to fire. "He fucking whines and doesn't get a goddamned thing done." Then he turned to me. "What do you think?" I said that the person in question had won major victories on Semisonic's behalf, but Lambert, setting down his drink, would have none of it. "Naw. I'm sick of his whining. I think I gotta fire him."

He got up to use the rest room, and his staff assistant put her hand on my arm. "Don't you love him? I mean, he talks tough, but his heart is in the right place." I smiled and nodded as I reflected on how much I missed Lambert's predecessor, Nancy Levin.

The rising tides that had preceded the explosion of "Closing Time," the hair-raising ionization of the atmosphere I had felt when stations across the country lined up to play it—in place of that hung an eerie calm. "Chemistry" lacked the powerful endorsement that K-ROCK programmer Kevin Weatherly had given "Closing Time" in the US and that Capital Radio's Richard Park had given "Secret Smile" in the UK. As our week of nationwide radio visits continued, I became increasingly impatient for good news. We flew to San Francisco, where our longtime supporters at Radio Alice gave us a friendly welcome, but across town, the program director of K-FOG refused to have his picture taken with us.

American radio, however, was only one front in an international effort. Soon we would travel to the UK and Europe. We spent an hour taping a long list of radio IDs.

"Hi, we're Semisonic and you're listening to Dank an Hank on three FM."

"We're Semisonic. Feel the heat rising from the streets of Istanbul with one-o-five point seven Hot Station."

"Hola, Somos Semisonic Y estas escuchando nuestro nuevo album *All About Chemistry* en Euskadi Gaztea."

We flew to London, where we felt more at home than in any city besides Minneapolis. So routine had our London visits become that after I checked into Mister Phelps's room, I put on my running gear for a brisk jog around Hyde Park, an invigorating scoff at jet lag. We made the rounds on English TV—*Top of the Pops, CD:UK,* and *The Big Breakfast*—and were splashed across the pages of the Sunday *Times* of London with another rave about our new album. We posed for some publicity shots underneath the giant sculpture of the beakers, still on display. As the traffic drove by, I was actually embarrassed by the amount of public space occupied by Semisonic.

Then we embarked on a two-week tour with the Scottish band Texas, opening for them in arenas across the UK and Ireland. Though we were the opening act, we were well known to the concertgoers. In the middle of "Secret Smile," Dan pointed at the crowd at Wembley Arena in London and commanded, "YOU sing!," and we were serenaded by 10,000 English voices. Little did they know that our stage moxie hid a growing uncertainty. The two major British stations, Radio 1 and Capital Radio, were not playing "Chemistry."

Drifting back and forth between the glory of arena stages and worried cell-phone conversations with Jim about our troubles at radio, I found myself in the presence of more and more celebrities. In the US, we had attended a banquet thrown by our publishing company, Warner Chappell. Others in the room included two of the members of Radiohead, Colin Greenwood and Ed O'Brien. No opportunity to gracefully engage either of them presented itself, though I offered my fumbling admiration to Ed, watched

Dan chat with Colin and his wife, and felt my stock bottom out when R.E.M. singer Michael Stipe breezed through the affair briefly to confer with the two Radiohead lads, perhaps arranging a later rendezvous far removed from the schmoozeoisie.

In London, Universal gave us tickets to the PJ Harvey Show at Shepherd's Bush, where Chrissie Hynde squeezed through the crowd and Dan chatted briefly again with Colin Greenwood, who offered a timely travel tip: "When you get to Manchester, make sure to visit Pelican Neck Records." We scored some highly sought-after tickets to a rare appearance by U2 at a London night-club, the Astoria. From where I stood, twenty feet from the stage, I looked over my shoulder to the balcony and saw Eric Clapton and Salman Rushdie sitting in the front row. In front of me, U2 proceeded to devastate the crowd of 2,000 with stadium-sized might. For the last half hour of the show, I stared at Adam Clay-ton, whose stage presence suggested a statue of a bass player that had been tipped to one side. He embodied the timeless rock-and-roll maxim "The less you do, the cooler you look."

After our show in Dublin, security guards unhitched velvet ropes for us as we walked into an exclusive party. Inside, John pointed out film director Neil Jordan while, in the corner, Dan shared a drink with pop stars the Corrs. The accumulation of star encounters felt like an omen. Perhaps I ought to get used to it. Perhaps this would be the year that we bubbled up to the top of the champagne glass and made a lot of celebrity friends. We walked out of the party and back to our hotel through streets of a city that resembled a carousel spun off of its base—a scattered mass of people swaying, stumbling, shouting, fighting, pissing, puking, falling, getting back up, and singing. A group of men tottered up to Dan and sang a drunken rendition of "Secret Smile."

Out of this dreamy fog of stars, fans, and critical acclaim, we returned to the US and the grim reality of radio resistance to our record. In New York, we played a show at Irving Plaza, produced by an influential New York City station and sponsored by Guinness. It was a standard arrangement, where in return for playing the station's event, the station agreed to add our single, "Chemistry," to their playlist in strong rotation. What we did not know until minutes before the show was that the show's sponsor, Guinness, planned to send a man dresssed in a giant Guinness beer bottle costume onto the stage during our set. We were expected to join this giant beer bottle in making a toast. "And it would be great if you could do it during 'Closing Time.' "

We were amazed that such a horrible requirement could have gone unmentioned until minutes before the show. "No fucking way!"

The MCA local insisted we cooperate, telling us that upsetting the station's sponsor could damage our relationship with the station, which in turn could cost us airplay and hurt our record. After fifteen minutes of intense pressure, we finally agreed to let the beer bottle make an entrance once we had ended our set and had left the stage. This one episode revealed how little clout we had to wield, how tenuous our status at radio was. Soon I began to ask Jim about phones and research, cursing myself for being swept up in the jargon and crass measurements of the business. It was too early to tell, but the initial signs were not good.

Hans blamed the difficulty at radio on the fact that, a year earlier, a top MCA executive had turned off a roomful of influential programmers with a demo version of "Chemistry." On the other hand, Jim had never thought the song was a hit. Whatever the reason for the resistance to the song, I became reacquainted with the familiar sensation of losing. The research came back: bad. Slow phones and bad research were things that "Closing Time" had overcome, but only because of the influential stations that had committed to it from the beginning. We had spent $300,000 on a video for "Chemistry," featuring a small steel ball rolling through the band and a series of Rube Goldberg contraptions. But the video was a dud, and MTV wouldn't play it. "Chemistry" was in serious trouble. I looked at Dan and John, who, as always, insulated themselves from talk of research, phones, spins, and so on. The wisdom of their detachment was now fully apparent.

The album was released on March 13. John and I did several interviews on Minneapolis television stations. "How do you handle fame and success without letting it go to your head?" By not challenging the interviewer's rosy preconceptions.

The next day, we flew to L.A. to play on *The Tonight Show*. Our previous appearance had felt like a reward for success; now it was a badly needed chance to remind the more than one million Americans who owned Semisonic's last album that our new album had just been released. The routine of rehearsal, taping, and watching the broadcast no longer amazed me. It only made me impatient.

More overseas promotion. Amsterdam, Cologne, Hamburg, Paris, and London. Universal continued the royal treatment—in Stockholm we stayed in the same hotel as Tony Blair, Vladimir Putin, and other European leaders convening for a summit—but the confident smiles that our hosts had worn a few weeks earlier had flattened. My own doubts were blurred by the swirl of interviews, shows, television appearances, and extravagant dinners with the Universal staff. To further intoxicate myself with hope, I logged on to the Semisonic message board to read what our fans thought about our new album. I waded through a pile of affectionate messages about Dan. One writer who saw an Internet broadcast of one of our shows wrote: "Jake, get some sleep." Another writer, noting the striped shirt I wore on the back cover of the CD, started a thread of messages titled "Does Jacob Slichter dress like a clown?"

Back home, the first week of album sales was nearing its end. Over the past three years, we had received thousands of e-mails about the quality and depth of our last album. Those fans would surely come back to hear more songs, but how many? Most? Half? I figured we'd get a strong first week—50,000 or so—and then fall to 20,000 per week for the remainder of the first month. Album sales might impress programmers, resuscitate our single, and restore the label's wavering confidence in the band.

We barely cleared 10,000 in the first week—a disaster. The second week was even worse. It was the inevitable result of being shut out on the airwaves. What use was our five-star review now? Was it the champagne bottle that christened an ocean liner's launch onto the rocks?

We played Letterman in early April. (I walked up and down the six flights of stairs to our dressing room several times, hoping to run into Renee Zellweger, only to learn that once again we had read the schedule incorrectly. The lead guest was actually Duke's basketball coach, Mike Krzyzewski.) We hit the road for a month of shows across the US and sold-out clubs full of enthusiastic fans. Record stores sponsored Semisonic soundcheck parties, and in city after city we signed hundreds of CDs. Mornings, we sat on the bus signing hundreds of posters at a time, trying to keep up with requests from the MCA promotion and marketing staffs. Certainly, this suggested a growing interest in our record. Hans told me, however, that the SoundScan numbers showed otherwise. Album sales in any particular city never increased after our shows. "You're preaching to the converted." Those who came to the concerts already owned the album; we weren't winning new fans, and our sales continued to sink.

Our friends and families beamed at us in the dressing rooms after our shows. In their minds, our success had been cemented since "Closing Time." They saw Semisonic billboards and rave reviews for our album, packed houses at our shows, and our appearances on network television. They had no idea of the unfolding disaster.

Between the flurry of constant attention on the one hand and the dwindling sales and airplay on the other, even I had trouble determining our altitude and trajectory. In Los Angeles, we checked into the Sunset Marquis, an exclusive hotel known for being protective of its celebrity guests. ("Do we protect the privacy of our guests? What guests?") I ate lunch by the pool as a young woman, apparently a supermodel mulling a career change to acting, listened to pitches from a series of prospective agents. "You want someone who can get you on the cover of *Rolling Stone*. That's worth millions in box office." I sipped iced tea and scanned the terrace for the members of U2, who were said to be staying there while on their US tour. After a while, Eminem rolled through, escorted by a pride of security guards. On my trips past the front desk, I smiled at the staff and wondered if my friendly praises of the fine service painted me as a yokel.

As for the MCA radio-promotion locals, they were exuberant— but not over Semisonic. "The Shaggy record's going nuts!" Shaggy, a Jamaican-born rapper, had a number-one record, and the story of that record's unlikely rise to the top of the charts presents an interesting case of an artist succeeding in spite of his label.

As Hans explained it to me, he and A&R chief Gary Ashley handed in Shaggy's newly finished album, *Hot Shot*, to their superiors, and the first two songs on the record they submitted were "It Wasn't Me" and "Angel." Remember those song titles and read on. The MCA bosses listened to the album and complained, "There're no singles!" The bosses demanded that Shaggy return to the studio and record new songs, and Shaggy agreed. This was exactly the scenario that Semisonic had faced in late 1997 when Jay Boberg and the other senior executives heard no hit potential in "Closing Time" and suggested we return to the studio to record more songs. Jim warned us that if we recorded a new batch of songs, the label would choose the single from the new batch and forget about "Closing Time." Fortunately, we heeded Jim's warning. When faced with the same dilemma, however, Shaggy accepted MCA's mandate to record more material, and no surprise, one of the new songs was selected as the single. The CD came out in August 2000, the single flopped, and within weeks MCA stopped working the album.

Meanwhile, a DJ in Honolulu, Pablo Sato of KIKI 93.9-FM, had downloaded Shaggy's album off of Napster and started to play one of the other songs, "It Wasn't Me." KIKI was flooded with calls and "It Wasn't Me" became a local hit. Bonnie Goldner and other Shaggy supporters at MCA seized on this success and advocated the song be pushed at other stations, and within a few weeks the song was a nationwide smash. By Christmastime, the album was on its way to number one, and after another hit single, "Angel," the album sold 12 million copies worldwide, no thanks to the people running MCA. It was Pablo Sato, his listening audience, and Napster—the dread enemy of the music industry—who pulled Shaggy's album from its grave at the Music Cemetery of America.

So with a chart-topping single, the MCA locals were quite excited about Shaggy. Of Semisonic and "Chemistry," however, they had little to report. Dan met with Jay Boberg, who said that Semisonic's inability to fit into any niche among the various radio formats continued to vex MCA, and that this in turn complicated the selection of a second single. On that matter, Dan had made up his mind. "I'd bet the farm on 'Act Naturally.' "

Jay nodded. "Yeah, but you should know that we've already bet the farm."

"Act Naturally" was a down-tempo ballad and therefore a harder sell at radio. At Hans and Jim's suggestion, we did a radio remix to spice it up with electronic elements and handed it to MCA. A week later, they reported back to Jim. "Well, we played it for a few radio folks, but they're saying they don't hear it." Jim viewed MCA's report as an elaborate bit of hedging. It was MCA who didn't hear the song. Plans for a second US single remained on hold, and given MCA's track record for not hearing hits, it was easy to give myself over to stewing about their refusal.

The UK company chose a different song as a second single—

"Get a Grip," an up-tempo ode to masturbation. "Get a grip on yourself you know you should / I've got a grip on myself and feels good." The song was so silly that we had questioned putting it on the album, but Hans had insisted. It had received a good audience response on our tour with Texas, and the UK company hoped the lyrics would appeal to the randy side of British humor. Perhaps the success of Shaggy's single "It Wasn't Me," a song about being caught "butt-naked banging on the bathroom floor" with the girl next door, lingered in the minds of those who were betting on "Get a Grip." The illustration on the cover of the CD single showed a hand gripping a frothing test tube.

Now our upcoming festival appearances in Europe and a tour of the UK appeared in the context of desperation. I did a number of early-morning phone interviews with the overseas press. In one instance, the UK publicity person miscalculated the transatlantic time difference, and I found myself on the phone, with no memory of having answered the call. It was ten past four in the morning, and it appeared I was in the middle of an interview. (Who knows what I said during the first ten minutes.) The reporters I spoke with that week seemed unaware that our album was tanking. "Are you excited about all the success you've had?" They were squinting at the sun, and I was looking back into a dark fog.

We flew to Germany to play two festivals, Rock im Park (Rock in the Park) and Rock am Ring (Rock at a Speedway). The Universal Germany staff told of some success with "Chemistry," but the crowd response suggested our diminished appeal. At the Pink Pop festival in Holland, I looked out from behind my drums and saw pockets of reverence from the few hundred people closest to the stage and distraction rippling back through the thousands behind them. After our set, we sat in an autograph booth and signed CDs and T-shirts. A few of the autograph seekers said they had traveled hundreds of miles just to see us, but most were simply filling in their festival T-shirts with signatures from every band on the show. As always, many could not hide their awkwardness at being in the presence of stars. Years earlier, I would have taken care to reassure them with a friendly smile. Now my smile was laced with the rage I felt about the miserable state of our album. The result seemed to titillate those autograph seekers even more. *They like to feel a little scared.*

When nightfall brought the headline acts onto the stage, I stood in the crowd and watched. Limp Bizkit front man Fred Durst pointed across the throng. "Link your arms together. Everyone. Link your arms. We're a big family. A big fucking family. No one can take us apart from each other, all right?" Seconds later, tens of thousands of fans unlinked their arms and pumped their fists in the air as they shouted along with Durst, "I did it all for the nookie!"

On to the UK for a headline tour. Our single "Get a Grip" was stopped dead on UK radio. Though our record was failing, we were still popular enough to embark on a series of theater shows, our biggest headline tour ever as measured by the volume of our production gear and the size of our team. Our crew expanded from six to fifteen, including drivers of the two trucks needed to haul the additional sound and lighting equipment. The crowning touch was a catering staff that cooked breakfast, lunch, and dinner for the band and crew. We had looked forward to this tour for months and at one point had considered spending an extra $30,000 to project films behind the stage for these shows. Now, however, grandiosity gave way to frugality.

At nightfall, the crowds lined up down the block. Once inside, the fans reveled in our music, screaming, yelling out the names of songs, showering us with affection and applause, and always requesting multiple encores. What a time for our best tour ever. I was pouring Champagne for the ocean liner's guests, keeping them unaware of the water flooding the lower decks. After the shows, fans crowded around the stage door for pictures, autographs, and conversation. "Jake, can I have a hug?"

I began to wonder whether this tour was the last chance to collect the souvenirs of a life we might soon lose. The London show was flat. Big-city audiences are always more distant, but now I feared that we were losing our performing touch. Nothing we did could rouse the fans from their comfortable seats. After the show, a Japanese woman introduced herself and told us she had flown all the way from Tokyo to see us. I was starting to regard such extraordinary expressions of adoration with impatience. Why were our fans a select group of considerate and sweet people who went out of their way to see us and bring us gifts from afar? Why couldn't they be the dull-witted masses who pumped their fists and shouted, "I did it all for the nookie"?

On our last day in the UK, we drove to the rain-soaked coast of Wales for an outdoor university ball. That night, men in tuxedos and women in evening gowns stumbled drunkenly through the rain, lining up for the bungee jump and more drinks, then cramming their way into a giant tent. At midnight, they hailed us with a drunken roar as we took the stage, but we wondered how much attention their alcohol-sopped brains were capable of giving us. As we played, a thousand tuxedos and gowns sloshed back and forth and the students sprayed one another with loud conversation and laughter. A woman in the front row draped her arm over her friend in an effort to remain standing and hauled out her cell phone, plugged her ears, and shouted into the mouthpiece. I fantasized about whipping a drumstick at her.

We returned to the States for some outdoor shows in the Midwest, ending with the Minneapolis block party behind the Basilica of Saint Mary. Our seventy-five-minute set was a nightmare of technical mishaps. The sound company had wired the stage incorrectly, and whenever one of us asked for more of one thing, we got more of something else. Dan couldn't hear himself sing, John couldn't hear Dan's guitar, and I drowned in the sound of my own drums. We never found our footing, and I didn't bother waving to the crowd as we left the stage. I cleared out of the dressing-room trailer before having to endure the smiles of friends who had just witnessed our worst hometown show ever.

MCA had no plans for releasing a second single in the US. Fortunately, a movie music supervisor for *Summer Catch*, a Warner Brothers film, had picked one of our new songs, "Over My Head," as being a perfect fit for the movie. (The song had been left off the album, but our publishing company had circulated it for possible use in film.) The film's music supervisor was especially excited about how aptly the lyrics described the trials of the main character, a summer-league baseball player portrayed by Freddie Prinze, Jr. Hollywood Records was releasing the soundtrack album, and they picked "Over My Head" as the first single. If the single connected, MCA could then reprint our album to include "Over My Head," and we'd finally get back on track.

I wondered if there was any cause for hope. Every soundtrack single we had ever released had received little promotional support and quickly fizzled. Hollywood Records and Warner Brothers studios agreed to pay for a video and sent us a box of director's reels. *There's the drummer close-up. I wonder if he whined and pouted to get that shot.* We discarded those reels and treatments and asked Chris Applebaum, the director of our "Closing Time" video, to take the job. The new video was shot in a baseball field east of Los Angeles. We lip-synched and stick-synched along to the track, first in the sunlight and later in darkness while being soaked by artificial rain machines. The finished video showed scenes from the movie, intercut with the glamorously dressed Semisonic, rocking in the sunshine and then in slow motion as raindrops rolled off the strings of the guitars and flew off of the cymbals and drums as the drummer smashed away in open-mouthed fury.

Our situation had now become so desperate that Jim suggested that I drop in on a conference of radio programmers who were gathered in Minneapolis. The idea was to hook up with a member of the MCA radio staff and work the room to win support for "Over My Head." Convincing even one programmer to play it might make the crucial difference, as Pablo Sato had proved with Shaggy's record. Miserable at the thought of this task, I pleaded with John to accompany me, and he reluctantly agreed. John and I were not alone in our distaste for this mission. Greg, the MCA rep whom we asked to escort us around the room, laughed in disbelief when I called with news of this plan. A few hours later, I stepped off the elevator at the Minneapolis Marriott and waded through a sea of programmers to find him, and when I did, he looked at me and winced, embarrassed to see me so willing to cast off any sense of dignity and come as an uninvited guest in order to beg for airplay. John, too, was unable to believe he had agreed to humiliate himself.

Greg spotted a programmer he knew and playfully put him on the spot. "Bob, this is John from Semisonic. Tell him why you're not playing his record."

The programmer was not amused. He looked at John. " 'Closing Time' was a great song. You should have followed it up with a hit." John nodded, showing appreciation for this refreshing insight.

A minute later, Greg grabbed a programmer from Kansas. "Hey, Brian, this is Jake from Semisonic."

"Nice to meet you, Jake. Do you know how to keep a six-pack cold?"

"How?"

"Stick it between two MCA records!"

Greg sipped his drink and shook his head at this ribbing. I looked back at the programmer. "Gee, Brian, that's kind of like telling a gas-chamber joke to a guy on death row."

That quip launched a more thoughtful but nevertheless depressing conversation about MCA's terrible reputation. As Greg drifted away, the programmer said, "You guys should have signed with Reprise. Look what they did with the Barenaked Ladies." Soon afterward, John grabbed me—"Let's get the fuck out of here"—and we slipped away.

"Over My Head" was the last hope to keep our record alive. I imagined, against all evidence and experience, that it might actually surprise everyone and become a hit, but it never had a chance. On its opening weekend, *Summer Catch* placed sixth at the movie box office—a bomb by Hollywood standards. The radio campaign for our single vanished. The video might have been played once or twice on VH1. Those who saw it would not have seen the fabulous $600 belt buckle that the stylist selected for John, because, of course, it was hidden behind his bass.

We skidded in every direction. Dan blew out his voice, and we had to cancel a show in Boulder, Colorado, and nearly canceled a trip to Japan the following week. Though we had never played in Asia, we had always viewed Japan as ripe territory for Semisonic and could not pass up this chance to play for Japanese fans. After two days of sightseeing in Tokyo, we drove up to the Fuji Rock Festival and played on a small stage for a few hundred listeners. Dan's voice was still trashed, and John and I had to sing the choruses of nearly every song in the set. It was our worst show ever, and all of us felt cheated. That night we stood in the wings of the main stage as Oasis lorded over 80,000 fans, who screamed out the words to every chorus. It was a panoramic reminder of the scale of success that only months earlier had felt within our grasp.

We limped back to Minneapolis for John and Penny's wedding, the one bright spot of the summer. John wore a mohair suit of purple, red, and blue, with a turquoise lining. He had purchased it in London with the assistance of—who else—Graham, who had taken John to one of his favorite Savile Row clothiers and helped make the selection. In honor of John's fashion suggestions to me over the years, I wore an orange tie.

Our final show of the summer was the Fash Bash, a Minneapolis fashion show fund-raiser for children's cancer research. Brooke Shields was the emcee, and in addition to Semisonic, the musical guests included Taylor Dane and Don McLean. The musical acts were rolled on and off on risers—palate cleansers between the main attractions—young women and men parading down the runway in Versace, Gautier, Donna Karan, and Dolce and Gabanna. Don McLean's time slot allowed only an abridged version of his classic, "American Pie."

Being shrunk down to a sideshow only added fuel to my raging frustration and self-disgust. As we ended the show with "Closing Time," the models walked on stage and crowded around us, lip-synching the words and shaking their bony frames with faux sexuality. They gathered more closely around the band, absorbing space, light, attention, and my resentment. But as Dan and John scrubbed out the final chord, I surprised the entire cast and crew by pushing back from my drum set, standing up, and walking through the models to the front of the stage. This departure from the script was Dan's idea. *Fashion show? I got your fashion show.* From the lip of the stage, I stepped out onto the runway and paraded my impression of a fashion model's catwalk. At the very end of the runway, I did a 360-degree turn and stopped. Fifty feet behind me, Brooke Shields and a stage full of models looked on while Dan and John sustained the final chord for my benefit. The spotlight poured its bright heat over me as I stared slowly across the room and took a deep breath, thinking about my final turn and the walk back to my drums.

Don't trip.

Chapter XVII

EL MATADOR

an, John, and I sat at a table outside a Minneapolis coffee shop on a beautiful late-August afternoon, shading our eyes from the sunlight, and sipping iced tea with the slow silence that bespeaks an epic hangover. It had been a terrible summer, a terrible spring, a terrible year.

A stranger walked up. "Hey, when are you guys gonna play in town again?" Soon, we said. How about Semisonic's next album, he asked, when would that be out? We reminded him that our most recent album was barely six months old. He smiled and waved good-bye, urging us to hurry up and get back in the studio so he could buy another Semisonic album in 2002.

It served as a strange reminder that at least a few people were waiting for our next album, even as we had gathered to ask ourselves if we would make one. Dan felt that as things stood there was no clear step forward for the band. He wanted to finish the solo record he had begun recording at the end of 2000. The songs he was writing did not sound like Semisonic, and there was no point in the band rushing to record new material that lacked direction. MCA was poised to drop us. Sending them a confused pile of songs would only hasten their decision to dispose of us. "So let's take some time off," Dan said. "I honestly believe we'll make another record, but I don't know when that will be."

Thus began a break of undetermined length and meaning. Friends asked me about the band, and the phrase "taking some time off" produced silent nods, searching looks, and more questions.

"So what are you doing in the meantime?" The band had absorbed the last eight years of my life, and hearing this question, I felt the camera pulling back from me, revealing the surrounding blank space.

John and Dan's brother, Matt, formed an acoustic duo, the Flops, playing shows in Minneapolis and the Midwest. Dan continued working on his record, calling in John to play bass and me to play drums on several of the tracks. As his solo album evolved into something purposeful and clear, I found it increasingly difficult to think about the band's future.

Dan proceeded with the recordings, and Jim asked MCA to clarify its position regarding the band. The word came back that our past successes in the UK gave MCA enough hope to hang on to us, even though the label was doubtful of our potential in the US. So then what about an advance on our next record? Those phone calls were not returned. Hans proposed some candidates to produce Dan's solo record, and after a few weeks of meetings and conversations with those producers, Dan made his choice. The issue of recording advances could no longer be ignored by MCA. Two days later, as Dan and I took a break from recording a drum track, the phone rang. It was Jim, calling to tell us that MCA had just canceled Dan's solo record and had dropped Semisonic. I stepped out for a walk, wondering if I was a fool to have been surprised. Now the camera had pulled back further, and I was but a dot in a wide white plain. A year earlier, my face had filled billboards.

Now without a record contract, we watched as the music business buckled under the weight of the Internet and growing listener alienation. The roof fell in at MCA, with more resignations and firings. Jay Boberg, gone. Gary Ashley, gone. Hans, gone. And then Craig Lambert, gone. Most of the familiar faces had vanished. Half the employees lost their jobs. Finally, the MCA name, thoroughly tarnished, was lowered into the ground. The remaining employees officially work for Geffen records, and albums by the remaining artists bear the Geffen label.

Dan, meanwhile, continued recording his solo album and recently signed a deal with American/Lost Highway, another of the record labels in the Universal Music Group. He's finishing the last few tracks and has even begun to look at artwork ideas for the CD cover. His current inspiration is a photo of an iceberg, an image I like because it suggests a distant world, beautiful and haunting.

Whatever artwork is on its cover, I look forward to seeing Dan's CD in my friends' living rooms and hearing it everywhere I go. The fan in me wants to share the experience of visiting the world of Dan's album, just as I enjoy standing in the crowd when John and Matt play at the 400 Bar. That's what I love about being a fan. When I walk down the street and hear "Beautiful Day" by U2 playing on a nearby radio and then see people around me mouthing the words, I feel connected to those strangers. We belong to the communion of all the other U2 fans, millions of them orbiting a bright center, all of us a part of the everlasting U2 show.

At the same time, whenever I go out to hear music, I long to be on stage, to be the one lifting all of the fans into their euphoric orbit. The strange thing is that sometimes, when I'm rocking on stage and see the staring eyes and swaying hips and hear the singing and cheering voices, I imagine being in the crowd. When we played in Mexico City and hundreds of lighters began to flick in time with the music, I was jealous of the crowd for the style with which it made the night so fun. I wanted to be the drummer *and* one of those people amplifying the drumbeat with their lighters. When we played at the Shepherd's Bush Empire in London, I wanted to be one of the people shouting at the band between songs, provoking laughter from the rest of the crowd and retorts from the stage, perhaps a playful scolding from the singer or a snarling pounding of the drums starting the next song.

The closest I've come to simultaneously living on both sides of the line between performer and audience is listening to a recording of a song I've written. For me, each hearing of a song is a trip inside the mind of the songwriter. When I hear Joni Mitchell sing, I don't picture her in front of a microphone in a recording studio, and I don't imagine her in her living room as she scribbles down and scratches out ideas on a pad of paper. I imagine the inner Joni, the one we can't actually see, the one behind her eyes who longs for "a river I could skate away on." I see the world inside Bruce Springsteen, the place where the "barefoot girl sitting on the hood of a Dodge drinking warm beer in the soft summer rain" lives. When I listen to "El Matador," I get to enter Jake's world from the outside, even as I look out from the inside.

Listening to my songs, I feel that the circuit between the performer and the audience is complete. But feeling the electricity arc across the line that separates the crowd and the band during a live performance never ceases to be a thrill. A month from now, I'll fly from New York to Minneapolis. When the plane comes down through the clouds, the entire world below me will be white with snow. My friend Pav will pick me up at the airport and drive me to Dan's, and I'll stay there for a few days as Dan, John, and I rehearse for the upcoming Semisonic shows at First Avenue. We've played fewer than ten shows in the past two years, so I'll be rusty. In the evenings, I'll visit my Minneapolis friends. In the mornings, I'll play piano with my six-year-old goddaughter, Coco, now in first grade.

Then the night of the show will come, and we'll drive down to First Avenue. I'll be nervous, as I always am when I walk through the hometown crowd as they mill about with their winter coats unzipped. All our friends will be there. Inside the dressing room, I'll pace back and forth as the door opens and closes and familiar faces peek in to wish us luck and our crew members pop in to grab spare guitars. Dan and John will warm up their voices, and I'll test my blood sugar and swill down cranberry juice to load up on calories. I'll pop a couple of Rolaids. Dave, our tour manager for the night, will walk in and tell us it's time. The door will open and Pete, our monitor engineer, will nod at us as a flashlight guides us up the stairs to the stage. A giant screen will hide us from the audience's view, but a few people in front will see our ankles and send up whoops that will quickly spread across the room.

The house music will stop, the houselights will go black, and I'll feel a huge rush of adrenaline as the screen in front of the stage lifts to reveal the cheering crowd. I'll look out at the faces in the darkness of the club, get a nod from Dan and John, shout out, "ONE TWO THREE FOUR," and the three of us will crash down with our guitars and drums. The music will flood the room. And the energy of the 2,000 people packed into the club will channel itself through the three people on stage and pour out again into the crowd, over and over, as we ride on waves of sound and light.

ACKNOWLEDGMENTS

I will begin by thanking my agent, Daniel Greenberg. I brought him a pile of ideas (mainly some road diaries off of the Semisonic website), and over several months' time, he helped me sort through and arrange these ideas into a proposal, which became the model for the finished book.

Gerry Howard, my editor, stepped forward with enthusiasm after reading the book proposal, waited patiently for the completion of the manuscript, and raised many useful questions along the way. I am lucky to have had such an engaged and supportive editor.

My friend Mike Miller spent hundreds of hours reading every page of every draft and then going over them with me during his lunch breaks. He took my calls late at night and first thing in the morning, and from beginning to end I relied on his perspective and encouragement.

Suzanne Wise took weeks away from her own writing to read every word of every draft and helped me untangle the most vexing chapters. Her poet's ears and eyes and the thoroughness with which she applied them were invaluable.

Liz Campanile and Carla Sacks of Sacks Communications played a decisive role in bringing this book into being by sending my road diaries to various people, including Neva Grant and

Maeve McGoran of National Public Radio. Neva and Maeve, in turn, put in long hours producing some of these diaries as commentaries for NPR's *Morning Edition*. This boosted my eagerness to write a book. I was further encouraged by Stephanie Cabot and Leigh Haber.

As I wrote, I relied mainly on my memories of various events. I was greatly assisted, however, by documentation from and conversations with dozens of people. Most of them have no remaining professional connection to Semisonic; they responded only out of their generosity. Hans Haedelt was kind enough to call me from beaches and highways across the country and contribute his recollections. Thanks also to Steve Ralbovsky. I kept Christine Wolff's phone ringing constantly, and she went out of her way to retrieve various tapes and interviews for me. Kymm Britton did the same from her home in Los Angeles. Leona Megerdichian's exhaustive compilation of interviews was a great help. The complete story of our international travels and success would have been impossible to recount without the help of Dana Collins. Ruth Flower, my favorite person in the entire music business, found the answers to numerous impossible questions. Dan Waite went out of his way to recover photos and documents. I am also indebted to Nina Hansdotter, David Quirk, and others in the London office of the Universal Music Group for their help.

Thanks to Rakesh Satyal, Elisabeth Wooldridge, Todd Gallopo, Dara Kravitz, Mike Regan, Michelle Saint Claire, "Bubba" Wayne McManners, Lillian Matulic, Lori Berk, Mary Lucia, Brian Oak, Shawn Stewart, Kevin Cole, Doug Gayeton, Karen Glauber, Ann Slichter, Stephanie Faiella, Johnny Temple, Chris Joyner, Ken Chastain, Frank Riley and High Road Touring, Mike Dewdney and ITB, Chip Hooper and Monterey Peninsula Artists, Greg Drew, Boo Bruey, Donny Brown, Eric Boehlert, David Russell, and Minneapolis weatherman Paul Douglass. Several people in various corners of the music business spoke about their experiences and the nature of their work off the record. I will not name them, but their insights were most valuable and much appreciated. Important pieces of advice, insight, comments, and other forms of writerly support came from Joey Brochin, Rebecca Carpenter, Rick Fabian, Lee Humphries, Renee Fladen-Kamm, Chris Hudson, Maggie Kent, Joe Lowndes, Sam Magavern, Pete McDade, Andrea Michaels, Hal Movius, Keith Page, Sarah Paul, Eugene and Jackie Rivers, Andrew Saxe, Donald and Ellen Schell, Maria Schell, John Slocum, Joan and Karl Stockbridge, Anne Vande Creek, Michael Welch, Matt Wilson, Craig Wright, and Priscilla Yamin.

In addition to the debt I owe them as a performer, the Semisonic crew, past and present, deserve special thanks. Our road managers—Chris Buttleman, Chris Hudson, and Chris Fussell—all took multiple phone calls from me and provided documentation of our travels. Our old bus driver, John Schott (known to us as Shooter), was another help. Soundman Brad Kern and our old guitar tech Toby Kutrieb answered my questions and never once called me a muso. I omitted the names of other crew members, and thus the book does not give proper accounting of the many people who have worked hard for Semisonic. Chris Pavlich and Pete Skujins appear briefly, an injustice in my mind given their multifarious efforts on our behalf. With this in mind, allow me to thank those whose names did not appear but whose labors were a big part of Semisonic's success: Tom Gorman, Gary "Gator" Fritz, Mike Riddle, Billy Smart, Charlie McPherson, George Aldrich, Ernesto Corti, Kevin Wegman, Greg Mandelke, Matt Kormann, Bill Latas, Michael Lavonte, Matt Johnson, Paul Kell, Mick Mullins, Jay Perlman, and Tom Crawford.

Thank you, Matthew Welch. Hairdresser Mimi Laubersheimer deserves extra thanks on account of the jacket photo, in which I am sporting one of the many free haircuts I received. Georgia-sized sacks of sugar to designer Delight Underwood of

Hyena Productions for outfitting me with the world's greatest scarf.

"Business manager" does not begin to describe all of the work Dave Ness has done for Semisonic over the years. He has been a rock-solid friend and source of indispensable wisdom. As I wrote the book, I called him constantly, and he went out of his way to help me retrieve various bits of information. Thanks to those on his team, especially Brian Wetjen and Laurel Gray.

We could not have had a better manager than Jim Grant, as readers of this book will know. Too bad Dan, John, and I cannot arrange a New York Knicks NBA championship in his honor, for that would be the only way to thank him adequately for his continuing guidance, encouragement, and hard work. During the writing of this book, he spent long hours digging up old reviews, tracking down sales reports, and making countless calls on my behalf. Thanks to the others in his office, especially Doug Smith and Heather Kolker.

Dan Wilson and John Munson, the true heroes of this story, contributed many of their recollections and dug through their storage boxes to help track down missing information. More important, without them, there would be no story to tell. If I have written it well, readers of this book will know that I owe Dan and John a lifetime of thanks, for the only thing more fun than rocking on the drums and traveling the world is doing it with such wonderful friends. Special thanks to Diane, Penny, and Coco.

Thanks to my family, to Hattie and Robert Marion, and Mrs. Davie Hill. Thanks to all the Semisonic fans. And thank you, Suzanne, for letting me be your lifelong fan.

Jacob Slichter is a native of Champaign, Illinois, and graduated from Harvard with a degree in Afro-American studies and history. He has read his road diaries (originally published on the Semisonic website) on NPR's *Morning Edition*. With his multiplatinum-selling band Semisonic, he has appeared on the Jay Leno, David Letterman, Conan O'Brien, and Craig Kilborn shows.